*Southern Biography Series*
William J. Cooper, Jr., Editor

Lillian Smith

Photograph by Leonard Skvirsky, Collection of Esther Smith

# Lillian Smith
## A Southerner Confronting the South
### *A Biography*


## Anne C. Loveland

Louisiana State University Press
Baton Rouge and London

Designer: Laura Roubique
Typeface: Bulmer
Typesetter: G&S Typesetters, Inc.
Printer: Thomson–Shore, Inc.
Binder: John Dekker & Sons, Inc.

10  9  8  7  6  5  4  3  2  1

Portions of Chapter III were previously published in "Lillian Smith and the Problem of Segregation in the Roosevelt Era," *Southern Studies: An Interdisciplinary Journal of the South*, Volume XXII, Number 1, Spring 1983.

LIBRARY OF CONGRESS CATALOGING-IN-PUBLICATION DATA

Loveland, Anne C., 1938–
    Lillian Smith, a southerner confronting the South.

    (Southern biography series)
    Includes bibliographies and index.
    1. Smith, Lillian Eugenia, 1897–1966—Political and social views.
2. Afro-Americans—Civil rights—Southern States—History.
3. Southern States—Intellectual life—1865–    . 4. Southern
States in literature.  5. Authors, American—20th century—
Biography.  I. Title.  II. Series.
PS3537.M653Z75      1986        813'.52        86-10641
ISBN 0-8071-1343-3

# Contents

# Illustrations

# Acknowledgments

I could not have written this book without the assistance of many people. Esther Smith, Paula Snelling, and Frank Smith granted me permission to use the Lillian Smith Collection at the University of Georgia Libraries, and J. Larry Gulley, Nelson Morgan, and Robert M. Willingham in Special Collections insured that my research was both pleasant and productive. I am also indebted to two of my colleagues in the Louisiana State University History Department, William J. Cooper, Jr., and Gaines M. Foster, for evaluating the manuscript and offering suggestions for improvement. I especially appreciated Gaines's sense of humor and his persistence in pointing out issues deserving consideration.

Many people helped with recollections or information about Lillian Smith: Anne Braden, Charles Bolté, Miriam Botnick, George Brockway, Arthur Ben Chitty, Carolyn Diffenbaugh, Virginia Foster Durr, Mairi Fraser Foreman, George Fredrickson, Rose Gladney, Doris Gold, Myles Horton, Faith Jackson, David Lifson, Barbara Livingston, Rollo May, Glenn Rainey, Frank E. Smith, Sara Terrien, Jane White Viazzi, William Warren, Joel Williamson, and Hilda Woodford. Pat Watters kindly allowed me to use in the title of this book his description of Lillian Smith in *The South and the Nation.*

For archival information and research I am indebted to Richard A.

Shrader of the Southern Historical Collection, Wilson Library, University of North Carolina, Chapel Hill; Carmen Russell of the Rare Books and Manuscripts Department, University of Florida Library, Gainesville; and research aides Linda McCurdy and John N. Wright. Paul Wonk of the Interlibrary Loan Department, Louisiana State University Library, was also very helpful.

I was aided financially by grants from the Louisiana State University Council on Research and the Southern Regional Education Board.

Lillian Smith

.

# Prologue

During the decade following the publication of *Killers of the Dream* in 1949, Lillian Smith insisted that book publishers and newspaper and magazine editors in both the North and South were smothering her by preventing dissemination of her controversial opinions on the race question in the United States. In 1967, the year after Lillian died, Margaret Sullivan charged in the *Mad River Review* that literary critics had aided the suppression, albeit in a different way. According to Sullivan, they punished Lillian for literary heresy by denying her "status as a conscious literary artist," refusing even to notice, much less evaluate, her seven books and numerous essays and articles.[1] Sullivan only echoed complaints Lillian herself had often made about the meanness of literary critics and book reviewers and the unjust treatment she received at their hands.

In recent years, however, an increasing number of historians have begun to call attention to the significant role Lillian Smith played in the social and intellectual history of the South. Of the small group of white southerners who enlisted in the civil rights movement in the 1930s, she is now hailed as one of the first to speak out publicly against racial segregation. As a writer she is regarded as an early example of the flowering of the Modernist tradition in the South. As Charles K. Piehl noted recently in *Reviews in American History*, historians now recognize Lillian Smith as "a pivotal figure in southern intellectual life as the region emerged from the renaissance years into the turmoil of the civil rights revolution."[2]

Nevertheless, the tendency so far has been to focus on her work in the civil rights movement and to neglect her literary effort. Both aspects of her career are important. More than anything, Lillian wanted to be recognized as a creative writer and thinker. Because historians have not fully appreciated how much her writing career meant to her, they have come close to stereotyping her—much as she claimed her enemies did—as "the nice little lady who did so much to help Negroes." Historians have also failed to recognize the difficulty she encountered in relating her writing and civil rights work (what she called the "Mary" and "Martha" sides of her nature), and the way the problem shaped her life and thought. To a considerable extent, Lillian's effort to abolish what she perceived as divisions and walls in the world of men grew out of her effort to eliminate them in her own life. She realized that her protest against segregation "did not have to do entirely with Negroes and whites, and the South" but with her own personal experiences. Segregation symbolized what she called "the splits and estrangements" in her own life.[3] Even in the public arena, racial separation was not her only concern. She defined segregation in the broadest possible sense, as encompassing all the modes of thought and behavior whereby human beings cut themselves off from alien ideas, emotions, or experiences. Thus in opposing segregation she protested not just racial separation but all forms of dehumanization that prevent mankind from realizing its full potential.

# I Growing into Freedom

A few little experiences can change a life. . . . Writing is often a way of trying to understand what one cannot even remember.

In writing about her childhood, Lillian Smith always emphasized what she called her Deep South upbringing. Although she lived virtually her entire adult life in the mountains of north Georgia, she was born and grew up in Jasper, a small town in northern Florida close to the Georgia state line. It was located midway between Tallahassee and Jacksonville in a region of small farms and rolling hills covered with stands of hardwood and pine. Lillian especially remembered the live oaks heavy with Spanish moss, the palmetto and sandspurs, the brown rivers edged with hot white sand. She was fascinated by the swampy areas that extended like fingers from the great Okefenokee Swamp in Georgia. The Indians called them "trembling earth" because of the sink holes and quicksand and bottomless ponds, and to Lillian, even as a child, they seemed symbolic of the uncertainty and mystery of life.

Jasper was the town on which Lillian modeled Maxwell, Georgia, the setting of her first published novel, *Strange Fruit.* The population of about one thousand was almost evenly divided between blacks and whites, and like its fictional counterpart, Jasper was rigidly segregated by race. But unlike Maxwell, Jasper had some redeeming features. Lillian described it as "a town of some economic wealth and culture."[1] Besides being the county seat, it boasted an opera house, a chau-

3

tauqua, and the Jasper Normal Institute, a teachers' college whose high
school the older Smith children attended. Although her family lived in
a small town, Lillian did not feel that they were isolated or provincial.
The Smiths frequently traveled to nearby Suwannee Springs and Jacksonville, and to Biloxi, Mississippi, and Saint Simons Island and Way-
cross, Georgia. When she was fourteen Lillian went with an aunt on
her first long trip to Manitou Springs in Colorado, visiting Chicago
along the way. Letters from older brothers away at college and from an
older sister living in China where her husband worked with the Young
Men's Christian Association offered glimpses of the world beyond
Jasper, and the cultivated talk of the Normal Institute teachers and
acquaintance with a family who had recently moved from Chicago also
afforded new and different perspectives.

The Smiths were a large family. Lillian Eugenia—or Lillie as she
was called—was born December 12, 1897, the seventh of nine children.[2] The four girls and five boys lived with their parents in a large,
comfortable house on "the street where most of the 'nice' houses were,"
across from the Methodist church, which they attended regularly.
Lillian's father, Calvin Warren Smith, made a good living in wholesale
lumber and naval stores. A deeply religious man who served on the
board of stewards of the Methodist church, he was also one of Jasper's
leading progressives—a member of various civic committees, chairman of the board of education, and a champion of public health, education, and prohibition.

Lillian described her father's people as Scotch-Irish farmers who
had migrated from North Carolina to settle in Ware County, Georgia.
Although they owned slaves, according to Lillian they believed slavery
was wrong, felt the Civil War was foolish, but "gave nearly all of their
menfolks in defense of what few really believed in." Calvin Smith's
mother, whom the children called Little Grandma, embodied for
Lillian the independence and fortitude of her father's people. When her
husband had returned from the Civil War a ruined and broken man,
she had taken over the management of the family farm and with her
nine sons plowed and planted and cultivated the fields. She had lived
through Indian raids and had braved the swamps and lonely stretches
of forest and wire grass. And she had killed a panther. Lillian never
tired of the story she told about it, wrapped in her shawl, stirring the

fire in her room while the Smith children roasted pecans and sweet potatoes in the ashes. "How did you do it, Grandma? we'd ask for the hundredth time. Her blue eyes would light up, she would laugh and say, You take aim straight at the head, and you pull the trigger, easy." To Lillian the story told by her eighty-year-old grandmother was "a legend of reassurance, a story of human strength able to deal with what comes to a person day by day."[3]

Lillian characterized her father as a man of keen intelligence and enormous physical and emotional vitality, full of curiosity about the world in which he lived. He seems to have provided considerable intellectual stimulation. Her mother, Annie Simpson, was more imaginative and introspective, and her gentle, quiet nature contrasted sharply with her husband's energy and tough-mindedness. She represented the aristocratic side of the Smith family, for her people had not been small farmers but wealthy rice planters in the tidewater region of Georgia. Lillian described her maternal grandfather, William Henry Simpson, as a romantic figure who was also a man of unusual erudition. He was different—born in New York City, he had been educated in a Canadian monastery to be a Jesuit priest, but had rebelled and, before saying his final vows, had escaped to the South where he married the young and beautiful daughter of a prosperous Georgia planter. When the Civil War came, according to Lillian, he fought with the Confederates "not for slavery but for States Rights and for his bride," and afterward he advised Yankees, white southerners, and Negroes during the difficult days of Reconstruction. Although they never met with him together, each group felt comfortable and welcome in his house and appreciated the "fair, honest advice" he dispensed. Lillian believed that her grandfather's judiciousness and learning had exerted a strong influence on the Smith family. It was symbolized by the library on the second floor of the house in Jasper, a room set aside by her parents to memorialize the grandfather's love of books. Actually, his books were not there, having been lost and scattered during the years of war, Reconstruction, and migration from one town to another. Lillian remembered that the few hundred books ranged on the shelves constituted "an odd assortment of truth and error," including the sermons of Dwight Moody and DeWitt Talmadge and fire and brimstone preachers like Sam Jones, the religious novel *In His Steps*, two terrifying books on hell, and an illustrated Bible. She also recalled *Pilgrim's Progress* and *Robinson Crusoe* and *Gulliver's Travels* side by side with Dante, Shakespeare, Goethe, Oliver Wendell Holmes, George Eliot, Dickens, Thackeray, Mark Twain, and Victor Hugo. She had read most of the books before she graduated from high school, some of them more than once.[4]

Lillian described her upbringing as southern-Calvinistic. In *Killers of the Dream* she remembered the lessons her mother taught her and the other children. The first one was about God.

> We were told that He loved us, and then we were told that He would burn us in everlasting flames of hell if we displeased Him. We were told that we should love Him for He gives us everything good that we have, and then we were told we should fear Him because He has the power to do evil to us whenever He cares to. We learned from this part of the lesson another: that "people," like God and parents, can love and hate you at the same time; and though they may love you, if you displease them they may do you great injury; hence being loved by them does not give you protection from being harmed by them.

The second lesson had to do with the body. She learned that the body was "a Thing of Shame" and that she should never show her nakedness to anyone except the doctor when she was sick, that she should never desecrate it by pleasures (except "the few properly introduced to you"), and that some parts of the body were "segregated areas which you must stay away from and keep others away from." They were to be touched only when necessary. The third lesson was that though the body was a thing of shame and mystery, a white skin was a source of strength and pride which proved one better than all other people on earth. The fourth lesson, on segregation, was "only a logical expression of the lessons on sex and white superiority and God. Not only Negroes but everything dark, dangerous, evil must be pushed to the rim of one's life. Signs put over doors in the world outside and over minds seemed natural enough to children like us, for signs had already been put over forbidden areas of our body." Indeed, the interlocking of the lessons contributed to their power. That and the fact that they were generally taught with love and gentleness, and less by explicit statements than by acts and gestures—"a raised eyebrow, a joke, a shocked voice, a withdrawing movement of the body, a long silence."[5]

The lessons on sin and sex, taught gently at home, were "welded together by the flames of hell" at the annual revival meetings Lillian attended with her family. She remembered the enormous terror she experienced under the revivalists' preaching. "By means of threats, hypnotic suggestion, and a recall of the earliest fears of childhood, they plunged into our unconscious and brought up sins we had long ago forgotten." Lying in bed at night after the revival meeting, she and the other children brooded over the preacher's threats. "Then, in the darkness, hell reached out bright long red fingers and seared the edge of our beds. Sometimes we would doggedly whisper to ourselves, 'we are saved too,' but even as we said it, we believed ourselves liars." She remembered that it was impossible for her to feel she was saved, even though she went to the altar numerous times, sometimes staying "until the revivalist pried me off my knees."[6]

At the same time they enforced the lessons on sin, sex, and segregation, Lillian's parents preached Christian and democratic values. In an article entitled "Growing Into Freedom," Lillian remembered becoming aware of contradictions in her parents' thinking and behavior. Her mother taught her tenderness, love, and compassion, but also schooled her in "the bleak rituals of keeping the Negro in his place." Her father preached the brotherhood of man and rebuked her for thinking herself superior to the children from the mill town, but he also taught her "the steel-like inhuman decorums I must demand of every colored male." He told his children that they were part of a democracy and should act like democrats, but he helped bring about prohibition by lining up his mill hands on election day and paying each one of them a dollar to vote liquor out of Hamilton County. Lillian wrote that by the time she had learned that God is love and that all men are brothers with a common Father, she also knew that she was better than a Negro "and that a terrifying disaster would befall the South if I ever treated a Negro as my social equal." She did not disobey her parents' teachings, but she was troubled by them. Even as a young child she was something of a rebel, always asking questions, always sensitive to "the dichotomies of our southern way of life."[7]

Bewildered and sometimes pained by the contradictions that surrounded her, Lillian also suffered feelings of rejection as a child. When she was two years old, her sister Esther was born, and Lillian was turned over to the care of the Smiths' black nurse, Aunt Chloe. She protested the loss of her mother's attention by refusing to eat. Aunt Chloe's loving ministrations soon convinced her that she was "once more the center of somebody's universe" and she abandoned her hunger strike, but she always remembered feeling wounded and hurt by her mother's rejection.[8] That early instance of rejection, coupled with her mother's seeming disapproval of her as a young girl, caused Lillian to have ambivalent feelings about her mother. "I was never like Esther who loved Mother purely; I loved her ambivalently," she wrote, and she once described her relationship with her mother as a love-hate relationship. She resented her mother for rejecting her, but at the same time adored her and desperately sought her approval.

Kathleen Miller has suggested that Lillian's feelings of rejection as a child also stemmed from her doubts about being saved. Lillian remembered that she found it impossible to feel saved. Nevertheless, wanting salvation so much, sometimes she would lie about it and stand up with the others when the evangelist asked all who were assured of salvation to arise and be counted. She sought salvation as desperately as she sought her mother's approval and felt unable to achieve either. And just as she envied Esther's congenial relationship with her mother, Lillian also envied her feeling of security regarding salvation. "My younger sister, more certain of her place in the family, was naturally more certain of her place in heaven, and rarely went to the altar [to seek salvation]. I remember how I admired her restraint."[9]

Lillian's ability to empathize with others also caused her pain as a child. "I could walk into a room (at age 9 or 10)," she remembered, "and feel almost instantly how each person in that room was feeling. I'd be almost overcome, sometimes, by my vicarious 'suffering.' And I often wondered why my younger sister, so sweet and gentle (while I was warm and quick-tempered) did not feel how people felt. I'd say to her, 'But that person is so sad!' and she'd say, 'How do you know?' And I would not be sure how I knew so I felt a little uncertain but I'd say 'I feel her sadness,' or 'I feel his good fortune,' or 'I know he is hating someone.'"[10]

People fascinated Lillian, even though her empathy with them sometimes caused her pain. According to her mother and others who knew her as a youngster, from the time she was five or six she seemed to think it was her vocation to watch people's words and actions and "put it all together."

> Mother used to say to me, "The whole world is one big novel to you, isn't it? People are not people, they are characters to you; you mustn't try to see all around them, the way you do; you can do that only in books." And I didn't answer her (I was about fourteen then) but I said to myself, "I can see all around them and it scares me to death to know I can do it." But I didn't want to worry Mother so I didn't say anything else. But now and then . . . she said softly, "There you go again; you just can't understand everybody." But I thought I could; and when I couldn't I loved to see how far I could go and when I reached that place where everything was dark and seemed simply to "end" about that person, I kept thinking "If only I were wiser I'd see more, and more and more—"[11]

Lillian's recollections of her childhood suggest that she was a rather precocious youngster: rebellious and questioning, aware of contradictions in her parents' thinking and behavior, sensitive to the pain and suffering of others. Granting that she may have exaggerated the extent of her rebelliousness and the intensity of her feelings, it seems likely that her behavior and emotions as a child were an important source of the moral outrage that impelled her to challenge segregation and other injustices. But her experiences as a young woman also helped to mold her.

Lillian graduated from high school in Jasper in 1915. That same year the Smith family moved to Rabun County in the north Georgia foothills of the Blue Ridge Mountains after Calvin Smith's business had failed. To make a living, he opened a small inn, the Laurel Falls Hotel, on Old Screamer Mountain, the site of what had been the family's summer home. Lillian and the other children helped him to run it.

Lillian loved Old Screamer, but Clayton, the nearby town, was a different matter. Jasper, though small, had offered an "open door to the outside world." Clayton, a muddy little mountain village, did not: it had no paved streets, only five or six stores, and poor schools. Its economy depended almost entirely on the summer visitors who stayed in boardinghouses and inns like the one the Smiths operated. On Saturdays the country people walked the five or six miles to town barefooted. Impoverished and backward, they made a meager living farming submarginal land or selling moonshine whiskey. Lillian missed in these poor mountain whites the vitality and spontaneity she had seen among the black folk of Jasper—their laughter, anguish and shame. Perhaps that is why she wrote so little of the mountain region in which she lived.

The summer after graduation, having obtained a teaching license, Lillian taught school at Dillard, Georgia. Homesick for Jasper and her friends, she was also anxious about the quality of her teaching. In the fall she enrolled at Piedmont College in Demorest. The little mountain school, all the family could afford at the time, impressed Lillian with its small classes and the caliber of the faculty, many of whom had been educated at prestigious northern colleges and universities. The small-town girl from Jasper also learned a good deal about rural, mountain people and saw poverty and ignorance she had not dreamed existed. She began to feel a desire to help people. The following year Piedmont offered her a full scholarship, but feeling that her parents needed her, she decided to assist them in operating a small hotel in Daytona Beach.

As a young girl, Lillian had deliberated between writing and music as a career. Having chosen the latter, she practiced the piano as many as six hours a day from the time she was eleven or twelve until she was in her early twenties. Her teachers and family thought her extraordinarily talented. Their praise, along with her experience in Daytona Beach playing with an orchestra, persuaded her to go to Baltimore in the fall of 1917 to study at the Peabody Conservatory. While staying at the Margaret Bennett Home for needy students and professional women, she worked as an accompanist to earn money for tuition and living expenses. Her instructor at Peabody, like her former teachers, thought her quite talented, and even gave her one free lesson a week in addition to those she received through the conservatory. However, Lillian was awed by the brilliant students she met and appalled by how little she knew in comparison. She was beginning to doubt the high estimate others made of her musical ability.

During the summer of 1918, which she spent with her family on Old Screamer, she decided that she "ought to be more patriotic" and "do something for the war effort." She volunteered for the student nursing corps and was accepted. Placed on call, she felt she could not return to Baltimore. The armistice was signed in November without her having ever served in the corps. At that point, although her first teaching job had been disappointing, on the urging of her father she decided to take a position at Tiger, Georgia, as the principal of a two-room school. Helped by her experience in Baltimore playing for classes at the Young Women's Christian Association and the Police Athletic League, she had a more successful time than at Dillard. Once again, though, she was dismayed by the primitive living conditions of the country people whose children she taught. She spent the weekends with her family, walking the three and a half miles home, but during the week she lived with a mountain family, sharing their frugal meals of coffee, hoecake, turnip greens, and sometimes a little fresh pork or "white side" (home-salted bacon). There was no toilet or running water; the washbasin was on the back porch, the privy outdoors. "People were poor, you know. I learned a lot that year."

The next three years spent at Peabody in Baltimore were also an important learning experience. She rented a room from a retired English teacher who taught her about literature; but until she found sufficient work, she nearly starved, and refused to tell her parents for fear they would insist she return home. She became acquainted with painting and sculpture, read many books, listened to fine music. Her work as an accompanist for classes at the American Can Company and the Bethlehem Steel Works brought her for the first time into contact with industry and with factory workers, many of whom were recent immigrants to the United States. She learned about "slums, poverty, factories—much I had known nothing about." Some of her artist and musician friends introduced her to the bohemian life, but she found it rather specious and preferred dating Johns Hopkins medical students.

Of all her experiences in these early years, Lillian ranked the three years she spent in China as the "most intense and profound." In 1922 she accepted a position as head of the music department of the Virginia School in Huchow, Chekiang Province, a Christian missionary school for wealthy Chinese girls. The young woman who had shocked Clayton by being the first to bob her hair and wear short skirts was completely unprepared for the cultural and intellectual shock of China. It was a land of sharp contrasts, of enchanting beauty and cultural richness alongside "dreadful disease and dirt and poverty and ignorance." China proved to be a "tremendous experience" that stimulated her aesthetically, philosophically, and politically. She began to read Far Eastern philosophy and the works of Rabindranath Tagore. She also began to take a new interest in world affairs. Her political consciousness was awakened for the first time as she observed the operation of European colonialism and the aftermath of the Chinese Revolution of 1911 and 1912 and as she heard and read about Mahatma Gandhi's fight for Indian independence.

Returning to Georgia in 1925, Lillian entered upon what she later characterized as a "miserable, even nightmarish" period in her life. In China her conscience had been stricken by the realization that her parents were unwell and in financial straits. Lillian decided that they needed—and they had apparently requested—her help. In 1920 her father had turned the hotel into a private camp for girls. Lillian had worked there as a music counselor during the summers of 1921 and 1922, but she had not cared for camp life or for the horseback riding, swimming, handicrafts, and other such activities Laurel Falls featured. Taking over the direction of the camp was therefore a painful, albeit self-imposed, duty. For one thing, the prospect of directing a camp bored her. Moreover, she disapproved of much that went on at Laurel Falls. In particular, she was concerned about the homosexual crushes and "over-emotionalized atmosphere" that some of the counselors encouraged among the young campers (and which reminded her of the unnamed yet passionate and forbidden relationships she had observed between some of the female missionaries and students at the Virginia School). She also objected to the emphasis on competition in sports and other activities and the patriotic ceremonialism that had been instituted while she was in China.

> There was a flag to be hiked up on the flag pole every morning; we were supposed to run out, make a circle and sing Oh say, can you see. I thought it was the damndest thing I had ever witnessed. Frogs in everybody's throat, everybody half asleep and here we were hoisting up Old Glory. Why? I asked. . . . Why all this sudden patriotism? Nobody seemed to know; one of the counselors had started it and Dad I guess thought it was about the safest suggestion these bewildering women had made. . . . But when I said Let's stop this foolishness, everybody stared at me, horror-stricken.

At night, walking down the road after the campers were asleep in their cabins, she wished she could "walk away and never come back."

She did fire all but four of the twenty-eight counselors and hire a new staff more to her liking for the summer of 1926. But something more was required than a change of personnel. She felt oppressed by the need to learn how to deal with the practical problems of running a camp—tending to leaking roofs, plumbing, electricity, sick children; soothing complaining parents; handling the kitchen and dining room and the domestic help. It was not just that her education and experience had not fitted her to be a camp director. Even after she had mastered the practical matters, she realized that the main problem was that in leaving China and returning home to help her parents, she had abandoned or suppressed the creative impulses she had been nurturing for many years. If she were to survive what had become a personal disaster, she would have to find some sort of outlet for them.

Many years later, in a reflective mood, Lillian described the experience of taking over Laurel Falls Camp in terms of a conflict between the "Mary" side of her nature and the "Martha" side, between her "creative daemon" and her conscience. In Baltimore and China she had indulged the Mary side. Then she realized that her parents needed a Martha to come home and help do practical things.

> So I sadly told the Mary part of my nature goodby for a while and went home to help. Those were miserable, even nightmarish years for me. I had to take over my father's camp for girls. What did I know about a camp? What did I care? Exactly nothing. Three dreary years of futility and failure, then Mary began nudging me: "you can make this camp experience as creative as a poem, a piece of music, a novel; try." Well, it was almost as trite and naked as that. I listened and I tried. And the nightmare began to turn into something quite clean and lovely, even wonderful at times.

She began by making some aesthetic improvements. Her father had built a new camp on Old Screamer (and turned the old one back into a summer inn), but it was "raw, unpainted, ugly, unplanned." Lillian initiated the transformation of the ugly red hill by building winding stone steps from the parking space to the ridge where the camp was located. Then, working with an old man who loved rock, she built a fireplace and chimney in the gym-theater. She painted the cabins and planted rhododendron, white pines, ferns, azaleas, and dogwood. "Mary was finding a little room for creating, if not poetry and music and literature, at least a little beauty."

During the next ten years, Lillian also changed the orientation of the camp. She eliminated much of the competition that had figured so prominently in sports and other activities. She instituted painting, sculpture, and etching classes and started a modern dance program. Creativity replaced competition. "Inch by inch I was setting up creative projects, new things, and in the new things I never let competition get to first base." There were reading and creative writing programs and a theater for which Lillian and the campers wrote and produced plays. Increasingly she made Laurel Falls a reflection of her own personality and interests. Under her father's direction, the camp had been little more than an extended house party, at which the campers made friends, learned to swim, ride, and play tennis, toasted marshmallows, and sang around the campfire. Lillian transformed it into a creative, educational experience. Perhaps most significant in this regard were her weekly talks with campers and counselors in the cabins or on Sunday mornings outdoors under the trees.

> We talked about the body and its functions and skills and talents and went into sex, especially the matter of babies, etc. (in younger groups— in older groups we discussed much more); we talked about our hopes and dreams, how hard a relationship can be between a girl and mother, sometimes girl and father, often girl and her sisters and brothers. We spoke of hate as though it is natural and to be dealt with by all of us; we talked of its getting twisted with love and how guilt springs, usually, out of such a twisting. We talked about envy, jealousy, the whys, etc., we talked about ideals and the difference in an ideal and a guilt feeling. . . . We talked about scape goats . . . about arrogance . . . and we went out into the world beyond our mountain and talked about war and peace, racial problems, poverty, class snobbery, conformity, acceptance of differences. . . . We didn't talk much about sin, here—although we knew all humans sin; and we didn't talk a great deal about "right" and "wrong" but we did talk about crude, stupid fun and imaginative fun; we talked about dull, insensitive relationships and tender, sensitive, honest ones.

Lillian's objective was to help the girls develop not only physically, but emotionally and intellectually. A reporter from the New York *Herald Tribune* who visited Laurel Falls in 1944 noted that at the camp nothing was considered right or wrong but rather babyish or grown-up, and that the girls were encouraged to be sympathetic and tolerant. Apparently race relations was a frequent topic at those weekly talks. The *Tribune* reporter described Lillian leading the campers in one such discussion and observed that "when they reacted violently against the people they thought were subjugating the Negroes, Miss Smith showed them that violence and intolerance toward the oppressors was not the answer. It is her belief that the South cannot change until the people in the South grow." As part of her effort to instill racial tolerance, Lillian proposed having Negro campers, but the white girls' parents objected. However, black children and adults did visit and eat with the girls in the dining room, a small step toward integration in the years before World War II.[12]

In 1927 and 1928 Lillian spent the winter semester at Columbia University Teachers College, taking courses in psychology, education, and history. She also did some course work in public school music that involved teaching three times a week in a Harlem school near 125th Street. Her pupils were Negroes, Jews, and Italians, nearly all very poor, many first generation immigrants. It was her first experience teaching Negro children, and though she found the ghetto children difficult to interest and control, she learned from the challenge. Her supervisor was "a fine, charming Negro man." She remembered that when other southern girls asked "How can you do it?" she merely laughed in response.

As in Baltimore, Lillian lived almost at subsistence level while studying at Columbia. She and a counselor from Laurel Falls shared a small room with housekeeping privileges. Having little money to spend, they did not see much of New York City. They went to a few shows and concerts, attended lectures at Columbia, and enjoyed bus rides up and down Fifth Avenue. Occasionally they splurged and took in a special sight, but only after counting out enough money to get home on the subway. They scrimped on food, often spending only thirty cents a day. Once when a lady spilled some potatoes while crossing the street, the two dashed into the traffic to scoop them up, taking their supper home in their pockets. Lillian was working part time for a mathematician, helping him to write an article on the metric system for the *Encyclopaedia Britannica*. On the days when Dr. Smith paid her, she and her roommate "had one Grand Meal—then starved the rest of the time."

In June, 1928, Lillian bought Laurel Falls Camp from her family, hoping that by managing the finances herself she might eventually be able to make a small profit. A week and a half after the papers were signed, the dam to the camp lake broke as a result of several days of heavy rain. The lake disappeared as a torrent of water roared down the valley. Lillian was frightened, half sick, worried about the loss of swimming and canoeing activities at the camp as well as the possibility of lawsuits for damaged fields and houses. Nevertheless, she kept her fears to herself and worked through the night with the Clayton people and state police handling the disaster. The following day her father praised her for the way she had responded. He told her that she was "a very brave girl and full of iron," and said that he had never been sure she could take such a hard blow, but now he was. His praise and her own efforts as the new owner in dealing with the disaster proved meaningful to Lillian. She not only survived the disaster but came out of it with "a sense of strength and confidence I had never had in myself before."

Two years later Calvin Smith died of cancer. Lillian and her father had grown very close since her return to Old Screamer. While she was taking over the direction of the camp, he had become a good and loyal friend who shared long mountain walks with her and praised her successes and forgave her mistakes. His death hurt her deeply, and she still had her mother to look after. Even though she was finding some satisfaction in managing Laurel Falls, she remained bitter about having to come home to help her parents. "I resented it even as I wanted to help, because I still had dreams about my music." She tried to realize something of those dreams through the music programs at the camp, but gradually she put them aside and turned her creative impulse toward writing. She was led in this direction partly by her experience writing for the camp: the catalog, which became more interesting and different every year, letters to prospective campers and their parents and to former campers, and the little newspaper called the *Laurel Leaf*. As she became aware that her craftsmanship was improving, she became intrigued with the idea of writing seriously. In 1930 she began in earnest, encouraged by Paula Snelling, a high school math teacher from Macon who was a counselor at Laurel Falls. The two women had become good friends as a result of a shared interest in literature, and when Lillian began writing, slowly and awkwardly at first, she found an honest, intelligent, receptive critic in Paula. She also got advice and criticism for about a year from a woman who had advertised as an editor-critic in the *Saturday Review.*

In the beginning the choice of an appropriate subject matter eluded her. She felt comfortable writing about the camp, but could not decide on a topic for serious writing. She attempted a story about a small Negro community but abandoned it before it was half finished. Finally, she decided that she would have to write about her own personal life or people she had known well, however much she might disguise them. She embarked on a novel based on her experiences in China, originally entitled "Walls," later "And the Waters Flow On." It was the story of six white women missionaries from the southern United States and their relationships with the Chinese girls who were their students. Lillian described it as "soft, warm, passionate, vivid, naked, honest, lyrical," and declared that "it scared the publishers to death." When two of them rejected it, she laid it aside hoping to publish it later. Her second novel, "Tom Harris and Family," was a rambling family chronicle that she decided was not good enough to publish, so it too was put aside. She also wrote three autobiographical novellas, but did not attempt to publish them because she thought that members of her family might be hurt by her portrayal of them. Significantly, in describing these five manuscripts, all of which were burned in the fire that destroyed much of her home in 1955, Lillian emphasized how shocking they were, even to her—which was one reason she hesitated publishing them—and implied that they were personal statements about herself and her experiences. She said that when she laid the China novel aside, she knew she "might never write so personal, so terribly honest a book again." Her first published novel, *Strange Fruit,* shocked some readers, but it did not offer the revelation of self that the earlier manuscripts apparently did. Nor did *One Hour,* her second published novel. However, from the fleeting descriptions she offered of "Julia," the novel she was working on when she died and which had grown out of one of the novellas, it would appear that in writing it she was returning to the autobiographical approach that characterized her early work.

Lillian wrote the first two novels and the novellas during the winters of 1930 to 1935 while living in Macon with Paula Snelling. She spent some of her time there handling camp business, but devoted most of it to reading, studying, thinking, and, above all, writing. She became engrossed in contemporary literature—including Hemingway who taught her something about talk in a novel; Faulkner, whom she did not like; and Virginia Woolf, whom she liked "only temperately" at the time. To help her with the craft of writing she read "the great novelists (especially the Russians)" and Proust and Joyce. She "analyzed, studied, brooded over how certain writers did certain things." She also joined a book club and, a little later, the Macon Writers Club. Neither organization taught her much about writing (though she did discover that she could talk as easily and entertainingly to adults as to children), but both provided the social life she felt she needed. She thought she was "becoming too much of a hermit."

The problem was that writing required one to be something of a recluse. Lillian recognized the necessity of working regularly, according to a strict schedule. Usually she was able to work uninterruptedly five or six hours a day during the time Paula was teaching. Gradually she developed her own procedure. She would "let things flow out crudely, roughly in order to get the passion and the deeper things that imagination (or mythic mind) will throw out if you open up wide." Then she would let her "critical mind take over to polish, question, etc." She rewrote extensively, even compulsively. Sometimes she found she had ruined the original by polishing too much. She said she "finally learned never to throw away anything until a book, or a piece was finished. After version #7, when maybe I had ruined it I could then go back to version #3 which was more likely to be right and use it."

The five winters in Macon were enormously productive and satisfying to Lillian. She was beginning to think of herself as a professional writer. She had also apparently worked through some personal problems. During the semester at Columbia she had begun an intensive study of psychology and psychoanalysis. Over the next decade she read all of Freud, as well as works by Sándor Ferenczi, Otto Rank, Carl Jung, Alfred Adler, and Karl Menninger. She said later that although she did not agree completely with Freud, his "books were a raft that I hopped on and escaped from the whirlpools by clinging to." Freudianism, she explained, "helped me to come to grips with many of my false guilt feelings, and with my Puritanic upbringing; it also helped me to loosen this awesome bond to my family which made me feel I must always be the 'Martha' in every situation, although I longed to get away from family."[13]

Like many of her generation, Lillian discovered in Freudian psychology a means of liberating herself from the fears and anxiety instilled during childhood. She had already, at age fifteen or sixteen, rebelled against her Methodist training; by the time she went to China she had become an agnostic. She found it less easy to throw off feelings of obligation and resentment toward her family. She had turned down a full scholarship for a second year at Piedmont College because she felt she should stay home to help her parents. Then, nine years later, in 1925, she had come back to Clayton from China to help them run Laurel Falls Camp. In the fall of that same year, when her older brother's wife died, she gave up a position teaching music and moved to Fort Pierce, Florida, to take care of his two-and-a-half-year-old daughter. When he made the request, she somehow felt she must say yes. But, she remembered, "I was stunned at the idea—I felt so young— how could I give up so much to do this!" Pressured first to help her parents and now her brother, she no longer felt her life was her own. "I was just carrying out other people's directives." She spent two winters in Fort Pierce, and although initially she resented having to forego her own plans, ultimately she found some satisfaction in helping her brother. After a sister-in-law took over the care of her niece, insisting that Lillian was too young and too radical to look after her properly, Lillian went to work for her brother, who was the city manager, and learned a good deal about city politics.

After her father died in 1930, Lillian felt she owed her first duty to her mother, despite the fact that from childhood her feelings toward her mother had been ambivalent. In 1935, when Mrs. Smith suffered a severe heart attack and the doctors offered little hope for her recovery, Lillian reluctantly gave up winter residence in Macon, where she had been pursuing a literary career, and moved permanently to the mountain. There she cared for her mother during the last three years of Mrs. Smith's life. Not only did she resent the move to Clayton, where she felt isolated and confined, but her mother's illness was painful to watch. Besides being an invalid, she was often mentally disturbed. Lillian's conflicting feelings toward her mother, and resulting guilt, increased. She remembered that although I did everything I could think of, rubbed her back each day, made cheery and real talk with her, told her the news, kept the radio going for her (when she wanted it) and even let her read the Bible to me now and then, still I suspect poor Mother felt my inner reluctance to live the life I was having to live. . . . my writing she was cautiously interested in (for my sake) yet she resented or was jealous of my interests. . . . My mind was shocking to her; my words sometimes stunned her sensibilities when I was even unaware that I was being shocking; I was naturally so honest and candid; and she had grown more Puritanic as the years passed and her mental condition had become so depressive and guilt-ridden. . . . my feelings toward Mother were mainly those of irritation and impatience and a compulsion to speak out my opinions about life, sex, etc. etc. instead of keeping them to myself (as Esther did). Es smoked more than I did; but she hid it; I felt it almost impossible to hide things from Mother. . . . Yet, she depended upon me; and nobody's judgment (in her opinion) was as good as mine; if I said it, OK; if others said it she might question them. When in pain or very ill she always wanted me near her not Esther; I could soothe her and dissipate her bodily anxieties. . . . But her death, although probably unconsciously or even half consciously looked forward to by me—as a release—was a shock and a dreadful hurt. Especially, of course, because of my ambivalence; I did more for her than anyone in the world did; yet I felt cramped and imprisoned and I imagine she at least guessed it.

Lillian later said she wished she had known how to work out her relationship with her mother, that she had always wished it could have been different. She had developed a close relationship with her father during their last ten years together, but, she said, "Mother always eluded me, somehow."

While directing the camp, nursing her mother, and working at writing, Lillian became aware of that deep split in her nature which she later described as a split between "Martha" and "Mary." The Martha side was her conscience that commanded her to give up her own freedom and interests to help her family. Lillian resented its demands, and felt guilty because of her resentment, but at the same time felt compelled to obey. She thought sometimes her conscience was self-destructive, as when it forced her to abandon creative or intellectual activities. The Mary side of her nature represented self-indulgence and freedom. It served as a standing rebuke to her overzealous conscience. Thus her music and, even more, her writing became a means of obtaining the freedom and pleasure the Martha side denied her. Lillian wrote that in the 1920s and 1930s, when she felt isolated and imprisoned, "this pressure of walls on me made me find a way out, a kind of 'bursting out' by means of my writing."

The Mary/Martha split continued to shape her life. Her childhood sensibilities—her empathy and feelings of rejection, her awareness of contradictions—may explain her later involvement in civil rights, but the Mary/Martha split, which represented an internal rather than an external contradiction, exerted even more influence not only on her attitude toward race and segregation but on the greater part of her life and thought. Lillian herself declared that much of her writing was an expression of what she called her fragmented life.[14] At the same time her writing was also part of a lifelong effort to reconcile the two sides of her nature. She saw writing as a way of helping people and thereby satisfying the demands of her conscience, but also as a way of indulging her creative impulses. *South Today,* the magazine she founded in 1935, and *Strange Fruit,* published in 1944, were the first of many attempts to eliminate the inner tension between conscience and creativity.

# II Editing *South Today*

My ideas about the South are purely existential ones: that is they became mine because of how I have experienced the South and its traumas and its exalting experiences, and lovable moments.

The year 1935 was "a mean bad year." Lillian had moved to Clayton to nurse her mother. A few months later, in the summer, Paula had a nearly fatal accident on a horse. Unable to return to Macon to teach, she stayed the following winter with Lillian and her mother on Old Screamer. "It was a terrible time," Lillian remembered. Paula gradually recovered from the trauma of her accident, but she and Lillian were almost overwhelmed by the difficulty of caring for Mrs. Smith. "We sometimes stared at each other, wondering how two lives which had seemed promising because each woman had a mind and lots of spirit, could now begin to peter out to zero." One day Lillian said, "Let's start a magazine. Don't say how; just tell me if you'd like it." Paula "swallowed hard" and said yes. They had only enough money to send out one hundred announcements of the magazine to friends. Twenty-four subscribed by return mail, and the two women were in business. What started out as a project to help them maintain their sanity during a difficult time lasted ten years and ultimately attained a circulation of nearly ten thousand.[1]

They called the magazine *Pseudopodia*. (In the spring of 1937 they changed the name to *North Georgia Review* and in the spring of 1942 to *South Today*.) The first number, published in the spring of 1936, listed Paula as editor and Lillian as associate editor. However, by the time

22

they issued the second number it was clear that Lillian was thinking up most of the ideas for the magazine and editing a major portion of it (besides financing it out of money earned from Laurel Falls); therefore, they decided to list themselves as coeditors. Their avowed purpose in founding the magazine was to provide an outlet for writers who had not been published by the large circulation magazines, though they also solicited contributions from those who had already attained national recognition. They were explicit about their intention to concern themselves mainly with the South, in particular "with whatever seems to us artistic, vital, significant which is being done by writers who have their cultural roots here whatever their present locale and interests may be, and by those from no matter where who have been grafted to us and are now bearing fruit nourished by our soil."[2]

*Pseudopodia* was not the first little magazine founded in the South. In the early 1920s, a number of journals trumpeted the beginning of what would later be called the Southern Renaissance. Three of the most significant were the *Double Dealer*, published in New Orleans; the *Reviewer*, printed in Richmond; and the *Fugitive*, devoted to poetry, founded in Nashville. In 1935, a year before Lillian and Paula started their magazine, Robert Penn Warren and Cleanth Brooks founded the *Southern Review* at Louisiana State University.[3] Like these four journals, *Pseudopodia* sought to encourage southern writers and raise literary standards in the South. However, *Pseudopodia* adhered more strictly to a regional perspective than the other journals.

Lillian wrote a regular column for *Pseudopodia* entitled "Dope with Lime" (referring to Coca-Cola, popularly called "dope" and sometimes spiked with lime juice to cut the sweet taste). She also published a number of fictional pieces in it, including excerpts from her first two novels and, in the winter of 1940–1941, from *Strange Fruit,* the novel she was working on while editing the magazine. Although Paula and outside contributors did most of the book reviews, Lillian occasionally expressed her own literary views in her column or in book reviews. In the first issue of the magazine, both she and Paula had agreed in condemning "that sterile fetishism of the Old South which has so long gripped our section." In a later issue Lillian took special delight in castigating southern writers for allowing themselves to become mired in some of the deep ruts of southern fiction. She was particularly scornful of two groups, the U.W.C., or United Writers of the Confederacy, who, she declared, "should . . . be plowed down under with the cotton," and the Manicurists who worked in "the Beauty Shop of Old Southern Culture." The latter were readily recognizable "among some well known Agrarians" and even more so among "the old Fugitive group."[4]

She reserved her most trenchant comments for the Dixie Dirt Dobbers, "the writers who are on the prowl for the filth of southern life, gathering their dirt where they may—and that is everywhere—plastering it on, going out for more, dobbing it, until there appears by virtue of sheer bulk, a book." Probably she was more critical of the Dirt Dobbers than the U.W.C. and the Manicurists because they had failed to realize their potential. They had abandoned the sterile fetishism and escapism that had so long characterized southern fiction only to fall into their own special rut and become mesmerized by one facet of southern life to the exclusion of all others. In criticizing them Lillian was no doubt thinking of Erskine Caldwell among others. Although she praised his writing skill and humor (despite its "strong chitlin' flavor"), she questioned whether "too much unconsidered fault-finding" was the best approach. Caldwell was trying to reform Georgia, but was going about it in the wrong way—trying to wean her from the sugar-tit by giving her an asafetida bag. "The stench is pretty awful for a little nose that has been used only to Cape Jasmine and magnolias," Lillian observed.[5]

Of all the groups that inhabited the southern literary landscape, only the Pips offered any promise. They were "the writers who have broken through restrictive mind-sets (and heart-sets), who have sloughed off racial and class and religious taboos, who give life a straight stare in the face." They were the only ones viewing the South honestly and realistically, but even they still had a way to go, for "they are a little wobbled from their effort at renascence and stagger around for the rest of their lives with feathers not quite dry." Lillian hoped they would be able to muster "enough vitality to survive the trauma of second birth and mature into full-feathered artistry."[6]

In exhorting southern writers to take an honest, realistic view of their region—to look at the South head on, without blinking—Lillian especially emphasized truthful treatment of the Negro. In 1937, as part of its effort to encourage and publish southern writers, the *North*

*Georgia Review* sponsored a literary contest. Commenting on the manuscripts she and Paula had received, Lillian was both appalled and amused at the "recrudescence of interest in Mammy stories, in dear old Uncle Ned and Uncle this-and-that, in little pickaninnies who sacrifice their lives (with what seems to us a lamentable lack of judgment) in an effort to save the life of their dear white Boss or their dear white Boss's child." She deplored the tendency of southern writers to focus on the mannerisms of Negroes instead of pondering "the secrets of their hearts and minds." Southern writers should "stop thinking of the Negro as a minstrel, a Laughing Man, a pathetic pet, a quaint objet d'art and begin considering him as a human being."[7] Significantly, that was exactly what Lillian would claim she had done a few years later in *Strange Fruit.*

Lillian's concern for honest, truthful treatment of the Negro and of the South as a whole was as much a product of her social conscience as of her literary viewpoint. She believed literature had a definite role to play in helping the South to solve its racial and economic problems. This was another point on which she was at odds with the Fugitive-Agrarians. Not only did she fault their nostalgic and escapist view of the Old South; she also disagreed with their critical view (that came to be known as the New Criticism) which located the fundamental value of a literary work in the work itself rather than in any ulterior social or ethical purpose. Lillian contended that fiction, especially novels, could and should assist southerners in facing up to the "personal, subjective, psychological implications" of human relationships. She was not unaware of the difficulties inherent in that position. The novelist who dealt with social problems was always in danger of slipping into one of those ruts that traversed the southern literary landscape—the one inhabited by the "Sandwich Men" who "trudge[d] up and down the back streets of the South constricting human nature to fit the dimensions of a Cause." It was a danger Lillian herself was confronting during the writing of *Strange Fruit;* in a couple of pieces for the magazine she volunteered some thoughts on ways of avoiding it. First, the novelist should see to it that even though he is writing propaganda "the propaganda is . . . obscured by the poet and artist." She complimented Fielding Burke for doing that in what she called two of the best of the proletarian novels of the 1930s. Second, the novelist should see to it that his characters are more than vessels holding or promoting a philosophy. They must be "real, alive people." Finally, the novelist should avoid focusing on abstractions or ideas "instead of flesh and blood and feeling." In Lillian's view the novel was not a form that could "successfully be lifted from the level of the concrete and emotional to the abstract and rational." It was the function of the novel "to arrive at truth by the more circuitous path of nerves and glands, by tapping the reader's unconscious memories, rather than by the more direct route of intellection."[8]

Lillian and Paula originally intended *Pseudopodia* to be a literary magazine that would publish and review southern writing, but they soon enlarged its scope to take in the whole of southern culture. When they changed the title to *North Georgia Review* in the spring of 1937, they added the subtitle, *A Magazine of the Southern Regions*. The magazine thus became part of what George Tindall has called the "literature of social exploration and descriptive journalism" that constituted the southern expression of a nationwide rediscovery of American culture. Lillian later explained the enlarged scope of the magazine as a response to the prompting of her conscience—the Martha side of her nature. As she and Paula worked on it, she recalled:

> Martha stepped in and said, pushing my conscience hard, "While you are doing this, you must face up to all the implications of what this southern way of life is. You must do something to change things." . . . I sighed. "Do I always have to stop my dreaming and creating to mop up messes? I've done the home messes, do I now have to do the South's dirty work?" Martha was adamant. The old conscience ached and pained and pushed me and I saw the light. Yes, I had to help. I could still create but I also had to help. . . . Not by organization work which I have rarely spent any time at, but maybe by giving insight, maybe by trying to "see the whole tree"—maybe I could show the roots now hidden by the old southern myths and half-lies and rationalizations and defenses. Maybe I'd better tear that segregating ground away so we all could see "the whole southern tree."[9]

The enlarged scope of the magazine was an outgrowth of several things. As Lillian's statement suggests, it was partly an effort to confront, understand, and perhaps eliminate the contradictions and ambiguities of southern culture that had troubled her as a child. It was also an outgrowth of her literary concerns. As a southerner and a writer she objected to the way other southern writers depicted the South. The mythical Old South of the Fugitive-Agrarians and Margaret Mitchell, Erskine Caldwell's benighted South, even William Faulkner's Yoknapatawpha seemed unauthentic. Determined to portray "the real South on all its many levels," she began to investigate the region and its culture.[10]

Like Jonathan Daniels and other southern journalists of the 1930s, she embarked on a program of discovering the South, by reading books and articles on it, traveling through all the southern states, talking with and getting to know a broad range of southerners. Exploring the South became an adventure, and she conveyed the excitement of her discoveries in the sketches and articles she published in her magazine.

She commenced her reading program on the South with all the books she could find by American Negroes, about 130 in all. They included such works as E. Franklin Frazier's *The Negro Family in the United States*, Horace Mann Bond's *Negro Education in Alabama*, and W. E. B. Du Bois' *Souls of Black Folk* and *Black Folk Then and Now*, all of which she recommended to readers of the *Review*.[11] She then branched out to consider other aspects of southern culture—history, economics, sociology—all the while continuing to read southern fiction and poetry.

As Richard King has noted, Lillian was one of a small number of southerners in the 1930s who questioned the conventional historical account of the Civil War and Reconstruction. In a review of four books on that period she criticized James G. Randall, Carl Russell Fish, and Paul Buck for writing from the viewpoint of the "better" white people in the North and South. She contended that Randall's unconscious bias led him to portray the abolitionists as fanatics, to minimize the evils of slavery, and, most important, to ignore the rights of the Negro and his role in Reconstruction. Fish and Buck were too conciliatory toward the whites of both sections, and she guessed no intelligent Negro would share Buck's enthusiasm for reunion. "What Negro can ever forget that one decade of this era of good feeling which produces Mr. Buck's lyricism also produced 1,035 lynchings of black men?" she asked. Like most white Americans the three historians were "color blind . . . from gazing too long and too unblinkingly at the garish light of White Superiority" and consequently unable to "see the black man, still with his hat in hand, waiting for his long over-due recognition." The fourth historian, James Allen, granted the Negro the recognition he deserved, though Lillian judged his treatment of Reconstruction less understanding than Du Bois'. Allen's Marxian viewpoint made her uncomfortable, and she thought he tended to find in Reconstruction what he wanted to find—but then so did the other three historians, except that they operated according to a "more conservative bent." Besides, Lillian noted approvingly, after two chapters Allen forgot his dialectics and became absorbed in "the drama of the Negro as a human being." Unlike the other three, his book focused attention, "as it should be focused, on the four million who were freed for one brief ecstatic moment only to feel again the old shackles snap back against their flesh."[12]

In the fields of economics and sociology Lillian praised Howard Odum's *Southern Regions of the United States*. It promised to supplant "vague intuitions" about the South and its problems with "detailed and comprehensive facts concerning our immediate, multiple-faceted and paradoxical dilemma interpreted against historical backgrounds." She was particularly struck by some of the facts garnered from the volume: The South was in the lowest quartile of the nation in terms of taxable income, yet "saddled with a dichotomous form of education" with more Negro students than there were white children in the Northwest, Far West, New England, or the Middle West. The South had a higher illiteracy rate than any other region, yet spent less money on schools. It had "more churches, more church members proportionately than any other region of the U.S., also more homicides, more lynchings, more crime." Lillian also lauded the University of North Carolina Press for publishing many of the studies produced by Odum's research institute on such subjects as race, farm tenancy, social-industrial relations, and public welfare. But she reserved her highest praise for John Dollard's *Caste and Class in a Southern Town*. He was "one of those rare sociologists who have been trained in the methods of psychoanalysis," she wrote. She thought his work was enriched by his Freudian viewpoint.[13] Her preference for Dollard is not surprising. Her wide reading in psychoanalysis inclined her to approach the South much as he did, from a psychoanalytical rather than a purely sociological or economic point of view.

When she began the magazine, Lillian had already done some traveling in the South as manager of Laurel Falls, and she continued this activity. Each spring for the twenty-five years she operated the camp she traveled from town to town in Georgia and Florida selecting campers and counselors. While her visits took her into hundreds of southern homes, they were mainly those of middle- or upper-class whites. Baltimore had provided her with a glimpse of another side of southern culture, but Lillian realized that she and Paula did not know the real South. In 1939 and 1940, they applied for and received fellowships from the Rosenwald Fund that enabled them to investigate the region. Lillian said they applied for the fellowships because they wanted to see the South that their relatively sheltered, well-to-do upbringing had prevented them from seeing. "Not because we were sociologists which of course we weren't . . . but because we were human, full of curiosity and concern, and wanted to see the 'real South' which the Agrarians and the Southern Review apparently knew nothing about. That was our wild and revolutionary desire—and the Rosenwald Fund, bless them, let us do it." During their two years of traveling, the two women visited places they had never seen and talked with people they had never encountered before. They attended sharecroppers' and miners' union meetings, visited schools and colleges (both Negro and white), mental hospitals, orphanages, homes for delinquent children, and the federal penitentiary in Atlanta. They talked with big planters and industrialists, with social workers and judges, with New Dealers working for the Farm Security Administration, the Tennessee Valley Authority, and the Works Progress Administration. They spent a month at the University of North Carolina in Chapel Hill, where they talked with English and history professors, attended several of Howard Odum's seminars, and renewed their friendship with William Couch of the University of North Carolina Press. Whereas earlier in the decade writing had offered Lillian a way to break out of the isolation and confinement of Clayton, now traveling through the South helped her to do so. She said that during her travels as a Rosenwald fellow, "I broke every barrier I could in the South to try to see 'things as they are.'" In exploring the South she consciously tried to broaden her experience and to break down some of the economic, social, and psychological walls that separated her from the people of the region.[14]

As editor of *Pseudopodia*, Lillian had corresponded with Negro contributors, but her travels provided her with her first opportunity to meet and talk face to face with educated Negroes. Then when she and Paula served on the Rosenwald Scholarship Committee in 1942, 1943, and 1944, she visited a number of Negro colleges and universities to talk with faculty members and to interview students. Sometimes she and Paula stayed in the president's home and were treated with "lavish hospitality." Other times, though their hosts were friendly enough, they did not offer meals. She and Paula "were never sure whether they dared not feed us (if it was a state supported college) or whether, because whites ordinarily did not eat with Negroes at that time, they were 'getting a nice revenge'—or what. But there were times when we went all day from breakfast on without food being offered us on a Negro campus; and once or twice we actually asked for a sandwich feeling unable to continue our strenuous walking and interviewing without a few calories."[15]

Fascinated by the different personalities and dialects she encountered during her travels, Lillian sought to capture them in sketches published in the winter of 1939–1940 under the title "So You're Seeing the South." She recorded conversations with a wide range of individuals. There was the truck driver who claimed to know every inch of the South: "Lady—you couldn't think up a question bout the South I couldn't answer fore it was out of your mouth." There was the old man sitting in the sun who remembered the "ten per cent, twelve, sometimes twenty per cent interest you had to pay the banker . . . how you hated him for it, hated him because he made you push your tenants hard as he pushed you, hard as somebody was pushing him . . . hated them cause you knew you sinned against them . . . feared them sometimes because you knew there was nobody neath em to push down hard on to ease the hate inside *them*." There was the white woman who explained why there was not a single union in the county: "Folks wouldn't stand for unions here. See we couldn't. Minute you let niggers start thinking they're running things . . . it'd be nothing but bad trouble." And there was the Negro preacher who called upon God to "break deh hearts" and "give um tears. . . . Don let um hush oh Gawd until dey feels deh sins. . . . When deh hearts is broke Gawd, tek yo white chile up. Tell im hush his frettin. . . . Tell im folks jes has tuh learn tuh treat his black brudder like a real fambly what belong tuh one anudder."[16]

In the fall of 1939, as part of their investigation of the real South, Lillian and Paula sponsored a contest for their readers, offering $250 for the best set of answers to one hundred questions about various aspects of southern culture. In the winter of 1941 they published an eighty-five-page supplement entitled "Across the South Today" in which they answered the questions themselves, drawing on the voluminous reader response. They were not content with mere description; they also criticized and advocated reform. They pointed, for example, to the inadequacy of mental health and penal institutions in the South. They also noted the ambivalent character of southern religion, which served at its worst as "a strong support of an exploitative status quo with no spiritual content" and at its best as "a means of achieving various ameliorations of society's surface ills and of giving mystical comfort to those who can take it." They were particularly encouraged by the emergence of a group of young southern preachers, mostly Baptist, Congregationalist, and Presbyterian, who were "felling by deed and word . . . soil erosion and waste, ignorance and disease, racial hate, starvation, apathy, unemployment."[17]

Lillian and Paula had visited union meetings and talked with organizers during their travels through the South. Now in the supplement they noted that though "the union label is not yet a badge of honor in the South," unions had begun to grow in the region. Of all the labor groups organizing in the South, they praised the Southern Tenant Farmers Union, the Textile Workers Union of America, and the United Mine Workers for having the greatest potential for raising the economic level of workers. All three were working where the most poverty, ignorance, ill health, and unemployment existed. The editors lamented the fact that unions encountered opposition not only from the leaders of industry and agriculture, but from "the uninformed public who, in the South, identifies itself with the dominant class, regardless of its actual ties."[18]

"Across the South Today" also featured a discussion of army camps. The editors noted that nearly all the camps set up for Negroes were in the South because, they speculated, white southerners did not want blacks to learn any "northern tricks" while defending democracy. Ironically, the camps only intensified racial conflict in the South. Whites resented the concentrations of large numbers of Negroes, while blacks resented the inequitable treatment they received. The editors thought that decent whites should not find it difficult "to understand why Negroes who are required by the government to kill and be killed in its defense are growing more sensitive to the undemocratic and bitterly cruel discriminations practiced against them, not only in civilian life but in the defense regime." They observed that "'For the duration' has been a long time already for Negroes"; they wondered, "how much longer can they endure."[19]

In the late 1930s, though they continued to focus mainly on the South, Lillian and Paula devoted increasing space in the magazine to the conflict in Europe. Lillian apparently did not consider herself an isolationist, but the views she expressed placed her in the ranks of those generally regarded as such. Indeed, on several occasions she commended articles in two prominent isolationist journals, the *Nation* and the *New Republic*, and singled out for special praise John T. Flynn, a columnist for the *New Republic* who was strongly isolationist. Unlike many isolationists, she did not oppose United States aid or intervention out of concern that it would lead to entanglement in world affairs; in fact, she argued that only by staying out of the conflict would the United States be in a position to use its influence and power to promote peace.[20] Her opposition derived first of all from a deeply felt abhorrence of war and second from a fear that intervention abroad would distract Americans, and especially southerners, from the urgent business of social reform at home.

Even before war broke out in Europe, Lillian worried that the American people were finding it difficult to remain detached from what was going on there. After the German invasion of Poland, she became even more fearful. She named the pressure groups and forces that were steamrollering the United States toward intervention: munitions makers, American imperialists, Allied propaganda, unemployment and poverty, big business, and "German hunger and madness." With a few exceptions, journalists were heightening the panic with their "asinine brays and paranoiac screams." Lillian seems to have thought that if only the American people were given a chance to think clearly about intervention and related questions, they would decide against it. Perhaps that is one reason she and Paula sponsored a number of essay contests in the magazine inviting readers to discuss such matters as the causes of war, the compatibility of the draft and democracy, the desirability of rearmament and military intervention and their likely result. Although they did not underestimate the power of the steam rollers, the response to the contests persuaded them that people in the United States were thinking seriously and that if they did decide to become involved in another world war, "blinders will not this time be so universally a part of the regulation uniform as they have been in the past."[21]

Of all the battle cries and slogans spawned by the European conflict, Lillian was most outraged by the one that urged United States intervention to save the democratic way of life—its own as well as that of the Allies. It reminded her of its "death-echo, 'Make the world safe for democracy.'" She dismissed both democracy and fascism as war cries, and she refused to view the conflict between the Allies and the Axis powers as a moral struggle between good and evil. While she condemned German aggression and anti-Semitism, she also insisted that "every people, including Germans, have virtues." And while she praised the courage shown by the British while under siege, she refused to close her eyes to the depredations visited upon China and India by British imperialism. Like many isolationists she was inclined to dismiss the conflict in Europe as one more round of its "eternal bickering" which bore little or no relation to the interests of the United States.[22]

Lillian's main objection to intervention was that it would distract Americans from the business of extending democracy at home. British propagandists, along with American journalists and government officials, were whipping the people into a mood of fear and hatred. But it was a hatred directed against the wrong enemies, against "a demonology composed of alien races and nations and political systems." Americans needed to learn to distinguish between authentic demons and fake ones. "Real demons never assume human form," she declared; and "real demons play no favorites among races or nations or classes but are as apt to torment one as another and are the common enemies of all mankind." The real enemies of mankind were poverty, greed, ignorance, intolerance, and cruelty, and as for Americans, "the authentic enemies which threaten us most are those within us and our own country." They were not fifth columnists or Nazis, but "soil erosion and unemployment, the poll tax and illiteracy, the aborted citizenship of the Negro and the undernourishment of little children, restricted speech and bad housing, low wages, and regimentation of thoughts and feelings, and . . . greed and hate." Besides, for Americans to talk of saving democracy abroad when they had not realized it in their own country was sheer hypocrisy. She attacked the "foreign-missionary zeal" of the interventionists in an editorial entitled "'Mr. Lafayette, Heah We Is—'" which appeared in the *North Georgia Review* in the spring of 1939. She directed it against "the proselyters of the Democratic Religion who are so anxious for us to give your bodies and our souls to spread the gospel in heathen Europe." Lillian said she was reluctant to distract them from their lofty objective or to shatter their illusions by "muttering about the need for home work." So she suggested that "we send our grimy home work to Europe."

> We suggest that we contribute toward the foreign mission fund—little mite boxes as it were—all the lives that are a blotch on our fair democracy, all the human beings who persist in casting their shadows on our gleaming purity: the sharecroppers, the unemployed, the slum-dwellers, the undernourished, and the Negroes. That would be a fair-sized "bit." And it should not be difficult to persuade them (remembering how readily propaganda turns all tricks), to sacrifice themselves in order to make democracy safe for the rest of us. . . . We'd send the Negroes as our shock troops, since they have the longest and most persistent record of being splotches. They could go, calling out in their deep mellow voices: "Mister Lafayette, heah we come! Leastways, all of us cept the 5,000 or so who was lynched a while back. Mr. Lafayette, heah we is. They don't call us mister back home and they don't let us ride in their railroad cars or eat at their tables or sleep in their hotels or let us vote;—and they gives us what scraps are lef as to jobs and we knows to say 'thankee Boss.' And we take what's lef over in the way of schools and hospitals and houses and sewer systems and sech liddle things like that, and tips our hats. But we live in Gawd's country en that's a fact, en it's a fine place to live in ef yo knows yo place, and we knows our place, yeah Lawd! Now we'se come to lay down our lives for those Jews Mister Hitler's been pickin on. We hear tell he takes their property and their money and kicks them about and spits on 'em and burns their books. An' all that makes our democratic blood about boil over. Yas suh! For hit sho must be terrible to live in a country whar yo has yo money tuk (our ways a lot better cause we has no money to be tuk—jus a little furnish which is et up and gone fo yo can say scat) and it sho must be a awful sight to have yo books burned—hit's a lot better never to learn how to read and write like us, we'se tellin you. And to be spit at in the face!

That just shows the awful wickedness of that fascism business. Now in our country things are worked out mighty well, a sight better'n that. Theah's plenty of back streets to walk on in every town and back doors what yo can go in and out of. And theah's always the Quarters. Yo don need to scrouge up close to folks, close enough for 'em to spit at yo! You kin always step off the side-walk. And if worse comes to worst you kin run yo tail off and make it to the Swamp. Yeah Lawd . . . there ain't nothin so plumb democratic as a good cypress swamp. . . . Ef them Jews hada jes had a coupla cypress swamps it'd sho helped them get rid of fascism. Yeah man. . . ."

The editorial, one of Lillian's first attempts at the use of irony, was not entirely successful, for in comparing the lot of the Jews in Nazi Germany with that of Negroes in the United States, she not only displayed a certain insensitivity to the plight of the former, but assumed a somewhat patronizing attitude toward the latter. As she readily admitted, she had gotten carried away by her impatience with those "loud speakers" who "jibbered" about saving democracy. Nevertheless, the editorial indicated her deep feeling on the matter and how early she had begun to make a connection between the conflict in Europe and the reform of race relations in the United States.[23]

Consistent with her prewar opposition to intervention on the grounds that it would distract Americans from promoting reform at home, once the United States entered the war Lillian continued to insist that it could not afford to put off such reform until the fighting was over. Both the right and the might to win the war depended on "our allegiance to democratic goals and our adherence to democratic ways of reaching them," she wrote in an article in *South Today* in the spring of 1942. Now was the time to go beyond the formulation of democratic ideals to translate them into reality, not only in the lives of minority groups in the United States but in the needier nations and among the "darker races" of the world. By such action the United States would regain moral leadership and at the same time win the support of "our allies of other color whose aid is indispensable and cannot be purchased at a cheaper price." Specifically, she urged "as a strategic war measure," abolition of the poll tax, the white primary, discrimination in defense jobs, and segregation in the armed services, public buildings and conveyances, and public education.[24]

Lillian believed that she and her fellow southerners had a peculiar

obligation—which the war rendered more pressing—to point out and
help resolve the contradiction between democracy and racism in the
United States. "In a very special sense," she declared, "America's failures are the South's failures, American sins are southern sins. The obligation rests heavily upon southerners during this war to see that the
wages of our sins against democracy is not the death of democracy."
She was especially concerned, as she had been before the United States
entered the war, to expose the hypocrisy of southerners who talked of
fighting to save democracy when what they really sought was to pre-
serve the status quo. In "Portrait of the Deep South Speaking to
Negroes on Morale," a monologue in the form of a poem published in
the spring of 1942, the orator alternately cajoles and threatens the "colored folks" on the subject of unity.

> Niggers—this is war!
> Don't you know we're fighting to keep a world free
> (for those who now own it—my folks and me!)

Colored folks should stop their "fifth-column talk about wanting to
vote," their "defeatist talk about Jim Crow." Voice blaring, snapping his
red suspenders, the orator shouts,

> THIS IS WAR! COLORED FOLKS!
> WHERE'S YOUR UNITY!
> This fool equality
>    you keep whining about
>       equal votes
>          equal education
>             equal chance for jobs and pay
>                equal chance for children to
>                   play—
> these little things you call America's foundations
> don't you know they're interior *decorations?* [25]

Lillian's opinions on the war, both before and after the attack on
Pearl Harbor, set her apart from most white southerners. Her views
were more in agreement with those of black Americans. When World
War II began, many of them had taken an isolationist position, arguing
that blacks should focus their energies on the war at home against exploitation and discrimination. After 1941, blacks supported the United

States war effort, but they continued to protest racism. Lillian's position was similar to that of the Pittsburgh *Courier* and other black newspapers which mounted a "Double V" campaign to win "victory over our enemies at home and victory over our enemies on the battlefields abroad."[26]

Lillian's views of the South had also evolved to a point where she was distinctly at odds with most of the whites in the region. The young woman who started out in the mid-1930s as a critic of the southern literary scene had become an outspoken foe of much of the southern way of life. By the early 1940s, she was devoting more and more attention to what turned out to be a lifelong battle against racial discrimination and segregation.

# III Segregation

Segregation is spiritual lynching. The lynched and the lynchers are our own people, our own selves.

Lillian recalled that she "gradually waked up to the problem of segregation while writing Strange Fruit and while at camp talking over human problems with the children. And with South Today through which I met many Negroes and began to meet union workers and their leaders and to see different phases of our life. I read during those years a lot of southern history and social science."[1]

In addition to her experiences of the late 1930s, there were earlier ones that influenced her. While they did not cause her to reject segregation, they planted doubts in her mind that persisted long afterward. One such experience occurred when she was a child. Some of the Jasper clubwomen discovered a little white girl living with a Negro family that had recently moved to town. Interviews with members of the family, who became increasingly evasive under interrogation, merely deepened the white women's suspicions; eventually they took the child away and brought her to live with the Smiths. Julie shared Lillian's room, sat next to her at the table, wore her clothes, and played with her dolls. The two little girls quickly developed a deeply affectionate relationship. Then one day there was a telephone call from a Negro orphanage. All afternoon there was a flutter of activity at the Smith house as the clubwomen came and went. In the evening there was a hushed conversation between Lillian's parents. The next day Julie was taken back to her

38

family in the Negro section of town. Why, Lillian asked her mother, did Julie have to return to a family she hardly knew, when she liked the Smiths and they had plenty of room for her? Because, her mother said gently:

> "Julie is a little colored girl. She has to live in colored town." "But why? She lived here for three weeks." "She is a little colored girl," Mother repeated. "She's the same little girl she was yesterday," I remember saying to my mother, "and you said yourself Julie has nice manners. You said that," I persisted. "Yes," my mother said, "Julie is a nice child but she is colored. A colored child cannot live in our home." "She did live with us," I said, "and she is the same little girl she was yesterday. Can she come to see me? Spend the day?" "No." "I don't understand." "You're too young to understand," Mother said and turned away.[2]

Perhaps Lillian was too young to understand, but she was not too young to feel "the pain of separation" from her new friend or to identify with her shame and bewilderment. Moreover, seeing her parents do something she believed contradicted their teachings about Christianity and democracy caused her to doubt their integrity. She remembered feeling "a profound reluctance ever again to accept something simply because it was told me by my elders." Although she ultimately forgot the incident, the doubt and hurt it caused left a lasting effect on her personality. When she recalled the experience some thirty years later she saw it as symbolic of other buried experiences no longer accessible to her which had collected around that "faithless day" and sharpened her awareness of what she later called a conflict between conscience and culture. She went on practicing the racial customs of southern society as she had been taught to, and she continued to love and admire her parents. Yet they were now under a cloud of suspicion. Although it would be many years before she would admit it aloud, she knew that something was wrong. "Something was wrong with a world that tells you that love is good and people are important and then forces you to deny love and humiliate people."[3]

Lillian's three-year stay in China in the early 1920s enabled her to see in bold relief the system of white supremacy she had more or less taken for granted in the South. At first she was enchanted by the elegance and beauty of Chinese culture. Then she became aware of the color prejudice among the missionaries with whom she worked and even more among British and American business groups in China. She could not see why Westerners thought their culture superior to that of the Chinese. There were incidents, too, in China that exposed the arrogance and cruelty of colonialism and extraterritoriality. Those incidents burned in her memory. In Shanghai: "British policemen beating Chinese coolies on the streets for not hurrying, maybe, or breaching some very minor traffic rule . . . and the big tall cruel faced, handsome Sikhs—brought in from India—to police Chinese." In the same city: "a beggar woman was lying on the street, her breasts exposed, a starving child nuzzling at breasts that were shrunken; . . . others were showing their sores, all were whining, screaming, pushing—and I made the 'mistake' of giving one or two of them money and was almost crushed before two or three 'white foreigners' and Chinese police extricated me. I have never been so frightened: frightened not so much about my danger as at this first big confrontation with naked, hideous, obscenely exposed poverty." A summer in Mokanshan with her eldest sister and family: "everywhere one found white arrogance, white colonialism in all its manifestations, smoothed over by Christian talk—and poisoned by unChristian acts. Always, always, we British and Americans segregated the Chinese—even the Christian Chinese from our 'fun' etc. We prayed with them but we didn't play tennis or swim with them."[4]

Seeing the white race do "so many ugly things" in China disturbed Lillian and raised questions about segregation in the South. "Seeing it happen in China made me know how ugly the same thing is in Dixie," she recalled. "For the first time in my life I was ashamed of my white skin. I began almost to believe that 'whiteness' cast an evil spell over all that it came in contact with." Her experience in China also revived the long repressed doubts and suspicions acquired during childhood. But now, Lillian resolved, "I would not try to 'understand' for I knew any 'understanding' of this was only a silly lie I must not believe." Still, at the time it was easy to push the questions and doubts into the back of her mind, to succumb to the "surface wonder and beauty" of China. "It was very hard to keep one's eyes on the seething, stinking rottenness at the core of this loveliness." Moreover, in the 1920s, Lillian remembered, such questions and doubts belonged to a different order of thinking from the one that dominated her at the time. It was "the novelist in me that was stirred by China," she explained. When she began writing about China in the 1930s, she took as her subject matter not the issues raised by colonialism and racism, but the personal relations between the missionaries and their students at the Virginia School.[5]

Lillian began her assault on segregation privately, on her own, several years before she publicly denounced it. Perhaps the word *assault* is too strong, for it implies a conscious effort to overturn the system of segregation. Initially, Lillian seemed not so much determined to overturn the system as to go her own way, according to her own convictions, despite it. Thus she invited Negro children and adults to visit the Laurel Falls campers, while acquiescing in the parents' objections to Negro campers. When she was in New York attending Columbia University she taught in a Harlem school, enjoyed working with her black supervisor, and got along well with black students at the university. She did not protest racial discrimination or segregation. She thought it was enough that she was not prejudiced. "I was decent; I did not bother about the others." Later she and Paula decided, when they began publishing *Pseudopodia*, that they would review books by Negro writers, would have Negro contributors, and would call them Miss, Mrs., and Mr., something no other white southern newspaper or magazine had done up to that time. The two women also made a point of visiting black colleges and universities and talking with black students and faculty during their travels throughout the South. When they attended the Eighth Annual Southern Tenant Farmers Union Convention in Sheffield, Alabama, where state law required segregated seating, they sat on the side of the hall reserved for the black delegates; and they accompanied H. L. Mitchell, STFU secretary, to the banquet provided for the blacks by the Central Labor Union.[6]

Of all Lillian's private efforts to erase the color line, at least in her own life, the biracial gatherings on Old Screamer were probably the most significant. The gatherings grew out of the dinners and house parties she and Paula began holding in the mid-1930s. These social occasions served at least two purposes. In the beginning they offered the two women another opportunity to burst, if only temporarily, the bonds that confined them to Clayton. If they could not leave the mountain because of the camp and Mrs. Smith's illness, they could at least bring some part of the outside world to it. At first they invited contributors to the magazine. Then they began inviting interesting people in business, publishing, and politics throughout the South and occasionally from the North. By the late 1930s and early 1940s, the occasions had evolved into a significant part of their effort to get to know and understand the South and its people. Over the years hundreds of famous and not-so-famous persons of all races, religions, and political persuasions were entertained on Old Screamer. Lillian described the range of visitors in a Chicago *Defender* column in 1948: "White Supremacists, old-line Democrats, Wall Street Republicans, Socialists, Communists, Jews, Gentiles, Progressives, Negroes, whites, Chinese, Japanese, Koreans, Nisei, French, Germans, CIO and AFL labor leaders, union men and shirt-sleeve farmers, great writers and men who cannot read or write their name, rural and city people, sculptors and painters, dancers, garage mechanics, and even a few Bostonians!"[7]

Guests stayed in the camp cabins and in the mornings and afternoons enjoyed tennis, swimming, hiking, and horseback riding. In the evenings Lillian and Paula turned Laurel Falls into a rustic salon. They served drinks (bourbon and scotch) and dinner, then gathered everyone in the library for conversation that was always interesting, often controversial, sometimes amusing, occasionally brilliant. The occasions combined "simplicity with sophistication, hilarity with good manners"—and they were fun for hostesses and guests alike. Charles Bolté, chairman of the American Veterans Committee, who spent a weekend on Old Screamer in 1945, remembered that "one of the diversions . . . was the old Georgia custom of burying three chickens, naming them after your unfavorite persons, and then baking and eating them." He and the other guests decided, after a "ferocious argument," to name the chickens Cardinal Spellman, Bernard Baruch, and Morris Ernst.[8]

The first biracial gathering was held in the fall of 1936 when whites and blacks drove from Atlanta together for supper on the mountain. Other biracial gatherings, including some for college students, followed. One of the most memorable was a house party in September, 1942, for twelve white southern women and twelve black women from the South and North. Lillian wanted to do something different from the usual women's biracial conferences and conventions. Making speeches to each other, she explained in her letter of introduction, was not conducive to the development of personal relationships between white and black women, which was her main objective. She thought the opportunity to engage in informal activities in the natural setting of the camp might enable the women to form "really warm and personal friendships." It would be a first step toward ending racial injustice. "All the movements in the world, all the laws, the drives, the edicts will never do what personal relationships can do—and must do," she wrote. Her idea proved to be a success, as she recalled some years later.

> They were here four days; we went swimming, we played tennis, we talked our heads off, some just roamed around on the mountain; we had as usual marvelous food. Our cook, an old-fashioned Negro lady from Atlanta, came up to do my party (she had been my cook at camp) and was very troubled, and a bit shocked, when she found it was bi-racial. . . . I sent Mrs. Paul Robeson in the first morning after breakfast to talk to her and persuade her to see that it was working beautifully. I handled things discreetly as I tend to do, and nothing happened. We were all a little scared—why not admit it?—and we watched our steps; we kept casual visitors away and we were discreet in every possible way. It apparently did not disturb anyone. The talk was very candid, and we had sudden arguments, sudden antagonisms rose to the surface and were then laughed away; it was a matter of raw nerves meeting raw nerves. . . . Mrs. Robeson had recently come back from South America . . . and taught us all the samba at the breakfast table. We had two or three elderly and slightly pious churchwomen there but they all took it in their stride—although one whispered when she left, her eyes twinkling, "I still don't see just why you chose *me* for your party. But I enjoyed it." [9]

In the early 1940s, Lillian began criticizing discrimination and segregation publicly, first in *South Today* and then in other magazines. She had, as she said, gradually waked up to the problem of segregation. Moreover, the success of *South Today* had given her a feeling of confidence as a writer and, no less important, assured her an audience likely to be sympathetic to, or at least willing to consider, her views. Three factors influenced her to take a stand against discrimination and segregation when she did. The first was the entry of the United States into the Second World War. Although skeptical of the battle cries of the war, she still saw the conflict as a test of democracy. As she observed in an article in *South Today* in 1942, long-standing patterns of discrimination and segregation took on a sharp edge as they were carried into the war effort.[10] She thought the war should be used as an occasion for persuading Americans to finally put into practice the democratic ideals they claimed to believe in.

The second factor was the blacks' own militant protest against discrimination and segregation, particularly in the armed forces and defense industries during the early years of World War II. Their effort, symbolized by A. Philip Randolph's March on Washington Movement of 1941, broadened and gave added momentum to the campaign already underway against lynching, educational inequality, and voting restrictions. As George Tindall points out in *The Emergence of the New South*, it also made segregation itself "at last, an open question." P. B. Young, a black Virginia newspaper editor, declared that "there never was a time in the history of the United States when Negroes were more united concerning the impact of segregation on their lives." Southern blacks joined northern blacks in confronting the segregation question head on. In October, 1942, for example, a conference of Negroes meeting in Durham, North Carolina, issued a statement declaring themselves "fundamentally opposed to the principle and practice of compulsory segregation in our American society." While traveling through the South in April of the same year interviewing Rosenwald Fund scholarship applicants, Lillian gained a firsthand understanding of black attitudes. She could not help seeing "something heartbreakingly valiant" in the eagerness of Negro youth "to prove to white Americans their willingness to die for a country which has given them only the scraps from the white folks' democracy." At the same time she noted "a quiet, strong resentment, running like a deep stream through their minds and hearts," something she thought few white Americans were aware of or wanted to face.[11]

The third influence on Lillian's thinking was her belief that the South was ready to respond positively to efforts to abolish segregation and discrimination. In February, 1942, she wrote to Walter White, executive secretary of the National Association for the Advancement of Colored People (NAACP):

> It is so apparent that the world's stage is set for a magnificent act on the part of the Anglo-Saxons! If the British people would today give India

her freedom, if Mr. Roosevelt by a proclamation justified by war would give the Negro in America his full status of citizenship, it would cause a mighty exaltation to sweep over the face of the earth. Mr. Roosevelt is afraid. He has no reason to be. Beneath the South's terrible dullness and prejudice is a deep sense of guilt. I believe white southerners would draw in a deep breath and thank God for what he had done. I believe this. And I know my South. The stage is set. People are sending their sons to die for something that in their hearts they know does not exist. It isn't a light thing to give your son to death. I believe there is an inertia, a profound lack of identification of the American people with the war aims—as those aims really stand today—that is similar, shockingly, disturbingly similar to the feeling among the people of France before its fall. . . . If Mr. Roosevelt is a great statesman, a great leader instead of merely a clever politician, he should be led to see this. I believe Henry Wallace can see this. I believe there are men and women North, South, East, West who will see this thing. This is the time. The South would "take" it today when in peace time they would not. Southerners deep in their hearts are cowards to public opinion. They play to a stage. They are the world's greatest actors. They would play up to this thing to the extent that race riots would be avoided. I do not believe southern people would dare have race riots over such an issue, although they are having race riots, as we both know, around the camps.[12]

Believing that the time had come to act, Lillian told White that she and Paula were sending out an editorial "to 5000 Southerners, newspapers, government leaders." The editorial, entitled "Are We Not All Confused?" and signed by Lillian, was published in the Spring, 1942, issue of *South Today*. It announced her unqualified support for Negro demands. She declared it was unjust to ask Negroes to pay taxes and serve in the armed forces while denying them their full constitutional rights and insisted that they had a right to share in "democracy's privileges as well as its duties." More important, the editorial focused not on the legitimacy of Negro demands—that, for her, was axiomatic—but on the fact that southern liberals who had supported the Negro cause in the past were now saying that the time was not right for those demands to be met.[13]

Lillian perceived and criticized a crucial limitation in the thinking of southern liberals. During the Rosenwald trip she had found many of them "giving up their liberalism 'for the duration,'" and she had noted that Negroes were "depressed and disheartened by the knowl-

edge that many of their white friends disappear when crises arise." As
Morton Sosna and others have pointed out, the wartime militancy
of Negroes severely tested the racial philosophy of liberals such as
Virginius Dabney, Mark Ethridge, Will Alexander, and Frank and
Jonathan Daniels. Before the United States entered the war, they had
been active in movements against lynching, the poll tax, and educational inequality. Now, when blacks directly protested segregation, liberals criticized them and their sympathizers for making excessive demands which they said only invited racial violence. Thus Dabney,
editor of the Richmond *Times Dispatch*, charged that extremist Negroes were "demanding an overnight revolution in race relations" and
thereby "stirring up interracial hate." He warned that "if an attempt is
made forcibly to abolish segregation throughout the South, violence
and bloodshed will result." Such statements led the NAACP's Walter
White to observe that "the highest casualty rate of the war seems to be
that of Southern white liberals. For various reasons they are taking
cover at an alarming rate—fleeing before the onslaught of the professional Southern bigots."[14]

In her editorial Lillian pointed to the cultural and psychological
factors that prevented southern liberals from supporting black demands for equality and an end to segregation. She explained that
under stress men tend to revert to early patterns of behavior. Under the
stress of the war as well as Negro militancy and increasing racial tension, liberals were capitulating to emotions and fears learned in childhood. Like all white southerners, she observed, they had been brought
up to believe in white superiority. As they grew to adulthood, common
sense and scientific knowledge persuaded them to reject much of their
early conditioning. "But no white child reared among Negroes ever for-
gets in his heart the sweet power of being 'superior.'" The belief in
white superiority was still there, "waiting for the propitious moment of
race-strain, to seize its old throne in the middle of reason from which
once it was firmly rejected." The confused response of southern liberals to black demands was a result of "a surrender under stress to the
pull of old childhood patterns of behavior."[15]

Lillian exhorted liberals to stop falling back on conditioned reflexes
and to engage in creative, constructive, intelligent action. Specifically
she urged them to create a public opinion in favor of racial equality.

By act, word, newspaper column, editorial, speech, sermon, in quiet reason with friends, public opinion can be created by liberals and labor to accept the Negro in democracy, as public opinon has been created to accept this war. Suggest that the old days have passed; that as war strategy it is the wise thing now, the "hard necessity" perhaps, but the only course to follow both for winning the faith of other peoples across the seas and for strengthening our inner defenses; that it is the inevitable direction which we must take to find a way out of our American troubles and the sooner we take it, the better.[16]

The 1942 editorial did not offer a comprehensive view of the problem of segregation, but that soon followed. By 1945 Lillian had formulated an explanation of the origins and function of segregation, why it was harmful, and how it could be eliminated. In "Two Men and a Bargain: A Parable of the Solid South," she explained the historical origins of segregation. It grew out of a bargain between Mr. Rich White and Mr. Poor White back in the late nineteenth century. If Mr. Poor White would let Mr. Rich White "boss the money"—by taking care of "jobs and credit, prices, hours, wages, votes and so on" (and managing them so as to turn a handsome profit for himself)—Mr. Poor White could "boss the nigger" and take satisfaction in being superior, at least to the Negro. Mr. Poor White could do anything he wanted to show folks he was the boss, but Mr. Rich White suggested that the best thing was "to Jim Crow everything"—streetcars and buses, trains and waiting rooms and movies, restaurants and hotels ("even if you don't have money to go inside one of them, it'll make you feel good to know you're sort of bossing things there"). "Jim Crow was the rich white's idea but the poor white got it working." He kept the Negro in his place by lynching and flogging and burning. He made sure other poor whites didn't break the bargain—for example by organizing unions or getting Negroes into unions. He kept the rest of southern society in line, too. He threw books out of libraries, decided what could and couldn't be taught, dictated folks' morals and manners ("when you could and when you couldn't use the word 'mister'; . . . who could come in your front door and who must go to your back door").

He told the newspapers what they could say and how they could say it—except about money. (The rich white told them about money.) He told

the preachers what they could preach and how they must preach it—
except about money. (The rich white told them about money.) He told
the teachers what they could teach and how they must teach it—except
about money. He was boss and he knew it. . . . boss of everything in
Dixie but the money. Boss of everything but the rich white's way of
making money . . . boss of everything but wages and hours and prices
and jobs and credit and the vote—and his own living. [17]

Although offered in the form of a parable, Lillian's explanation of
the origins and function of segregation was similar to that presented in
a number of scholarly works that she had read and in some cases
praised in *South Today*. These included the works of historians such as
W. E. B. Du Bois, C. Vann Woodward, and W. J. Cash, as well as social
scientists such as H. C. Nixon, John Dollard, Arthur Raper, and Ira
De. A. Reid. All of them emphasized the influence of the connection
between class divisions and economic exploitation on one hand and
racism and segregation on the other in shaping the twentieth-century
South. [18]

Lillian contended that in the 1940s powerful forces continued to
support the bargain between Mr. Rich White and Mr. Poor White.
Southern politicians and "a lot of Yankee Republicans" were part
of the larger group of vested interests in the South who found it ad-
vantageous to maintain tension between the races. Others Lillian
identified as among the vested interests were planters, industrialists
(northern and southern), financiers, bankers, and creditors (and their
lawyers), and certain leaders of the American Federation of Labor.
They worked together to keep wages low and unions weak and "to
maintain prestige-value in cheap jobs reserved for whites only." [19]

The vested interests were powerful, but numerically they constituted a small minority. Why then did the majority of southern whites
allow themselves to be controlled and exploited by them? Why did they
follow their lead instead of looking out for their own interests? Lillian
believed the main reason was the desire for self-esteem. In the South,
where the old planter families insisted on their superiority to other
whites, the desire for self-esteem on the part of poor and middle-class
whites was a hunger. "The white southerner," Lillian wrote, "not a
proud man as he so often claims, but one torn by feelings of inferiority,

is therefore continually driven to assert his superiority to the Negro and his identification with the 'gentleman'."[20]

Although Lillian believed that economic factors were responsible for the rise and continuance of segregation, she did not think they were the only or most important influence. Psychological and cultural factors outweighed them. The root of the problem was the notion of white superiority. Even "Two Men and a Bargain" suggested as much in showing how Mr. Rich White cleverly exploited Mr. Poor White's desire for self-esteem. In other writings of the 1940s, Lillian formulated her psychocultural explanation of segregation more explicitly. She described the white man's overesteem of his skin color as a kind of infantilism, a continuation of the child's self-centeredness and appetite for self-importance. She referred to "the white man's infantile desire always to be first, always to sit on the front seat, always to have the biggest and best of everything—a desire that makes a nuisance of a child but makes a menace of a man who has the power to get what he wants." Lillian attributed such infantilism partly to childhood training, observing that white children were brought up to believe in white superiority, which actually reinforced their childish sense of self-importance. However, she also thought that certain aspects of white culture encouraged the infantile stress on superiority, citing Calvinism, monogamy and the small family, the high esteem placed on "sex purity," and the dominance of "the Protestant God-the-Father image" as opposed to "the Catholic Mary-Mother-of-Christ" image. "Over-esteem of one's skin color," she wrote, "whether in individuals or in masses of men is a regressive narcism, a symptom of psychosexual maladjustment that involves sex, religion, family life, and yes, money also."[21]

Lillian recognized the harm segregation and the notion of white superiority did to blacks—"the quiet killing of self-esteem, the persistent smothering of hope and pride, the deep bruises given the egos of young Negro children; the never ceasing humiliations which Jim Crow imposes upon human beings who are not white." However, she placed even more emphasis on the harm segregation did to whites. In an article in *South Today* she pointed to the damage segregation had done to the personalities and culture of white people, noting that "it is more than poor wages, wasted soil, poverty, race riots," more even than "the

damage done to Negroes themselves." She contended that growing up
and living under segregation inhibited the emotional growth of whites.
Segregation and the notion of white superiority on which it rested
produced stunted, crippled, emotionally immature people who were
not able to become fully human (or to view Negroes as fully human)
because they cut themselves off from human relationships and therefore from human growth. She explained:

> In trying to shut the Negro race away from us, we have shut ourselves
> away from the good, the creative, the human in life. The warping dis-
> torted frame we have put around every Negro child from birth is
> around every white child from birth also. Each is on a different side of
> the frame, but each is there. As in its twisting distorted form it shapes
> and cripples the life and personality of one, it is shaping and crippling
> the life and personality of the other. It would be difficult to decide
> which character is maimed the more—the white or the Negro—after
> living a life in the southern framework of segregation.[22]

Viewing segregation as a psychocultural problem, Lillian sought to
eliminate it through an approach based on psychotherapy. She contended that the first step in eliminating segregation was for whites to
recognize that it was not a Negro problem as so many insisted, but the
white man's problem. Whites must recognize that their "sick obsession
with skin color" was destructive and give it up. This psychological
change was fundamental to the speedy elimination of segregation.
Lillian did not agree with liberals who insisted that segregation could
only be abolished gradually. She insisted it could be eliminated "as
rapidly as each of us can change his own heart." In addition to changing their racial attitudes, Lillian urged whites to make efforts to get to
know and understand Negroes better. Among other things, she suggested reading books about blacks and subscribing to their magazines
and newspapers. She also advised whites to "seek out among the Negro
race a few individuals with whom you can become good friends." She
was clearly writing from her own experience, remembering her need
to break out of the confinement of Clayton and thinking of her visits to
black colleges and of the biracial gatherings on Old Screamer. She was
urging whites to take the steps she had taken when she began her private assault on segregation. She emphasized developing comfortable,
even friendly relations between whites and blacks for several reasons.

She thought that if whites got to know Negroes better they would overcome their irrational fear and dislike of them. She also believed that better relations between whites and Negroes would promote emotional growth and maturity. "All emotional growth has to do with [the] ability to love and identify ourselves with more and more people," she declared. In this regard she seems to have been influenced by Karl Menninger, whose works she had recommended on several occasions to readers of *South Today*. In *Love Against Hate*, published in 1942, Menninger argued that the power of love, an expression of the life instinct, could be used to sublimate aggression and hatred, channeling destructive impulses into creative ones so as to bring about better human relationships. Lillian believed that "nothing but human relationships can break down segregation." Although she favored such legislative and judicial action against Jim Crow as abolition of the poll tax and the white primary, removal of Jim Crow laws from state codes, a federal antilynching law, and an end to segregation in the armed forces, in the early 1940s she did not anticipate quick action on such matters. Besides, she believed that segregation laws would not be removed from the statute books "until enough people form relationships despite the laws, and insist upon their removal." Good human relationships were crucial, for even if (and after) segregation laws were eliminated, the "custom of racial segregation" would still isolate people from one another unless they worked at building "personal bridges across the chasm."[23]

Lillian emphasized the importance of individual efforts to abolish segregation. In an article in *South Today* entitled "Addressed to Intelligent White Southerners," she listed "the simple, undramatic things we all can do," such as calling Negroes Mr., Mrs., or Miss, paying cooks and maids more and shortening their hours, and sitting by Negroes on buses or streetcars. People who were in a position to lead public opinion could make speeches, write editorials, or preach sermons against segregation. Everyone could do something, she insisted. Some things even the most timid could do; others would require courage and intelligence and resourcefulness.[24]

Lillian also favored collective action to abolish segregation. She praised the various religious and labor groups and interracial committees working to eliminate racial discrimination in the South and the nation, and urged readers of *South Today* to support and join them.[25] Although she did not consider herself an organization person, she did work with one organization in the early 1940s, the Southern Conference for Human Welfare (SCHW), serving on its executive board from 1942 to 1945.

Formed in 1938, the SCHW was a coalition of liberals and radicals representing various groups in the South: workers, youths, farmers (including tenants and sharecroppers), politicians, educators, newspapermen, and other professionals. The leadership was mainly white, urban, and middle-class professional, but Negroes and unionists accounted for the majority of the delegates at the annual meetings. At its first meeting, the conference advocated a wide range of reforms, from improved labor conditions and expansion of Farm Security Administration programs to uniform federal and state voter-registration procedures and federal aid to education. During the early 1940s, however, it concentrated most of its effort on the abolition of the poll tax.[26]

As a delegate to the second annual meeting in 1940, Lillian expressed high hopes for the organization. She was particularly impressed by the fact that the conference sessions were unsegregated, which she saw as "a symbol of a changing South, a good South." When she became a member of the executive board in 1942 she wrote to James Dombrowski, the executive secretary, that while she expected to "disagree with many about much," she believed she could "work with the board pretty fully on almost every kind of aim and objective."[27] Increasingly, though, she found herself at odds with the policies and practices of the organization. In May, 1945, she resigned from it, but not without regret.

Chief among her grievances was what she saw as a lack of democracy in the SCHW. She felt that policies were formulated and decisions made, not by the mass of delegates or even by the entire executive board, but by the officers or a small number of board members. Writing to Dombrowski in May, 1945, she declared, "The organization is run by very few people: you and Clark [Foreman], mainly; Miss [Lucy Randolph] Mason has a lot to do with it, Virginia Durr, several of the CIO folks and one or two people whom I do not know. Things happen, new policies are initiated, that I know nothing about until I read it in the newspapers." She urged Dombrowski to have more frequent, regular meetings of the executive board scheduled a year ahead of time so that all members would be able to attend, and annual rather than biennial meetings of the conference as a whole. "The executive committee needs the strong light of group criticism on it," she wrote. "It is the only way that any group is kept democratic. It doesn't keep itself democratic; it has to be kept so by pressure from the members at large and by public opinion even of those who are not members."[28]

Lillian thought the SCHW was also undemocratic in its composition. Certain groups were not represented in the conference, while others were overrepresented or had a disproportionate influence. In 1942 she noted that the conference had "no representation of public health workers, psychiatrists, physicians, child welfare workers, penologists, juvenile judges, physical scientists, technicians, artists; few creative workers in any field; few educators; few lawyers; few industrialists; few social scientists—whose techniques, points of view, scientific knowledge, objectivity are tools so valuable that the conference cannot wisely attempt to function without them." She called for the representation of cooperatives, for more rural people, for a larger proportion of Negroes, and for a broader spectrum of interests and occupations within the youth group. In 1945 she reiterated her complaint about the lack of professional people. She also expressed the opinion that the SCHW had discriminated against Socialists as well as "pacifists, conscientious objectors, and those who do not label themselves but who take a strong stand against the violence and stupidity of war." "The Socialists have had no chance to get into the conference either as individuals or as groups," she wrote. "I do think there has been discrimination there."[29]

Whereas Socialists were excluded from the SCHW, in Lillian's view Communists or those who "follow[ed] the Communist line very closely" exerted undue influence. She thought four or five such persons served on the executive board. She particularly resented the Communists' tendency to glamorize Soviet Russia and to emphasize "American-Soviet Friendship (why not American-China Friendship, American-Indian Friendship, even American-British Friendship?)." She also thought they had influenced the conference to adopt a "'get there no matter how you get there' philosophy." To Clark Foreman, chairman of the SCHW, she wrote, "I know it sounds like 'old stuff' to be afraid of the

Communists. But I *am* afraid of them, Clark. I am afraid of their op-portunism, of their easy habit of using questionable means to bring about good goals; of their reliance on authoritarianism, of their lack of intellectual integrity." Virginia Durr and Myles Horton, who knew Lillian in the 1930s and 1940s, attribute her hostility to Communists to the influence of Frank McCallister, the leader of the Socialist faction of the SCHW. Lillian was devoted to him, according to Durr. He advocated barring Communists from the organization, and his influence may also explain Lillian's complaint about SCHW discrimination against Socialists. Of course Lillian was not alone in worrying about Communist influence in the SCHW; at various times Howard Kester, H. L. Mitchell, Frank Graham, and Roger Baldwin, among others, shared her concern. However, Thomas Krueger, the author of a recent history of the organization, argues persuasively against the notion that Communists or fellow travelers dominated or tried to dominate it.[30]

Lillian also complained that labor groups were overrepresented in the conference and that there was a disproportionate number of union leaders to union members and nonunion workers. Following the 1942 meeting she suggested to Dombrowski that more people be brought into the conference in order to "rub off a little of the earmarks of its being simply a labor conference." She was sympathetic to unions and labor, but she seems to have felt that their representatives tended to be partisan and inflexible in their views. "The labor folks have had to struggle against such horrible odds in the South that it has made them intolerant fighters though brave ones," she observed. Although she was much more sympathetic to unionists than to Communists, she criticized both groups for following a narrow union or party line. If the conference were to survive, she told Dombrowski, it would have to "have a broader purpose and more people in it who know the art of 'sweet reason'. . . . We have somehow—all of us—got to find enough things we all believe in and want, to be willing to overlook each other's theologies."[31]

Lillian's remark about the exclusion of pacifists, conscientious objectors, and other critics of war was related to her long-standing disagreement with the conference's focus on winning the war. The 1942 meeting in Nashville, organized around the theme of "The South's Part in Winning the War," stressed the need to mobilize the South behind the war against fascism. Writing to Dombrowski following the meeting, Lillian confessed that she was "not much of a war person." She was not a pacifist and she wanted the war to end quickly, she added, but thought the conference was wrong in promoting its ideas and justifying its actions "by saying they are done to win the war." Three years later she reiterated her concern that winning the war had been the primary goal of the conference. "I have never been able to follow the line that we must get rid of racial discrimination, for instance, or unemployment, for instance, in order to 'win the war,'" she wrote. "I think we must get rid of these evils because they are cancers in human culture and bring on wars. A war cannot be 'won'. Some day we shall all learn this, but God only knows when."[32]

In explaining her decision to resign from the SCHW, Lillian emphasized that it stemmed more from a feeling of being philosophically at odds with the organization than from disagreement with particular policies and actions. The SCHW had not turned out to be the sort of organization she had hoped it would. "My dreams of the Conference were so different," she wrote to Foreman in 1945.

> I saw it as a great coming-together of Southerners who had been blocked off from each other for centuries by race and poverty and religion and ignorance. . . . I hoped it would be a group who could hold on to issues, not personalities; who would see things not from the prejudiced viewpoint of labor, nor from the prejudiced viewpoint of industry or of Russia or of any interest group. I hoped it would not turn into a pressure group working for special ideologies and special interests but something more profound, more inclusive.

By the middle 1940s Lillian thought that the conference had lost sight of "the interests of all people." Moreover, it appeared to be "turning into a political group" and "playing politics." She cited its promotion of Ellis Arnall, governor of Georgia, as an example of this tendency. Arnall was no better than Eugene Talmadge, she insisted. "He simply has better manners. . . . Everyone in the South knows he is a small man, an opportunist, a 'compromiser', if there ever was one, a man of little social knowledge and almost no social vision. . . . He has never done anything to promote the Negro's rights in Georgia." She particularly deplored the conference's crediting him with eliminating the poll tax in Georgia. In promoting Arnall, Lillian believed, the SCHW focused on personalities rather than issues. It was "this opportunistic nature of the Conference" that she objected to most of all. By becoming political, it was bound to "compromise big ends for little ones," and that was something she was unwilling to do. "I ain't made that way!" she wrote to Foreman. "My talent is that of clarifying issues; is that of telling the stark truth as I see it, with as much compassion of spirit as I am capable of." To Dombrowski she wrote:

> I am often called an idealist because I refuse to give up big ends for little ones. I *am* an "idealist", but a pretty tough one, I think, who believes that just to be smart isn't enough nor is it enough to be right. One must be both right *and* smart and one can be both. I think the world needs people who are willing to stand for what they believe without compromising. I think the world is sick to death of the little strategists, the little compromisers. And it is this philosophy of the Conference, more than any specific defect in its organization, that I find myself completely out of sympathy with.[33]

Lillian also thought that the SCHW had narrowed its focus from human welfare broadly defined to a few economic and political objectives. In a letter she sent to the members of the executive board explaining her resignation, she argued that human welfare encompassed more than improved material conditions. "It is so easy to forget that a man's self esteem, his dignity, his feelings about himself, his thoughts and his freedom to express these thoughts are what give him his human stature—not the new shoes on his feet, nor his new house, nor his increased wages, nor the ballot, although these are essential to his humanity also and goals that every one of us must work unceasingly for." She urged the board to "remember that human beings are our end, that their creative growth is our end. The ballot, the job, the wages, the housing are simply *means to this end.*"[34]

In addition to her other reservations, Lillian may have withdrawn from the SCHW because it failed to take a forthright stand against segregation. Conference meetings were unsegregated, which branded it as a racial equality organization in the eyes of many, but before 1946 the SCHW never went on record as opposed to segregation in all aspects of southern life. (The resolution passed at the Birmingham meeting in 1938 that evoked so much controversy merely condemned forced segregation at conference meetings.) On several occasions Lillian urged the conference to be more forthright in opposing Jim Crow, but to no avail. In her letter of resignation, she praised Foreman for never wavering in his fight against segregation, but said she thought a statement on segregation recently issued by the conference "was very mealy-mouthed." She wondered if the SCHW were getting cautious as it started out on its "big money campaign."[35] Although Lillian did not make it a major issue, her more radical position on segregation undoubtedly influenced her decision to resign from the SCHW.

Lillian criticized another interracial organization, the Southern Regional Council, for some of the same reasons she criticized the Southern Conference for Human Welfare. The Southern Regional Council (SRC) was formed in 1943 by a group of southern liberals led by Jessie Daniel Ames. Howard Odum served as the first president of the organization, which was concerned with race relations, economic affairs, education, and community life in the South. In January, 1944, the editor of *Common Ground*, Margaret Anderson, invited Lillian to write something on the council to appear alongside a critical article by J. Saunders Redding, a black professor of English at Hampton Institute. Anderson had originally invited Howard Odum and Virginius Dabney to do the white angle, but they had demurred. Lillian's statement was more restrained than Redding's, but like him she took the SRC to task for holding to "a regressive belief in segregation, a belief announced with the flourish of trumpets." Although she did not accuse the council of hypocrisy or evil motives, she did fault it for promoting itself as a movement for racial democracy when in fact its aim was merely to improve the social and economic life of the South without disturbing segregation. "Not much is going to be done to bring about racial democracy by this group until its leaders accept and acknowledge publicly the basic truth that segregation is injuring us on every level of our life," she wrote. She ranked herself with "other leaders in the South who believe segregation must go before any people can find a good life for themselves; who cherish with their minds and their spirits the concept of human equality; who prize it so highly that they are not willing to give up big ends for little ends."[36]

As Lillian noted in the *Common Ground* article, she had not been asked to participate in the SRC because, she believed, of her public stance against segregation. Shortly after the article appeared she re-

ceived an invitation from Executive Director Guy B. Johnson to become a member of the council's board of directors. She replied to him
early in June, 1944, sending copies of the letter to the SRC board members, other individuals, and thirty or forty newspapers. The *New Republic* published portions of the letter, in somewhat altered form,
under the title "Addressed to White Liberals." Lillian declined to join
the council. "I would not feel comfortable as a member of any organization working for racial democracy that does not deem it important to
take a firm and public stand in opposition to segregation and in defense of human equality," she explained. Elaborating on her disagreement with the SRC, she returned to the point she had made in the
*Common Ground* article and in some of her criticisms of the SCHW.
The approach of the Southern Regional Council to the problem of race
relations was inadequate.

> Racial segregation, political and economic isolationism cannot be
> considered apart from man's whole personality, his culture, his needs.
> Neither can man's needs be considered apart from the destroying effects
> of segregation. Nor can the South's major problems be solved by trying
> to put a loaf of bread, a book, and a ballot, in every one's hand. For man
> is not an economic or political unit. To believe that he is, is to ignore
> personality and cheapen the human spirit. And by ignoring personality,
> we over-simplify a complex, subtle, tragically profound problem. It
> helps us sometimes to see this in perspective if we will look at the re-
> stricting frame of segregation in terms of the needs of children. A child's
> personality cannot grow and mature without self-esteem, without feel-
> ings of security, without faith in his world's willingness to make room
> for him to live as a human being. . . . No colored child in our South is
> being given today what his personality needs in order to grow and ma-
> ture richly and fully. No white child, under the segregation pattern, can
> be free of arrogance and hardness of heart, and blindness to human
> need—and hence no white child can grow freely and creatively under
> the crippling frame of segregation.
>
> I personally, would prefer that my own child do without shoes than
> do without the esteem of his fellows and I would prefer that he never
> look into a book than that he look down upon another human being. We
> simply cannot turn away and refuse to look at what segregation is doing
> to the personality and character of every child, every grown up, white
> and colored, in the South today. Segregation is spiritual lynching. The
> lynched and the lynchers are our own people, our own selves.[37]

Lillian's statement underscored her conviction that segregation was above all a psychological and cultural problem, something she had insisted on since the early 1940s. At that time she had regarded segregation as a social mechanism for adjusting relations between the races, but by 1944 she was defining it more broadly and in such a way as to suggest even more profoundly than before its crippling effect on human beings. She formulated the new definition in two articles published early in that year, but expressed it more clearly and succinctly in the letter to Johnson. Segregation, she wrote, was not just a southern custom or an attitude of white people toward Negroes. It was "an ancient, psychological mechanism used by men the world over, whenever they want to shut themselves away from problems which they fear and do not feel they have the strength to solve. When men get into trouble they tend to put barriers between themselves and their difficulties." Earlier she had condemned segregation as an arrangement that cut men and women off from human relationships; now she condemned it as a device used to shut out new or alien ideas, emotions, and experiences. Either way it prevented men and women from becoming fully human, from developing their full emotional and intellectual potential.[38]

Lillian's letter to Johnson also indicates how far removed her view of segregation was from that of most white southern liberals. The liberals sought improved race relations, but they did not challenge segregation directly, as she did. Moreover, they did not see race relations as a psychological or cultural problem, but as an economic, political, or social problem. Some of the liberals, particularly those associated with the New Deal, believed that improving the economic status of whites and especially blacks would diminish white prejudice and ultimately lead to the abolition of segregation. But this was a long-range, not an immediate, goal to be accomplished through economic and social planning. Indeed, most liberals were concerned with problems other than segregation—educational inequality, lynching, poverty, the poll tax. They refused to confront the problem of segregation, arguing that southern folkways could not be changed overnight and that any attempt to eliminate Jim Crow would lead to violence.[39]

Lillian saw the last argument as a rationalization southern liberals used to resist Negro demands for equality. Their stock response to those who sought to eliminate segregation was, "But it will only cause violence, it will lead to race riots." The fear of doing harm was "basic to the psychology of the southern liberal," she wrote. It was partly a rationalization of his fear of change, "for the southern liberal in common with liberals the world over is conservative in temperament, fearful of sudden changes on all levels of his life." It was partly a result of his succumbing to the "skillful and persistent propaganda" of the vested interests who sought to maintain tension between the races. But the root of the southern liberal's fear of doing harm was to be found in those ambivalent and guilt-ridden feelings toward Negroes that grew out of his painful childhood experience of having to disavow the black nurse and playmates to whom he had given his first love and friendship. Lillian argued that the southern liberal had twisted such feelings into "a fear of himself, doubt of his capacity for doing good, even to the group to whom he owes it most" and "a dread—a kind of prophetic fore-knowledge of failure and disaster that will certainly attend any attempts he (or his group) makes in the area of racial reparations."[40]

Lillian's position on segregation also differed from that of Christian radicals and socialists in the South—men such as Howard Kester and Claude Williams of the Fellowship of Southern Churchmen and H. L. Mitchell of the Southern Tenant Farmers Union. Like them she sought full racial equality and democracy. Like them she recognized the class and economic origins of segregation and the way the vested interests fostered racial prejudice as a means of exploiting poor whites and blacks. But while she sympathized with their efforts to organize agricultural and industrial workers, the development of a radical southern labor movement was not one of her major concerns. She insisted that the radicals' economic solution was just as limited and partial as the liberals' economic solution. Neither went to the root of the segregation problem, which was the notion of white superiority. Another important difference between Lillian and radicals like Kester was that they preached "a biblical message of human liberation"—what Anthony Dunbar terms a "radical social gospel"—whereas her message was overwhelmingly secular, grounded not in the teachings of Jesus but of Freud and Karl Menninger.[41]

Although she thought of herself as leftist and "all for the underdog" in the 1930s and 1940s, Lillian avoided working with Communists even during the Popular Front years when other southern reformers such as Lucy Randolph Mason and Claude Williams cooperated with them. She was not sympathetic to or even very familiar with Marxism, and as her comments on the Southern Conference for Human Welfare indicate, she was repelled by what she viewed as the Communists' rigid adherence to the party line. From what she said about them, it appears that her antipathy was as much personal and emotional as ideological. It derived as much from her dislike and distrust of them as individuals as from her disagreement with their politics. She wrote in the 1960s about her feeling during the Second World War that "most American communists seemed to me to be psychic problems; they seemed full of hatred for their families which they took out against their country; they usually showed very poor judgment, they seemed to like to be furtive and secretive; they were always against something, and not often for something; and I just didn't trust them."[42]

Lillian's position on segregation was closer to that of black civil rights leaders and white northern liberals than to any white group in the South. She advocated the same things that Rayford Logan, Roy Wilkins, W. E. B. Du Bois, Mary McLeod Bethune, and other Negroes did in a book published in 1944 entitled *What the Negro Wants.* Logan's statement was representative: "In the name of democracy for all Americans we ask these irreducible fundamentals of first-class citizenship for all Negroes: 1. Equality of opportunity 2. Equal pay for equal work 3. Equal protection of the laws 4. Equality of suffrage 5. Equal recognition of the dignity of the human being 6. Abolition of public segregation." These were the goals of interracial civil rights organizations such as the National Association for the Advancement of Colored People (NAACP) and the Congress of Racial Equality (CORE), as well as liberal journals such as the *New Republic* and the *Nation.* Lillian supported all these goals.[43]

However, there were important differences between her views on the race problem and those of black civil rights leaders and northern liberals. She was skeptical of their reliance on such political and economic solutions as ending discrimination in voting rights, housing, employment and education, and on court decisions and legislative action to achieve such objectives. Nor did she agree with their tendency to discount the intensity of white prejudice against Negroes. In this regard, and in relying on political and economic solutions, black leaders and northern liberals shared the opinions expressed by Gunnar Myrdal in his classic work, *An American Dilemma*. Lillian did not oppose the position taken by Myrdal, black leaders, and northern liberals. She simply thought it partial and inadequate. She also differed from them in contending that segregation did as much or more harm to whites as it did to blacks. At the same time, she was not especially sympathetic to A. Philip Randolph's plan to use mass direct action—the March on Washington Movement—to win black demands. Although she described the proposed march as "a non-violent and democratic way of protest" and contended that blacks had a right to use such means, she hoped "it would never be necessary for the Negro race to have to resort to it."[44] That was in 1943. Two decades later she changed her mind and supported the nonviolent protests of Martin Luther King, Jr., and his followers.

Lillian agreed with black civil rights leaders and northern liberals on ends but not means. Indeed, her emphasis on the notion of white superiority as the root of discrimination and segregation, her stress on the damage segregation did to whites, and especially her conviction that a psychological approach was the best way to eliminate it by changing white attitudes and behavior set her apart from most individuals and groups concerned with the race problem in the 1940s.

# IV The *Strange Fruit* Controversy

We, the people, white and colored, are the strange fruit which our culture has produced.

During the years she was moving toward taking a public stand against segregation, Lillian was working on her third novel, *Strange Fruit*, which was published in February, 1944. In the midst of the controversy that erupted over it, and long afterward, she denied that her intention had been to write "a race book." She insisted that *Strange Fruit* was "a story about human beings and their relationships with each other," not about social problems. It was "not about racial prejudice and lynchings—though these evils do appear in the book—not about poverty and low wages, sharecropping, wasted land, ignorance—though these, too, are there." She claimed that the characters in the book could have lived anywhere, but since they happened to live in the South, they had learned to walk in the way of segregation. As a result, their lives "were shaped and twisted by their learning as if their personalities had been placed in a steel frame within which they could grow, but only according to the limits defined by the rigid design of the frame." *Strange Fruit* was concerned with that "restricting, rigid frame of segregation, . . . but far more with the children who grow up in it, who are forced to bind their feeling, their love and their fear, their hate and their dreams to this pattern." She observed that it was a pattern found not only in the South, but "in every corner of the earth, wherever men because of their deep trouble try to shut themselves away from each other, from a reality which they feel too weak to face and

63

identify themselves with, a reality which seems too full of danger for them to dare to face. And in shutting themselves away, they shut out creative rich forces of life also and live in loneliness with their deep fears that destroy them as they live."[1] *Strange Fruit* was about segregation defined in the broad sense Lillian had employed in her letter to Guy Johnson.

*Strange Fruit* was partly autobiographical. In writing it, Lillian drew on her childhood experiences in Jasper. "I was trying to put down the South as I had personally known it to be," she explained. Because many of her most profound experiences concerned white and black people, she thought it was only natural that she should write about the two races. She also thought the book reflected the splits and estrangements in her own life. She described the characters in the novel as "torn and ambivalent" and said that each of them "was myself or a mirror in which I looked at myself," that "every tension was an echo of a tension in my own life."[2] Thus she claimed that she was not writing about racial segregation itself, but was using race conflict and segregation as symbols of the tensions within and between human beings and of the walls that separate them from each other and from new ideas and experiences.

Whatever her intentions, it is difficult not to regard *Strange Fruit* as a book about the South and racial segregation. Indeed, in 1942 when she was still working on the novel, she told Walter White of the NAACP that her theme was the effect of the southern concept of race "upon not only lives but minds and emotions." *Strange Fruit* dramatized the effect of segregation and the notion of white superiority on all the inhabitants, white and black, of the fictional town of Maxwell, Georgia. All of them are crippled or stunted by the system of segregation. While stationed in Marseille during World War I, Tracy Deen, the principal white character, realizes that he loves Nonnie Anderson, a black woman. But upon his return to Maxwell he is unable to relate to her except in terms of the racial beliefs and customs he learned as a child. There are moments when he and Nonnie escape from the world of segregation to a world without racial barriers—a world comprised of just the two of them making love in a deserted cabin. But Tracy is always pulled back into the world of segregation by some thought or word that triggers deep-rooted feelings of prejudice. *"Colored girl. Negro.* Spoiling every moment, like a hair that's got into your food. Why under God's heaven did he keep on thinking those damned words! Why couldn't he— Jesus!" The evening of his return home, before he has really settled back into Maxwell's ways, he happens to meet the town's black minister and his wife. Tracy has just been with Nonnie discussing plans for the future. "We might go back to France—I made friends—I could work in a bank there—we—." The encounter with the Reverend and Mrs. Livingston somehow forces him to realize that his and Nonnie's world is an illusion. He cannot explain his feelings after the meeting. All he knows is that

> thirty minutes ago he had been with the woman he loved. Now there was a colored girl named Nonnie. That was all there was to it. . . . Why it was so, why the accidental meeting with the Reverend and Roseanna could have done this, he did not know. All he knew was, as he stood there looking at them, a door slammed in his mind, shutting out the new world, shutting out Nonnie with it. He was just there on the sidewalk, where he had always been, feeling the feelings he had always felt. He had been somewhere . . . in a dream maybe; maybe crazy. Maybe it had been shell-shock. . . . Or plain amnesia. . . . Maybe he'd lost, not his memory, but his white feelings. . . . Well, he was sane now—the dream was over. Whatever he had forgot how to feel, Roseanna had made him remember. He had come back to Maxwell. Yes, the Reverend had said it, he had come back home.[3]

Psychologically crippled as he is, Tracy is unable to resist the pleadings of his mother and Brother Dunwoodie to join the church, marry the girl next door, and live a respectable life. Tracy pays Henry, the Deens' Negro houseboy, one hundred dollars to marry Nonnie, who is pregnant with Tracy's child. His decision to do all these things is presented as foreordained: he had "started on a road whose map had been drawn long ago, so long ago he could never remember."[4]

Nonnie, a college graduate who works as a nursemaid, is also psychologically crippled. Her sister and brother accuse her of pretending she is not a Negro, but they misunderstand. Nonnie simply does not recognize the existence of racial distinctions. Race, like social position and ambition, is for her something made up, unreal. Her way of dealing with segregation—denying its existence—is no more satisfactory than Tracy's acquiescing in it. Nonnie is presented as an escapist (the other characters call her a "sleepwalker") who has withdrawn into "a remote and secret place of safety," a dreamworld of her own making that bears little relation to reality.[5]

Although it dramatizes the debilitating effects of segregation, *Strange Fruit* proposes no solution. None of the characters in the novel is free of or able to overcome the crippling effects of race prejudice. By portraying all the characters' lives as conditioned by the system in which they have grown up and by emphasizing the role of unconscious fears and desires in shaping human behavior, the novel seems to preclude any solution. At the conclusion of the story, the lynching of Henry, erroneously charged with Tracy's murder, is presented as unpreventable, the inevitable consequence of a whole host of wrongs, misconceptions, and disasters. Thus *Strange Fruit* illustrated one side of the argument Lillian had developed by the early 1940s, that racial segregation and the notion of white superiority were maintained by the training children received in the South—and the resultant fears and anxieties—as well as by the region's special brand of evangelical religion and Victorian morality, and that segregation did as much harm to whites as to blacks. Lillian said she had no "short-range 'purpose'" in mind when she wrote the book, but hoped it would give readers a better understanding of human relationships and the complexities of personality and "arouse their imaginations so that they will think of our people, white and colored, as human beings, not as 'problems'."[6] Perhaps she thought the novel would induce the psychological change she believed was a prerequisite for the elimination of segregation.

Lillian had submitted the manuscript, originally entitled "Jordan Is So Chilly," to ten publishers, all of whom rejected it. She wrote to Walter White that she thought it was because of "my complete frankness about the racial ambivalence of the South." Then in 1943 Frank Taylor, an editor with Reynal and Hitchcock, heard of her, *South Today*, and the novel from Frank McCallister and asked to see the manuscript. His firm accepted it within four days but wanted a change of title; Lillian agreed, suggesting "Strange Fruit." She had first used the phrase in 1941 in an article for the *North Georgia Review* describing the strange fruit produced by southern old-time religion. Then in "Two Men and a Bargain" in the Spring, 1943, issue of *South Today*, she used it again. Mr. Rich White is lamenting the breakdown of his bargain with Mr. Poor White and dreading the time when he will begin "filling his unions with niggers, keep right on filling them, making them bigger and stronger, and first thing you know he may not even *care* whether he's better than niggers." Something whispers not to worry. "Long as you have segregation none of these things can happen!" it says. "Just keep saying *nothing can change it, nothing!*" When Mr. Rich White complains that everybody's against him, Something reassures him. "I'm for you, I'm for the guy who wants to be first, I'm for the guy who loves his own image, I'm for the guy who rides the front seat always the front seat and won't let others ride with him." "Who are you?" asks Mr. Rich White. "You know me," Something replies. "Every man from the womb knows me until death stops the knowledge. But some won't make me a bargain. You did. . . . Who am I? Listen, I'll tell you. I'm that which splits a mind from its reason, a soul from its conscience, a heart from its loving, a people from humanity. I'm the seed of hate and fear and guilt. You are its strange fruit which I feed on."[7]

In between writing the two articles, during the summer of 1942, Lillian heard a recording of the song "Strange Fruit" by Billie Holliday. In the song the phrase refers to a lynching, but Lillian had used it to refer to a people and a way of life, and that was still her sense of it when she suggested it to Reynal and Hitchcock. In the summer or fall of 1943, after the manuscript had been accepted and she was working on revisions, Taylor phoned to ask her about giving the writer of the song credit for the title of the book. As Lillian remembered the conversation she said, "'Frank, I didn't get the title from that song; etc.' He cajoled me, 'Oh be generous and give him the title; it'll do him good and won't hurt you, etc.'" So she did, and the book had a credit line on the copyright page: "(Title from song of same name by Lewis Allan, courtesy of Edward B. Marks Music Corp.)." Lillian said she always regretted her decision. She thought that the result of linking the novel with Billie Holliday and the song was to distort the theme of the book. In her view, *Strange Fruit* was not about a lynching. It was "about the 'strange fruit' of our racist culture and how that 'strange fruit'—Tracy, his sister, his mother, and Nonnie of course and all the *people* came out of our twisted way of life," she wrote. As for Taylor, "I should not have trusted him as I did," she declared many years later, explaining that he "was lovable; he did for a time admire me and love me tremendously, but he always had this little slickness about him." She claimed to have discovered afterward that Taylor felt the credit line would influence a leftist group with whom Lewis Allan was associated.[8]

*Strange Fruit* was published February 29, 1944. Reviewers for the well-known literary magazines and journals of opinion praised the author's honesty, sincerity, and compassion and characterized the novel as powerful, moving and destined to have a terrific impact. They disagreed in their estimate of its literary quality, however. Orville Prescott, writing in the *Yale Review*, called it "a very considerable achievement," citing Lillian's use of stream of consciousness and "deft time shifts." Malcolm Cowley, on the other hand, contended that she lacked "the specifically literary gifts of William Faulkner . . . or Carson McCullers" and suggested that her talents pointed to "some other field than the novel." Reviewers focused most of their attention on characterization and generally agreed that Lillian had done a superb job of rendering the whites of Maxwell. Although Struthers Burt felt the novel offered "a genuine and penetrating insight into the colored mind," and Prescott characterized its portrayal of blacks as masterly, other reviewers found the Negro characters unconvincing. Cowley thought Nonnie "the least successful character in the novel" and criticized the "false dialogues" between her and her sister. He charged that in trying to show that the two women were well educated, Lillian had put "words in their mouths that no sisters, Negro or white, would use in private conversation." Diana Trilling, writing in the *Nation*, observed that "in conflict with each other, or in family or affectional relationships, her Negroes carry great psychological conviction, but when Miss Smith is inside their minds or trying to characterize them as personalities, they tend to fade or fall into stereotypes." Trilling excused the weakness by declaring it to be "a common failing in books about Negroes by white people. With the best will, it seems to be impossible for a member of the dominant group to imagine the way of thinking and feeling of a people who for so many generations have been taught to hide their thinking and feeling."[9]

Trilling was unique among reviewers in contending that Lillian had done more than describe the lives and emotions of southerners growing up, living, and dying under segregation.

In her hands the Negro problem turns out to be not only the problem of the whole South but, by implication, of all modern society. To say, for instance, that "Strange Fruit" anatomizes a small Georgia town at the end of the last war would be to regionalize and particularize in time a social study which is applicable to any number of other American communities and moments; or to say that Miss Smith's book is concerned with racial conflicts would be to ignore her knowledge that in the degree that race is set against race, man is set against himself. "Strange Fruit" is so wide in its human understanding that its Negro tragedy becomes the tragedy of anyone who lives in a world in which minorities suffer; when it ends in a lynching, we are as sorry and frightened for the lynchers as for the victim. Indeed, we are terrified, for ourselves, at the realization that this is what we have made of our human possibility.[10]

Like most other reviewers, W. E. B. Du Bois viewed *Strange Fruit* as a regional novel. In a front-page essay for the *New York Times Book Review*, he praised its explicit depiction of "the tragedy of the South. . . . On each page," he declared, "the reader sees how both elements [white and black] in Maxwell are caught in a skein (economic, ethnic, emotional) that only evolution can untangle or revolution break." Another black reviewer, Theophilus Lewis, writing in the *Crisis*, echoed Du Bois' high praise for the novel. Other blacks disagreed. A reviewer in the Baltimore *Afro-American* contended that the black characters in the novel were "untrue to type" and worried that white readers would judge blacks by the distorted portrayals given in the book. Like Trilling, she thought Lillian's failure to accurately portray blacks was a consequence of her "not being one of us." Dean Gordon B. Hancock, a contributing editor of the Associated Negro Press, was even more critical. The *New York Times Book Review* quoted one of his columns in which he wrote, "It is difficult to imagine a more subtle yet scathing indictment against the Negro race in general and Negro womanhood in particular than that presented in 'Strange Fruit'" and predicted that it would do "irreparable damage to the cause of race relations." He explained, "When Miss Smith portrays in Nonnie Anderson, a young Negro woman college graduate, no higher ambitions than to be the mistress and concubine of a dissolute poor white man, she stabs at the very heart of the hopes of the Negro race." Hancock called the popularity of *Strange Fruit* "ominous" and contended that it derived largely from the fact that it cast the Negro in a subservient role.[11]

Not all of the Left regarded *Strange Fruit* as positively as Du Bois had. Myra Page, writing in the *New Masses*, questioned what seemed to her an overemphasis on early childhood conditioning of racial attitudes. While she conceded the influence of early experiences, she declared that "there is nothing final or fatally determining about these attitudes gained in early childhood. People can change. New experiences, new contacts with people, and fresh ideas gained through reading or shift in environment, can break down old sets, help new ones form." A common complaint of leftist reviewers was that Lillian was unsympathetic, even unjust (Cowley's term) in her treatment of southern poor whites. Cowley criticized her for implying, "though by indirection, that the 'best people' in the South could take steps toward solving the racial problem, if only the poor whites wouldn't interfere." She didn't realize, he wrote, "that the poor whites have been made to suffer almost as much as the Negroes." Cowley and other reviewers on the Left were disturbed at the impression they thought *Strange Fruit* gave, that poor or working-class whites were chiefly responsible for racial violence, especially lynchings, in the South and that educated middle- and upper-class people in the region had little or nothing to do with it.[12]

Southern reviewers generally reacted negatively to the novel, which they assumed was an attack on the southern system of race relations. An exception was Gwen Davenport, who reviewed *Strange Fruit* in the Louisville *Courier-Journal*. She emphasized the importance of reading and criticizing the book "as a novel about people and their passions, rather than as a social document." Davenport thought *Strange Fruit* a good novel, though she predicted that "a whole lot of people aren't going to like it one little bit. Maxwell, Georgia, is too much like Maxwell, Alabama—or Tennessee, or Louisiana, or Carolina, Mississippi, Kentucky, U.S.A."[13]

Most southern reviewers criticized Lillian's difficult style, her romanticism, her obsessive concern with sex, and what seemed to them an "unreal love story." The most vitriolic attack on Lillian, the novel, and the cause it supposedly promoted appeared in the Hapeville *Statesman*, whose associate editor was the former governor of Georgia, Eugene Talmadge. A front page story in the newspaper charged that Lillian's purpose was to portray "a romantic love affair between a white Georgia boy and a negro girl . . . in such glamor that will make court-

ships between negroes and whites appear atractive [*sic*]." A few southern reviewers contended that the picture *Strange Fruit* drew of race
relations in the South was outdated and distorted. The events of the
book took place immediately after World War I, but the South had
changed greatly in the twenty-five years since then, they asserted. Indeed, a reviewer in *Social Forces,* published by Howard Odum's institute
at Chapel Hill, thought Lillian should have omitted the lynching, arguing that "the decreasing rate of lynchings [in the South] has made this
climax a little stale as literature and reality."[14]

Even before *Strange Fruit* was released, Reynal and Hitchcock were
anticipating a best seller, having received advance orders for more than
20,000 copies. By the end of April it had gone through seven printings
for a total of 140,000 copies, and on May 14 it moved to first place on
the best-seller list of the *New York Times Book Review.*[15]

On March 20 the novel was banned in Boston after police had received complaints about its obscene language. Two weeks later *Harper's
Magazine* columnist Bernard De Voto instituted a court test of the ban
by buying a copy of the book from Abraham Isenstadt, owner of the
University Law Book Exchange in Cambridge, in the presence of
policemen who had been notified in advance. The case went before
District Court Judge Arthur P. Stone who found the novel obscene and
fined Isenstadt two hundred dollars for possessing and selling it. The
novel was already selling well before the banning, and the publicity
helped boost sales even further. Not only De Voto but other nationally
known columnists, including Eleanor Roosevelt, commented on the
banning. The American Center of PEN protested it. And Pathé News
did a newsreel on it, showing De Voto and Isenstadt being arrested and
featuring a five-minute talk by Lillian about why she wrote the book
and why she was unwilling to delete the objectionable parts.[16]

In mid-May the Post Office Department barred *Strange Fruit* from
the mails and advised newspapers and magazines not to advertise it. A
few days later the department abruptly lifted the ban to the extent of
allowing the publisher to mail the book at the risk of prosecution under
a law prohibiting the mailing of lewd books. Although it was not generally known at the time, the reversal was a result of quiet intervention by
President Roosevelt. Curtice Hitchcock, the publisher, had flown to
Washington for a conference with Eleanor Roosevelt. She in turn had

talked to FDR who ordered the ban lifted. One other effort to ban the novel occurred in Detroit. There the book was banned by a "gentlemen's agreement" after a police sergeant visited booksellers and persuaded them not to sell it, but resistance by the United Auto Workers and the Detroit Public Library prevented an official banning by the city.[17]

With the banning in Boston, Lillian began to feel the full impact of the controversy that was developing around the book. She recognized the value of the publicity for sales, and she enjoyed being a celebrity, at least in the beginning. "Everyone recognized me, everyone was nice to me in stores, shops, hotels, restaurants." The proceeds from the book enabled her to do all the little things she had wanted to do, including staying at the Pierre or the Plaza, taking friends and relatives to places like "21" and the Colony Club, and buying wine and whiskey and "garlic olives (which were delicacies in those days) and caviar, too." But soon all the publicity began to have a debilitating effect. "I felt my sense of identity slipping away from me," she remembered. Being a celebrity became "a dreadful thing." "You are called bitch and saint, whore and heroine, you are praised for your courage and sneered at for your obscenity; you are made into stereotypes, no one sees you as a person, not even those who admire your book most; you are turned into images which please them or appeal to their feelings of hate or admiration, to their fears or their hopes." She returned to Clayton as often as possible to rest and get her "psychic bearings." She also took time out that spring to conduct interviews for the Rosenwald Fund, as she had done in previous years. Traveling was difficult (often by day coach at night, since berths were not available), but she felt she owed it to the fund. The *Strange Fruit* controversy intruded briefly: she found that she could not return to Spelman College in Atlanta because Nonnie was a Spelman graduate and the president said Lillian had disgraced the college and was not welcome.[18]

In the summer she returned to Old Screamer for camp. For the first time she had enough money to do some of the things she had always wanted to do, such as buying equipment for the theater and craft shop and, most gratifying, paying off the mortgage on Laurel Falls and on the family home. The camp was full when it opened. Only four campers had withdrawn after the banning of *Strange Fruit* and more than forty had asked for their places. The parents who brought their children to camp did not mention *Strange Fruit*—"as though it had never happened," Lillian remembered. But when they came to Parents' Day at the close of camp they talked freely. It was as if they felt relieved that nothing had happened to their children. They were "now ready to tell me the cuts they had received, the nasty phone calls, etc. Many talked quite frankly to me—especially the men who had (some said) been 'defending Miss Lil all summer'."[19]

In the late spring of 1944 Lillian had signed a contract with José Ferrer and Arthur Friend to make a play out of *Strange Fruit*. She spent the summer in Clayton managing the camp and writing the script with the advice of her sister, Esther, a dramatics professor who had had a good deal of experience producing and directing college plays. Lillian wanted the play to focus on the destructive effect of segregation on whites, so she omitted the lynching scene. The play was to be done on a stage without curtains and with just one set, using blackouts and spotlights to move from one scene to another. When they saw the script, the producers declared it too experimental. Lillian thought Ferrer, the director, liked it, but he would not help her fight the "old-fogy" producers. For a time she considered breaking the contract rather than changing the script. Then one night Ferrer telephoned her from San Francisco (where he was playing Iago in *Othello*) and talked for almost two hours, begging her to stay with the contract and revise the play. Lillian feared that if she made the desired revisions, including restoring the lynching scene, the emphasis of the play would shift from the dehumanizing influence of segregation on whites to the unjust treatment accorded Negroes in the South. She said Ferrer "cajoled, flattered, talked sense, injected humor and imagination" and finally persuaded her against her "hunches" and "deep intuitions." She called Esther to ask her to come up to New York to help with the revisions, found an apartment, and began reworking the script. In November Esther suffered a head injury and the next month she and Lillian returned to Clayton. During Esther's long and difficult convalescence Lillian continued working on the play, occasionally traveling to New York to discuss it with Ferrer and George Jenkins, the stage designer. In August she and Esther, now recovered, moved to New York to begin casting and rehearsals. *Strange Fruit* had become a heavily staged, two-act play, with many large sets and twelve scenes (which required thirty-five stagehands, as many as some musical shows). The cast was also large: thirty-four actors and actresses, about half of them Negro.[20]

The play opened in Montreal where it was well received, went on to Toronto, Boston (where the official censor approved it), Philadelphia, and then to New York City. Lillian described the opening at the Royale Theatre on Broadway, November 29, 1945, as "very smart, very fashionable: everybody who should have been there was there: big actors and actresses . . . big name society people." The audience was warm and responsive and called her to the stage to take a bow. But the early morning reviews were "mixed & some were mean" and, she remembered, "we knew we were in trouble." The New York drama critics praised Lillian's honesty and sincerity (as the book reviewers had), but they criticized her stagecraft as sprawling, rambling, verbose, confusing, and "lacking in sustained force and continuity." In trying to dramatize the life of an entire southern town, Lillian had cluttered the play with too many episodes and too many actors. "All too often," Wilella Waldorf wrote in the New York *Post*, "Mr. Ferrer, as director, seems to be more of a traffic control officer than anything else."[21]

With so large a cast and so many stagehands, *Strange Fruit* needed a full house for almost every performance to meet its payroll and other expenses. When audiences dwindled, the cast became depressed, Ferrer stopped coming to the show, and finally he gave notice that it would close in a week. Lillian used her proceeds from the play, fifteen thousand dollars, to keep it running for another two weeks. She had been cutting and improving it all along, and she now realized that drastic revisions would be necessary to save it. However, she felt too discouraged and exhausted to make them. The play closed on January 19, 1946.[22]

Lillian did not take kindly to criticism of *Strange Fruit*, but her reaction varied depending on the source. She was able to dismiss the fulminations of what she referred to as "the lunatic fringe of the fascist groups and the white supremacy crowd." She admitted being hurt by the cold treatment she received in Atlanta and elsewhere in the South. "I was . . . frozen out; people were rarely nasty-rude . . . just froze me out, stared through me, wouldn't wait on me in stores, etc." On the other hand she was able to see the humor in the way the Clayton library reacted. She told Charles Bolté "that it was unthinkable for the Clayton library to shelve the book, equally unthinkable for it not to catalogue the book by Clayton's leading citizen, so she and the librarian did a deal: Lillian gave the library a copy and then checked it out herself, and never returned it. Never got an overdue notice."[23]

The Clayton library, even the "Dixie demagogues" and white supremacists were, after all, home folks, fellow southerners. Lillian had expected the novel to anger and possibly shock many people in the South, and she was able to deal with their reactions. She felt similarly about the "Boston banners." They were like the Dixie demagogues, mindless and rather silly—and, it turned out, harmless.[24]

The reviewers for the eastern literary magazines and journals were another matter. Lillian insisted they had misunderstood her and did not hesitate to express her dissatisfaction. In an article for the *Saturday Review*, published in February, 1945, she complained that even the most generous of the white critics had failed to treat the novel as literature. Instead they had viewed it as a social problem novel written for the purpose of bettering race relations. If she felt white critics had misunderstood her, she believed she had suffered worse treatment from many Negro critics and all of those on the Left. In her view, their response constituted nothing less than betrayal. She thought she had portrayed blacks honestly and realistically and could not understand the black reviewers' criticism, especially the insinuation that she was prejudiced against Negroes. She became even more resentful when she decided that Walter White, a man she regarded as a friend and ally, shared their views. White had helped her during the writing of *Strange Fruit* by suggesting publishers who might be interested in it, but he was unhappy with the novel and quite critical of the play. He explained in a letter written after he had seen the play in Boston that his main concern was the character Nonnie. "I can understand a girl who had grit who goes through college and, because of having fallen in love, being willing to go back to a town like Maxwell and nurse a fretting child because she wants to be near her lover," he wrote. He could understand her having a child by her lover, though he doubted a girl coming from a family like the Andersons would be as indifferent to public opinion regarding illegitimacy as Nonnie was. But, he continued, "the scene on the ridge where Tracy asks Nonnie if she would live in the house near the one where Tracy and his wife-to-be would be living, to which question Nonnie replies, 'I love you', made me writhe. I just don't believe that a girl like Nonnie under those circumstances would be willing to do this." White admitted he was distressed by the play partly for personal reasons; his daughter Jane was playing the part of Nonnie. But also, as executive secretary, he was concerned about the effect on the NAACP. He feared that because Jane was his daughter, her playing a character who was "almost like a sleep walker in spots can and possibly will cause repercussions" harmful to the civil rights organization. Lillian had little sympathy for White's "fierce resentment," which she attributed solely to his concern for Jane and which she felt was directed not only at the play but at her personally. She seems to have put him in the same category with the "embittered Negro racists" who she said met Jane nightly at the stage door before the play "to tell her she was disgracing the Negro race."[25]

In the *Saturday Review* article Lillian complained about charges by "the lunatic fringe of the C. P." that *Strange Fruit* was unfair to the Negro and to labor. According to her later recollections, her controversy with the Left began with the publication of the novel, when she discovered that her editor, Frank Taylor, was trying to "insinuate to the Commies in New York" that she was a fellow traveler. When she realized what was going on, she made "a big speech taking a clear stand against communism." As a result, she claimed, the Communists were furious with her. They had been pushing the book, but now they turned against it. She was especially bitter about the response of the *Daily Worker* and the *New Masses*. She remembered that initially they gave the book "glowing reviews" but then they published reappraisals in which they took back everything they had said. "They said in review #2 that I was a very sly, shrewd 'charming' defender of 'Capitalism'. They said 'Look how interesting and likeable she made the mill owner etc. etc." Actually, the initial reviews were not so glowing as Lillian remembered some twenty years later. Mike Gold in the *Daily Worker* praised *Strange Fruit* briefly for its "high moral fervor" but admitted he had not read it and was basing his estimate on others' reports. Samuel Sillen in the *New Masses* emphasized its "seriousness of . . . purpose" and declared it a "rich and challenging novel," though not a

completely successful one. Nor were the reappraisals exactly as Lillian
later described them. About two weeks after he had praised the novel,
Gold published a letter he had received from an old college professor
whom he described as "one of the best progressive elements in the
South." Professor X objected to Lillian's picture of a southern lynching.
"She conveys the impression that only poor whites do these horrible
things," he wrote. "The good, respectable, educated members of the
community, doctors, merchants, lawyers, etc. wouldn't soil their hands
or stoop to such vile things, she indicates. The respectables even try to
prevent working class whites from lynching." Professor X also wondered why the novel needed "to be smeared with what the enemy calls
lewd and vulgar language." He thought such language kept the people
who most needed to read the novel from reading it. In the *New Masses*
reappraisal, Myra Page criticized Lillian for failing to develop the character of Nonnie and for being unsympathetic to poor whites, present-
ing them as "spineless, complaining pawns," but she also praised
Lillian's compassion, seriousness, and realistic style.[26]

The controversy with the Left over the novel set the stage for an
even nastier confrontation over the play. In later years Lillian went so
far as to charge the Left with sabotaging the play. She admitted that
other factors contributed to its failure. She conceded that there were
problems with the script, that the play moved too slowly and clumsily,
though she tended to shift the blame to the producers who had urged
her to revise the original script, "to make it over into somebody else's
idea." She blamed José Ferrer's "careless amateurishness," his "lack of
craftsmanship and expertise." She also thought the play had been affected by the dropping of the atomic bomb, after which, she said, "no
one wanted to look at American sins and troubles." But she put most
of the blame on the fact that "the communists . . . decided to kill
Strange Fruit" in order to promote "their official play," *Deep Are the
Roots.*[27]

Lillian claimed that Communists and fellow travelers in key places
on some of the New York newspapers engineered a complete news
blackout of the attempted banning of the play in Philadelphia. "Had
this news appeared in NYC," she declared, "our theater would have
been full and the play made for six months anyway." On opening night

in New York, she contended, "the commie stage hands (everybody knew they were commie-dominated) began to fight me; at every hushed moment they deliberately dropped something big backstage. . . . they slowed down in changing scenes, they made horrible noises, they did all they could to ruin that play." She also claimed that in favoring *Deep Are the Roots* over *Strange Fruit*, New York leftists were following the Communist line that "a white girl must be in love with a Negro man and best of all a Negro from 'the masses.'" This may have been so, but the reviews of the play provide no substantiation for her opinion. The two opening-night critics who compared *Strange Fruit* with *Deep Are the Roots* praised Lillian's play as the better of the two. So did Stark Young in the *New Republic*. Samuel Sillen, writing in the *Daily Worker*, called *Strange Fruit* "a disappointingly poor play" and argued that unlike *Deep Are the Roots* it failed "to focus on a central theme" and consequently failed "to illuminate the grave problem it sets out to describe." But several weeks later the *Worker* ran another article by Eugene Gordon. He admitted the play's weaknesses (especially "its assertion that the 'riffraff' and the 'millworkers' are the chronical lynchers, while 'respectable' men like the millowner are the Negro's protectors"), but he thought it "definitely worth seeing" because "it attempts to say important things which warrant support." And about a week after he had reviewed the play and though he admitted he disagreed, Samuel Sillen quoted a statement in his column by Paul Robeson saying he "'wish[ed] that every American could see this moving and prophetic play.'" Robeson had seen the play about a week after it opened. Lillian remembered that afterward he came backstage to speak to the cast.

> Paul Robeson made us the most poignant, deeply touching speech I have ever heard; he began calmly but in a moment he was weeping as he said he had been looking at his life; that he never expected to see such a truthful, honest, deeply understanding play in his lifetime; but here it was; he stopped and sobbed for a moment; then he went on telling us about his childhood; and by this time we were all crying, whites and blacks together, holding each other's hands, sometimes suddenly putting our arms around the person next to us. It was so beautiful, so real, so genuine, so quietly dramatic. Here was one man who was a different kind of Communist—not a silly American Commie following a stupid Stalinist line; he was a Communist because he loved the Russian people who had treated him and his wife and their son as real persons all the

time they lived in Russia; you can't blame a man for that. He was truly great that night.[28]

In her controversy with the Left over the play, Lillian was resentful, bitter, even slightly paranoid. Her feeling of betrayal was profound. When the play closed she was hurt, baffled, exhausted. "It was all over but hard to let it go. Two or three mean months ensued," she remembered. She spent the spring of 1946 "trying to get out of the doldrums."[29]

# V A Southerner Talking

Underneath all our troubles, our blindness, there is a good South a-growing, a creative people who are beginning to lift themselves out of their old defensiveness and are coming to terms with the world they live in. . . . Yes, I am pro-Southern.

As editor of *South Today* Lillian had achieved considerable recognition by the middle 1940s, not only in the region but in the nation at large. By 1943, circulation of the magazine had reached 5,000, and reprints of some articles sold in the tens of thousands. One of the most popular, "There Are Things To Do," which had appeared in the Fall-Winter, 1943, issue, sold 250,000 copies. In February, 1943, Lillian was named to the 1942 Honor Roll of Race Relations compiled by the Schomberg Collection of the New York Public Library. One of six whites so honored (including Wendell Wilkie and Franz Boas), she was cited for maintaining "a consistent liberalism in a land where it takes courage to be liberal."[1]

As the author of *Strange Fruit,* she received the 1944 Page One Award given by the Newspaper Guild of New York, and in 1945 was awarded the Constance Lindsay Skinner Award presented by the Women's National Book Association "in recognition of meritorious work." She remained disappointed that *Strange Fruit* was recognized more as a race novel than a literary achievement, but she was not unwilling to accept the role it conferred on her as an authority on the South and race relations—and to avail herself of the wider forum now open to her. She and Paula suspended publication of the magazine with the Fall-Winter, 1944–1945, issue, and during the next several years

Lillian engaged in a rather strenuous program of article writing and speechmaking. She went on several radio programs, including the popular "Town Meeting of the Air," spoke at such colleges as Yale, Harvard, Smith, Mount Holyoke and Queens, and to many religious or interracial groups. She also lent support to various organizations, including the American Veterans Committee, the Southern Conference Educational Fund, the Workers' Defense League, and the National Citizens' Political Action Committee. For the last-named organization, created in 1944 by the CIO Political Action Committee to reelect FDR, Lillian wrote a public letter which appeared in newspapers throughout the country, including the New York *Times* and the Atlanta *Journal.*[2]

She was also active in the Americans for Democratic Action (ADA) during the late 1940s and 1950s. She served on its national board, spoke on its behalf in Chicago, Columbus, and Philadelphia, published several articles in the *ADA World,* and wrote letters requesting contributions to the organization. One of her letters, urging support of a federal antilynching bill, gained over one thousand dollars in contributions from some two hundred people. In March, 1948, she appeared before a Senate committee to testify on behalf of the ADA in favor of abolishing the poll tax. When *Killers of the Dream* was published, she persuaded W. W. Norton to contribute fifty free copies to the ADA to distribute to politicians, publicists and, she suggested, "a few rich old ladies."[3]

In the articles she wrote after *Strange Fruit,* Lillian elaborated on the themes she had developed in the early 1940s. She discussed the effect of segregation on the intellectual and emotional development of children, white and black. She reiterated her opinion that segregation was as damaging to whites as to blacks, and that it was not just a means of regulating relations between the races but, borrowing from her letter to Guy Johnson in an article she wrote for the *New Republic,* a "psychological mechanism used by men the world over whenever they want to shut themselves away from problems which they fear and do not feel they have the strength to solve." Far from being "merely a Southern tradition," segregation was "the most conspicuous characteristic of our entire white culture," she declared in another article. Those who insisted on viewing race relations in terms of "the Negro problem" were at a dead end. The problem, she asserted over and over again, was the

white man and his need to feel superior to other races. There was no
Negro problem. It was something conjured up by white people who
were afraid or unwilling to look inside their own hearts and minds. As
she declared in an address to the New York *Herald Tribune* Forum, "We
have not yet faced the painful fact that whatever the problem is concerning white people and colored people, it will be found in the ideas
and feelings which we white people have about ourselves and our
color."[4]

In an article for the *New Republic* entitled "Addressed to White Liberals," Lillian criticized those who maintained that segregation must
change slowly. "I believe it can change as rapidly as each of us can
change his own heart," she wrote. "I believe it will never change until
we look at what it is doing to the personality and character of every
child, every grown-up, white and colored, in the South today—and to
a less bitter degree throughout the country." The time had come for
those who did not believe in segregation to say so, to break "the conspiracy of silence which has held us in a grip so strong that it has become a taboo." It was the same prescription she had urged previously
in *South Today:* whites must first recognize the nature and effects of
segregation, then give up allegiance to it, and finally speak and act
against it. Although Lillian believed that segregation and the notion of
white superiority were the product of psychological maladjustment,
she also insisted that they could be eliminated by an act of individual
will. Giving up a belief in segregation involved giving up racial hatred
and prejudice that supported it. Each individual must rid himself of
"his personal need to hate, his need to feel superior to other human
beings, his arrogance." She thought Negroes would have to help, too,
in bridging the chasm between the races. They would have to "discard
their suspicions of whites, *their* need to hate other people, *their* need to
feel persecuted." She demanded of blacks the same act of the will she
demanded of whites. How it might be elicited she did not explain. She
did say that it was not something that a mass movement or laws could
achieve, and that to cleanse one's heart and mind of destructive impulses was "the hardest job a human being can undertake, and the
easiest."[5]

Even before prejudice and suspicion had been eliminated, there
were bridges that could be built across the chasm separating the races.

Here, apparently, was the place for legislation and collective action. Lillian suggested working for a national and permanent Fair Employment Practices Committee (FEPC), for state FEPCs, and for all kinds of laws outlawing discrimination in jobs and wages. She urged efforts to rid the South of the poll tax and the white primary. She called for justice in the courts for all people and for public works to produce jobs that would be "a fine insurance against riots, against racial and religious violence, against labor-industry fights." She urged efforts for federal aid to education and exhorted whites to join interracial groups, to make friends with people of other races and religions and nationalities, to "sit by people of other color whenever it is possible to do so," and to refrain from telling race jokes or using derogatory names. She had offered these suggestions earlier in *South Today* to "intelligent white Southerners." Now, in the *New Republic,* she addressed them to "white people . . . wherever they may live." She was convinced that segregation was a problem confronting all Americans, not just southerners. Moreover, she thought that action to abolish it would have to come first in the North. At a Hunter College conference on racial and religious prejudice, she declared, "The North will have to take the initiative in abolishing racial segregation. With the pace set, the South will find the courage to follow. As long as the North has its racial barriers, the South has a wonderful excuse for continuing with the same policy."[6]

While writing and speaking about segregation as a national problem, Lillian became involved in the politics of her home state, Georgia. Since the early 1940s she had been an outspoken critic of the governor, Eugene Talmadge. During the 1946 gubernatorial election she wrote a piece opposing his campaign of fear and hate and offered it to two anti-Talmadge newspapers. Both refused it, though it was subsequently published in the *Nation.* One of the editors who rejected it called it "one of the most beautiful things" Lillian had ever written, but explained that publishing it would probably help Talmadge and only hurt "the cause of decency and democracy in Georgia."[7]

Such thinking reinforced Lillian's skepticism regarding the anti-Talmadge people, particularly Ellis Arnall. In a 1943 article in *Common Ground* she had expressed doubts about Arnall's recent victory over Talmadge. Granted, Arnall was an intelligent, energetic man who would probably give a few reforms to the state, would "keep his nails clean and not spit on floors," and would "not directly incite race riots." But, she pointed out, during the campaign Arnall had defended segregation and repudiated racial equality as zealously as Talmadge. Arnall and his men defended themselves by saying that nobody could have won the election had he espoused racial equality, an argument Lillian dismissed as a variation on the time-worn refrain, "*This isn't the right time.*"[8] Because Arnall's performance as governor confirmed her initial view of him, she criticized the Southern Conference for Human Welfare for promoting him as a friend of the Negro and democracy.

Her opinion of Arnall and his people improved slightly in early 1947 when they fought the take-over of the governorship by Herman Talmadge, Eugene's son. She wrote in the *Nation* that Arnall "spoke out for democracy more firmly than ever in his political career. He spoke eloquently for constitutional law and order. He thrilled many people by his words and by his wise acts." But, she contended, Arnall and other Georgia liberals would have to do more than offer good government to counteract Herman's appeal. They would have to give up their condescension toward rural folk and show some interest in rural needs. White Georgians, especially the country people who constituted a majority of the population, suffered from "a profound sense of social inferiority" and neglect that Herman was able to exploit by preaching white supremacy and by promising them "the many little things" they needed. Arnall and his supporters would have to supplement their talk of monopolies and freight rates (which Lillian admitted were important but not of much concern to rural folk) with talk about hospital care for children, aid to education, and economic security for the elderly. If Arnall "would go 'all-out' for everyone's right to be human, to be well fed, well employed, healthy, secure, and esteemed, he could substitute these fundamental rights for the phony right to be 'Cracker and white' that the rural folks now cling to," she wrote. "He could tap great sources of energy in the state, for these people have boundless energy that will be used either for good or evil." Arnall and the liberals must learn "the fundamental principle of politics: you have to give the people something to believe in with all their hearts, or something to hate with all their hearts; and plenty of bread."[9] Just as in earlier writings on race relations and the South, Lillian was reiterating her notion that economic improvement was important but that the psychological dimension of the race problem must also be addressed.

Lillian also became involved in the politics of Rabun County. In 1947 and 1948 her brother Frank was running for a fourth term as county ordinary. Lillian was proud of him and the reputation he had earned as a progressive by promoting, among other things, a county library and maternity home, both of which admitted blacks as well as whites. During the campaign his opponents sought to defeat him by linking him with Lillian and her ideas about racial equality. She described the smear campaign in a letter to Edwin Embree: "taxi cab drivers told how hundreds of 'niggers' came to my hill, how I rushed out and embraced each one of them." She and Frank decided to say nothing in response. "But the people did it for us," she wrote.

> The old female gossips of Clayton riz up and defended me, yeah by God they did! I never expected them too [sic] but they did. Most of them said it is ridiculous and let it go at that. "Of course she has a few Negroes out there at conferences," they said, "why not?" they said. "But she can't have hundreds, she doesn't have that much room." "As for kissing," one of them said, "Lil doesn't kiss anybody except an occasional child whom she's fond of. I've always said she didn't show enough affection. So I know she hasn't started a new habit in her old age." It really was very funny. One poor old sister who was determined to do her part in my defense said "I bet it was Jews she kissed anyway; Jews and 'darkies' (her words) looke [sic] a lot a like [sic] in the twilight. I bet it was that."

Within a week, all of the talk had stopped. "It was all hushed up in one week. Simply stepped on, as if one stepped on a louse." Lillian was almost incredulous. "I could not believe it myself; with all my faith in their essential decency I could not quite believe it could happen like that." The lesson she drew from the experience was that "where you are known, your whole life is known, your every-day acts and words are known, you can take any decent stand you want to take. It is only people who are 'ready to be hated' who get the other treatment in a small town."[10]

Lillian's appreciation of Clayton, and the South generally, had been growing steadily since the publication of *Strange Fruit*. In an article written for the Atlanta *Journal,* she had remarked on "the wonderful loyalty of friends throughout the South and especially in my home town of Clayton" and "the good humor and tolerance of Rabun County neighbors, who accept my strength and my weakness as simply as I accept theirs." During the middle 1940s she maintained an apartment in New York City, but disappointed by the northern reaction to *Strange Fruit* and finding life as a celebrity increasingly hectic, she found more and more satisfaction in her visits to Clayton. "How good it was . . . to get back on the mountain again" and "to return to the old way of life," she wrote in the *Journal,* adding that she sometimes thought it would be a relief if her career as a best-selling writer were over.[11]

In 1947, after what she described as three years of "a kind of long-drawn-out troubled night," Lillian returned to Clayton. "I came 'home', literally and psychologically," she explained to Edwin Embree of the Rosenwald Fund. Although Clayton had remained her legal residence, she realized that she had been "away in mind and body and spirit much too long." She wrote:

> I came home, dismissed my big staff that had been trying to handle my strange notoriety and all the queer, artifical [*sic*] demands it had made on me, and settled down in my same little rock house, exactly as I lived when you first visited me here. I did as much of my own typing as possible, I put on old slacks and lived in them, I stopped answering the telephone (for a dreadful while I had as many as 20 long distance calls a day) I worked in the fields with the men, I read, I talked to Paula, and gradually I found my soul again—its muscles a little shrivelled from disuse but still healthy I believe and pray.

She felt more and more accepted, more and more at home, in Georgia and the South—except for Atlanta. "It is only Atlanta that stills [*sic*] snubs me in Georgia," she wrote. "Here in Georgia the rural people have treated me with more esteem than the so-called liberals in Atlanta." Other southern cities had invited her to speak, but not Atlanta. "It is only Atlanta that is still afraid to invite me to speak; only Atlanta papers that will not mention my name in the news or when they do only to pass on a bad rumor; only Atlanta. . . . They have taken a stand against me and do not know how to crawl down from it, I suppose."[12]

Feeling more accepted by her region, Lillian was perhaps more inclined to assert her identity as a southerner. In the late 1940s she continued to speak out on southern as well as national issues, but she made it clear that she was speaking as a white southern woman living in Clayton, Georgia, who loved what was good in the region but who also feared and sought to eliminate the poison that infected it. On March 22, 1948, she wrote a long letter to the New York *Times,* prompted by the burgeoning southern revolt against President Truman and his civil rights program. In early February Truman had sent an unprecedented special message to Congress calling for civil rights legislation, including an antilynching law, an anti–poll tax law, a permanent Fair Employment Practices Committee, and the prohibition of discrimination and segregation on interstate trains, planes, and buses. Truman declared that he would soon issue an executive order "containing a comprehensive restatement of Federal non-discrimination policy," and he indicated that he had instructed the secretary of defense to eliminate discrimination in the armed forces "as rapidly as possible." Although Truman's proposals were more moderate and less comprehensive than those of his Committee on Civil Rights (whose report, *To Secure These Rights,* had been published in October, 1947), they intensified resentment and foreboding among white southerners.[13]

According to Robert Donovan, "Truman's message touched off such an outburst of comment on Capitol Hill from members from Mississippi, Alabama, Louisiana, South Carolina, and Georgia as often exceeded the standards of what was printable in the newspapers of those days." Georgia's Senator Richard Russell became the spokesman of southerners determined to defeat civil rights legislation in the Congress, and Truman's program became the principal issue in the state's special gubernatorial election. The two leading contenders were Herman Talmadge, who emulated his late father in championing white supremacy and states' rights, and the incumbent Melvin Thompson, who also defended segregation. A resurgent Ku Klux Klan joined in attacking Truman and his program. Throughout the state, the Klan had been using county elections as occasions for cross burnings, parades, and demonstrations. In early March, the Atlanta *Constitution* reported a Klan demonstration in Wrightsville at which Dr. Samuel Green, the Georgia Grand Dragon, criticized Truman's civil rights program, declaring that "The Klan will not permit the people of this country to become a mongrel race." Those who did not want the United States to be "a white man's country" as the founders intended, should move elsewhere, Green said. "We want to see the Negro treated fairly, but whenever the Negro takes a place at the side of white men through force of Federal bayonets, blood will flow in streets of the South," he warned.[14]

Lillian began her letter to the *Times* by identifying herself as a southern woman who was "deeply shocked that our liberals are putting up no real fight for human rights in the South." For weeks, she observed, the newspapers had been full of "demagogic race fear, Yankee hate, affirmations of the 'great belief' of White Supremacy." Nevertheless, "Southern liberalism maintains its old grim silence." Once again, as in the early 1940s, Lillian criticized the conservatism and timidity of southern liberals, but the development of the Cold War provided a new twist to the argument. The timidity of southern liberals was not hard to understand, she wrote, if "we remember that Georgia, U.S.A., still has a lot in common with Georgia, U.S.S.R. Totalitarianism is an old thing to us down home." The authority of white supremacy and the one-party system, both nourished on poverty and ignorance, had "solidified the South into a totalitarian regime" long before the Russian Revolution of 1917. Political demagogues in the South "used and still use the same tricks Stalin uses today: an external enemy to hate (the damyankee), an internal enemy to fear (the Negro), an iron curtain which was first forged out of the reluctance of the democratic few to take an open stand against such powerful forces."[15]

Whereas in the early 1940s, in articles like "Are We Not All Confused," Lillian had viewed the conservatism and timidity of southern liberals as an outgrowth of childhood training and unconscious fears and anxieties over which they had little or no control, now she criticized their self-imposed censorship. Southern liberals had not only allowed themselves to be hypnotized by demagogic oratory; they also indulged themselves in an "awful if unconscious snobbery." She was referring to the belief of the southern liberal that "everybody is prejudiced but me." It was easy to think so, she admitted, "because we hear nothing to the contrary," but that was because liberals themselves failed to speak out. Lillian placed more responsibility on southern liberals because she thought it was less dangerous to challenge segregation in 1948 than previously. Then, to speak out "was truly the dangerous act of a fool (though a great fool); to speak out today is a mildly dangerous act of great wisdom." It was hard not to conclude that "we just don't love human freedom enough to take real risks for it."[16]

Lillian conceded that it was impossible to change the views of southerners overnight (though she called the notion that "everybody is prejudiced but me" a "vast, though unintentional, libel against the whole South"). But liberals could and must change overnight. They must give up silence, which was a poor way of changing people, and begin a concerted effort in the newspapers, on radio, from the pulpit to "break the back of demagoguery . . . by giving Southerners something else to believe in and making them fall in love with their new beliefs." This could be done in a year, she declared. Long-range rural programs to combat the poverty and ignorance that nourished prejudice were important, but they would take ten years even with hard work. "We don't have ten years now," she insisted. The South was at a watershed. Liberals were faced with their only chance to save human freedom. Her sense of urgency derived partly from her appreciation of the influence southern demagogues continued to wield, but also from her fear that some southerners might be attracted to another, equally pernicious brand of totalitarianism. The Communists were not waiting for liberals to decide what to do, she observed. Drawing on her earlier comparison of Georgia, U.S.A., and Georgia, U.S.S.R., she noted that "people long used to one authority find it easy to accept another. The Solid South founded on the authority of White Supremacy, held firm by one party and a hatred of 'those enemies outside,' might not find it too hard to accept the authority and one-party system of the Solid Soviets." She did not explicitly equate the Communists and the Progressive party, but the implication was there. "Already," she noted, "the Wallace Party is gathering up many of our young idealistic Southerners while their elders are still saying 'This isn't the right time,' and the demagogues are still screaming about 'our enemies in the North.'" Southern liberals were caught up in the "drama being played on stages all over the world today: liberalism squeezed to death between the Right and Left reactionaries."[17]

In October, 1948, Lillian began writing a weekly column for the Chicago *Defender*, a black newspaper. Welcoming her to a distinguished group of columnists that included Langston Hughes, Walter White, and Mary McLeod Bethune, the editors described her as "a dis-

tinguished daughter of the white South who has risen above the prejudices of her class and section."[18] Appropriately, her column was entitled "A Southerner Talking." In it she ranged over personal matters
(planting a garden on Old Screamer, books she was reading, a visit to
an art gallery, reflections on her world view) as well as national and
international events.

The week before the 1948 presidential election she explained why
she planned to vote for Truman. "I am voting for him because I am a
white Southerner and I am proud of the magnificent thing that he has
done in taking so brave a stand for the civil rights of all Americans,"
she wrote. Besides praising Truman's civil rights program, she also
lauded his support of anti-inflationary controls, the European Recovery Program, federal housing, and aid to education and health, as well
as his opposition to red-baiting and the Taft-Hartley bill.[19]

In a number of columns Lillian discussed political and social issues
growing out of the Cold War. For example when the controversy over
the "loss" of China erupted in the United States, she recalled the three
years she had spent in the Far East. It was not events or policies since
World War II that had determined the fate of China, she argued, but
"the errors . . . committed by us long before this last war began." For
one hundred years Americans and British had preached and practiced
white supremacy in China. The "little touches of arrogance," the "false
airs of superiority," the "poisonous words" and "terrible acts" that she
herself had observed were now "coming back to the Western World,
heavy-laden with dread and death." She did not see how anybody
could be surprised by the Communist victory in China. On the other
hand, she believed that "in the long run totalitarianism hasn't a chance
in China." The Chinese "would merely turn communism to their own
uses." The immediate danger was that acceptance of communism
in China would "open wide the door to its acceptance in India and
throughout Asia." She thought that only "a big moral gesture" by the
United States would prevent this. "We can save the rest of the Far East
only by laying down white supremacy as a way of life," she declared.[20]

In her column Lillian praised the newly founded Americans for
Democratic Action, describing its members as noncommunist liberals,
which is how she regarded herself. She had been suspicious of Communists and fellow travelers before and during World War II, and in

the postwar period she included in the group members of the Progressive Citizens of America and the Progressive party, people she described as still believing that "the best way to work for peace is to defend everything Russia does and to criticise everything the United States does." On the other hand, she refused to endorse the militant anticommunism of so many postwar liberals and ADA members. When Sidney Hook and others organized the Americans for Intellectual Freedom to hold a counterrally protesting the Cultural and Scientific Conference for World Peace on the grounds that it was a communist front organization, she explicitly dissociated herself from them. She said she had no sympathy for the conference because she did not believe "its motives sincere or its backers as clear-thinking as they should be"; and she said she shared the liberals' desire for peace, their concern for human rights and their fear of a police state and authoritarianism. "And yet," she wrote, "I cannot go along with them in this protest. . . . we, who want to bring about our new world have got to find a better way of doing it than wasting our time protesting the Commies' slick little doings. Why don't we get busy and have our own World Conference on peace? And why couldn't we have thought of it first? Do we always have to tag along snapping at their heels? . . . Don't we have any ideas that we might thrill the world with?" In another column she expressed the wish that the white press would stop heckling Paul Robeson and his wife. "I know them both and like them," she wrote. Whatever the truth about the Robesons (she did not believe the whole story, in all its complexity, was being revealed), she did not "see how any white person who has a grain of sportsmanship in him can criticize any Negro, who, in confusion, has turned to communism for the answer that democracy has not yet given." Communism was a poor answer, she thought, "but we white folks have not yet given Negroes in the South a better one. Until we do, I wish we had the grace to keep our mouths shut."[21] Underlying her impatience with the militant anticommunists was her conviction that communism did not pose a significant internal threat to the United States and that liberals should concentrate on the positive goal of promoting democracy rather than wasting time criticizing their opponents. This was, after all, the strategy she had urged on southern liberals in her recent letter in the New York *Times*. Neither silence nor criticism of the opposition was as effective as persuading people to believe in something, whether it was peace or human rights.

As "a Southerner talking"—and writing for a predominantly black audience—Lillian devoted the majority of her columns in the *Defender* to the subject of civil rights. In December, 1948, following Truman's surprise victory, she was optimistic about his civil rights program. As a southerner she knew only too well that the Dixiecrats were "stubborn, shrewd, thoroughly selfish men . . . out to wreck the President's program." She hoped Truman recognized this, that his "great triumph" would not "mellow him too much," and that he would not now weaken on civil rights. She looked primarily to the ADA to fight the Dixiecrats, and she believed "for the first time in many months . . . that the liberals of our country have a real chance to make themselves felt and felt in a powerful way." They now had allies in the Congress, she pointed out, newly elected men like Paul Douglas and Hubert Humphrey "who are wholeheartedly behind the President's program and are really great liberals with a courage and talent that too rarely find seats in Congress." By early spring, however, her anticipation had turned to disappointment. The Dixiecrats seemed immune to attack. By engaging in several weeks of filibuster and voting with conservative Republicans, they were able to defeat an effort by administration leaders to change the cloture rule so as to facilitate the passage of Truman's civil rights program. As Lillian recognized, the Dixiecrats' victory effectively scuttled the president's civil rights program in the Senate and eliminated the possibility of any major civil rights legislation during his second term. In her column she proposed setting aside a "day of public mourning to show the world how deeply we feel this disgrace that filibusters (and their Republican aides) have brought upon us."[22]

Lillian continued to praise the efforts of the ADA and especially Hubert Humphrey to secure passage of federal civil rights legislation. But remarks by Paul Douglas on the last day of the filibuster fight caused her to revise her earlier, admiring view of him and probably other northern liberals. Responding to a question from Georgia's Senator Richard Russell, Douglas declared, "We are not proposing to abolish segregation in the South. We are not proposing to abolish it in housing, or in the Federal aid for education bill. We are not proposing to abolish it in the schools." He went on to say that those favoring the new cloture rule were simply "saying we should give equal opportunity to all the people in the South, black and white." When Russell cited the recommendations of the President's Committee on Civil Rights as attacks on segregation, Douglas replied: "We of the North are only urging the Democratic platform which was adopted in Philadelphia. We are not urging the program of the President's Commission on Civil Rights." He listed the four civil rights planks in the platform: abolition of the poll tax, a federal antilynching law, nondiscrimination in the armed forces, and a Fair Employment Practices Committee law, and asked, "What is wrong with the four planks in the Democratic platform to which I have referred, for which, I believe, the Senator from Georgia has something less than a burning enthusiasm?" Russell admitted having no great enthusiasm for them, adding, "but if the platform were all construed as the Senator from Illinois is construing it, I should feel much better about the future."[23]

"The old familiar phrase: 'We are not proposing to abolish segregation in the South; we just want—' sounds evil enough at home in Georgia, but when said with a Yankee accent it makes one feel sick all over," Lillian wrote. She was shocked that Douglas would "stoop to a double-talk that fools no Southerner" and she noted that "Russell's reply was edged with sarcasm. He knows, as every Southerner knows, that to work for civil rights is to work to get rid of segregation in the South. Every Dixiecrat has this much sense; every demagogue knows this fact of life; it is only we liberals who get confused about such matters." Although she reminded readers of Douglas' honorable record, she contended that although he did not realize it, he had not yet sloughed off "the psychological priorities and economic advantages of White Supremacy." Despite his honorable record, "in racial issues he is still a white man," she wrote. He was like many other northern liberals who sincerely thought they were for civil rights but who had not "thought their way skin-deep into the problem." They still did not see that segregation was the fundamental problem and that legislation on what Douglas called "proximate issues"—such as lynching and the poll tax—was not enough. The main problem, segregation, not just its symptoms, needed to be attacked. Northern liberals did not see segregation for what it was. "They are too concerned with the noise, the violence," she wrote; "it is the pus running out of the sore that offends

and not the sore itself." In this regard they were not very different from
southern liberals like Hodding Carter and Ralph McGill who spent
their time fighting the "foul drainage" from the "sore of segregation"
rather than segregation itself.[24] Although she continued to refer to herself as a liberal (as in "we liberals"), in her view of the race problem
she was not much closer to northern liberals like Douglas than she was
to southern liberals. In the 1940s neither group saw segregation as the
principal problem or advocated an immediate, frontal attack on it, as
she did.

The filibusterers' victory and Douglas' double-talk persuaded
Lillian that change could come in the South only and primarily as a
result of the efforts of southerners themselves rather than the federal
government or northern liberals. "For us to work to pass federal legislation and do so little to change men's beliefs back home is not only
futile but dangerous," she wrote. Newspaper editors, preachers, and
politicians—as well as school board members (thinking perhaps of her
father) and doctors—must be persuaded to speak out against segregation and for human rights. Some way must be found to "go straight to
the people," especially the rural people. "We have got to get to the side
streets and alleys in the cities and to the tobacco roads in the country
with our lesson in human rights and our belief in human dignity," she
insisted. "We have got to reach the cross-roads stores and filling stations." Here she cited the example and achievement of Gandhi, who
had walked from village to village in rural India talking quietly to the
people. She did not minimize the importance of federal legislation, for
she believed in government protecting human rights and filling human
needs. "But I believe more in Gandhi's way. I believe individuals not
connected with politics can do far more than politicians can do. It is
more urgent to change men's beliefs than to pass legislation though I
think both necessary."[25]

Changing men's beliefs was a matter of selling democratic beliefs—
acceptance, dignity, mutual esteem, human rights, freedom and responsibility—to the southern people. Rural southerners, especially,
because of poverty and isolation, had never felt "this mutual esteem of
people, one for another," she wrote. They had taken the drug of white
supremacy when it was offered to them, because they were starving.
Now some were taking the drug of communism when it was offered.

Meanwhile, "we, who have the real food, the real beliefs that increase the stature of men, refuse them to the starving."[26]

Despite the power of Dixiecrats in Congress and demagogues at home, despite the timidity and confusion of northern and southern liberals, despite the scuttling of President Truman's civil rights program, Lillian was optimistic about the direction in which the South was moving. Georgia's new governor, "Hummon," was trying to turn the calendar back to "the evil days of his father's regime," but the old way was not going to come back, she wrote. All over the world, even in the South, freedom and human dignity were on the march. She felt impelled to point out evidence that the South was changing for the better, not only because as a southerner she loved "the sweet and the good" in the region, but also because she thought it helped the cause of civil rights. "We need to hold on tightly to every good, hopeful sign of recovery in this field of race relations," she emphasized. "There is no one more willing to point out evil than am I, nor more willing to criticize the South or North when there is need to do so. On the other hand, we who work with human beings know that while criticism is necessary, so is praise. So is encouragement. So is hope. And we can destroy our chances of recovery, we can actually delay the coming of the good, by too much criticism and too little praise." Perhaps, too, Lillian devoted many of her columns in the *Defender* to the positive changes in the South because she wrote for blacks, many of whom had emigrated from the South before and during World War II in the Great Migration. She noted that many Negroes hated the South and refused to admit there was any goodness or any good person in it. While she agreed and sympathized with a black friend who told her, "'It still isn't legal to be human in Georgia,'" she saw signs that the situation was improving, however slowly.[27]

Ten years ago, Lillian pointed out, segregation was not an issue and "a heavy conspiracy of silence" covered the South. Now some of the southern states, including Georgia, had abolished the poll tax and the white primary, and a number of Supreme Court decisions had paved the way for desegregation of graduate and professional education. Interestingly, Lillian's optimism derived not so much from these major achievements as from other, less publicized indications of a change in the minds and habits of the South. There was Joe Rabun, the Baptist minister who had run for governor of Georgia in 1948 on a platform against the white primary and the poll tax, for the FEPC, and against segregation in the armed services. Another minister, Charles Jones, had welcomed Negroes to his Presbyterian church in Chapel Hill despite protests from the church board and threats from the Klan. And there was Mrs. Dorothy Tilly of Atlanta, who had been working for civil rights for two decades and had gradually reached the point where she was "completely opposed to every form of racial segregation." Besides prominent people like Mrs. Tilly, Joe Rabun, and Charles Jones, there were, according to Lillian, "hundreds, thousands of whites, in the past six years [who] have met with, worked with, eaten with Negroes in full friendship and democracy." In many cases, she admitted, they were doing so secretly or "so quietly that next-door neighbors are not aware that Jim Crow is being flouted," but this was out of necessity rather than choice.[28]

In the past two years, Lillian noted, the churches had finally "broken their silence." Although most ministers were still too scared to challenge segregation, the Fellowship of Southern Churchmen had challenged it. The Methodist women in the South had spoken against segregation in higher education, the Virginia Council of Churches against segregation in public carriers, the Methodist Ministers' Association of Atlanta against the Klan. Even the Southern Baptists had protested against racial injustice, though they had not come out against segregation. She admitted that the pronouncements of the church organizations were "just words." But "good words are spoken before good acts are done." The biggest obstacle to change in the South was the fact that few good words had been said in public against segregation and for human rights.[29]

There were acts, too—not just the quiet, secret acts of the whites who flouted Jim Crow, but more public incidents, like Jackie Robinson's playing ball in Atlanta. Or the fact that the Atlanta papers, promptly and "without hiding one ugly fact," reported the lynching of Caleb Hill. "And every one reading, must have felt less comfortable when he went about his business that day," Lillian wrote. "Women drinking their morning coke at the town drugstore must have felt less pleasure as they sat there. Politicians must have been less sure of themselves and their words." She also pointed to the full-page advertisement in the *Constitution,* run by Atlanta's largest department store, showing pictures of two young Negro graduates in caps and gowns. "That ad went into 187,000 homes and was looked at by at least one fourth of all Georgia's population, many of whom had never before 'seen' a Negro college graduate," she observed. It was a first step in the "mass breaking of stereotypes" so necessary to improved race relations in the South.[30]

Those were minor events to be sure, but taken together with other changes in thought and behavior they seemed to Lillian to promise significant improvement. Although her white friends insisted it would take fifty years, she was much more sanguine, predicting in June, 1949, that "in five years there will be little legal segregation left in the South." There would still be hate and prejudice, she admitted, but she had never believed they could be legislated out of existence. The effort to change habits, values, and attitudes would have to be prosecuted alongside and even after any legislative action against segregation.[31]

Since 1944 Lillian had been thinking about doing a nonfiction book on segregation and the notion of white supremacy, and in 1947 she began working on it. The impulse to begin came while she was at work on a novel, "Julia." She was writing about the suicide of the main character, a clergyman, when she "suddenly saw the South, and the USA, and all 'white culture' in a different and more profound way." She had used the phrase "I have killed my dream" in the clergyman's suicide note, and she suddenly realized that "the killers of the dream are ourselves as well as 'the others' and we kill our dreams on so many levels of being." That became the theme and supplied the title of the new book, *Killers of the Dream.*[32]

In the foreword Lillian described *Killers* as "a story made of memory and historical fact." Elsewhere she referred to it as "an autobiographical account of the Southern way of life as one Southerner understands it." Drawing partly on her own experience and observations, partly on other sources (she said she had learned much about race relations from Gilberto Freyre, John Dollard, E. Franklin Frazier, Hortense Powdermaker, James Weldon Johnson, Walter White, Richard Wright, and W. E. B. Du Bois), Lillian described what it was like to grow up in the South and to live in a segregated culture. She did so not just to understand the South and segregation, but to find the answer to an old question, "Why has the white man dreamed so fabulous a dream of freedom and human dignity and again and again tried to kill his own dream?"[33]

The killers of the dream were the evils and abuses Lillian had been writing about since the 1930s: poverty; ignorance; the political bargains struck between North and South and rich and poor whites (one chapter was a slightly revised version of "Two Men and a Bargain"); timid and confused liberals; and especially the "haunted childhood" of white southerners, the topic Lillian devoted most of the book to. "The white man's burden is his own childhood," she wrote. "Every southerner knows this. Though he may deny it even to himself, yet he drags through life with him the heavy weight of a past that never eases and is rarely understood, of desire never appeased, of dreams that died in his heart."[34]

Lillian did not deny the "velvety texture" of southern childhood, woven out of "sugar-tit words and sugar-tit experiences"—names like honey, sugar, and sweetie, and "kisses and big hugs . . . and tea cakes and bread 'n' butter 'n' sugar," and the warm and melting air, and "everywhere the sweet smell of flowers." This was the childhood she thought most southern whites remembered. But there was a dark and fearful side of southern childhood, too, that Lillian dredged up out of her own and the South's collective unconscious. It grew out of the lessons on sin, sex, and segregation white children learned from their parents, from custom (southern tradition), and from the southern church.

> We learned the intricate system of taboos, of renunciations and compensations, of manners, voice modulations, words, feelings, along with our prayers, our toilet habits, and our games. I do not remember how or when, but by the time I had learned that God is love, that Jesus is His Son and came to give us a more abundant life, that all men are brothers with a common Father, I also knew that I was better than a Negro, that all black folks have their place and must be kept in it, that sex has its place and must be kept in it, that a terrifying disaster would befall the South if ever I treated a Negro as my social equal and as terrifying a disaster would befall my family if ever I were to have a baby outside of marriage. . . . I was put in a rigid frame too intricate, too complex, too twisting to describe here briefly, but I learned to conform to its slide-rule measurements. I learned that it is possible to be a Christian and a

white southerner simultaneously; to be a gentlewoman and an arrogant callous creature in the same moment; to pray at night and ride a Jim Crow car the next morning and to feel comfortable in doing both. I learned to believe in freedom, to glow when the word *democracy* is used, and to practice slavery from morning to night. I learned it the way all of my southern people learn it: by closing door after door until one's mind and heart and conscience are blocked off from each other and from reality.[35]

The haunted childhood of white southerners also included three traumatic relationships—"ghost relationships" Lillian called them. They had "left a lasting impression on all of our people, though few of us, actually, have suffered them directly." They continued to arouse so much terror and anxiety that many urgent problems could not be dealt with rationally. These ghost relationships, like the childhood lessons, needed to be brought to the level of consciousness before they could be finally laid to rest.[36]

The first of the ghost relationships grew out of "the backyard temptation"—the attraction of white men to black women and more generally to the "laughter, song, rhythm, spontaneity" of Colored Town— and the feelings of guilt and hate the illicit relations produced. The second referred to "the South's rejected children," the children of the secret white-black unions, rejected by their white fathers and white kin. The mass rejection of these children was a heavy weight on the southern conscience, Lillian believed. Repressed, it lay "deep in the ooze of the old and forgotten, but when talk of change is heard, it stirs restlessly as if still alive in its hiding place and is felt by minds innocent of participating in the original sin but who for involved reasons have identified themselves with it." The third ghost relationship was the relationship between the white child and his black nurse. Loved by and loving his mammy, the white child ultimately learned to disavow her, but not without shame and anxiety. "Stifled, sometimes forced into the unconscious, though betrayed ingenuously by the bathos of the 'my old mammy' theme, this ambivalent and tragic relationship of childhood . . . has powerfully influenced the character of many southerners of the dominant class," Lillian wrote. Although small in number, the class included politicians, newspaper editors and journalists, college professors and presidents, doctors, preachers, industrialists, bankers, writers, governors and their wives, and many prominent officials in the national government. Thus many of the dominant class in the South "suffered not only the usual painful experiences of growing up in America but this special southern trauma in which segregation not only divided the races but divided the white child's heart."[37]

Lillian's purpose in describing the haunted childhood of white southerners and life in a segregated culture was therapeutic. She explained in an article for the *New York Herald Tribune Weekly Book Review* that she wrote *Killers* to bring to light "hard, bitter facts of life" and to uncover experiences that needed to be understood if the South were to become a healthy society. She said she hoped the book would "bring back not dust and spiderwebs, but important things we need to know, from its search into the dark corners of the past which we have locked our minds in."[38]

By becoming conscious of long-repressed experiences and beliefs, Lillian seemed to be saying, southerners would be able to relieve themselves of their burden of fear, anxiety, and guilt and arrest its movement toward destruction. Although not as optimistic in *Killers* as in many of her *Defender* columns, she did point out that the process of recognition had already begun. Some people in the South "were beginning to see at last what the white man's false beliefs about sin and sex and segregation had done to the minds and spirits of the most powerful nation on earth." A few southerners were "strong enough, mature enough, objective enough to endure such stark knowledge." However, others resisted the new insights. Most people in the region had not yet "found the strength to make the stark decision to give up segregation, though more and more southerners had begun to see it as a crime against the human spirit, and more and more church and religious organizations have taken a stand against it." Liberals, in particular, who were supposed to be "the carriers of the dream," had not given enough thought to the philosophy and practice of segregation. Moreover, they were destroying themselves by factionalism, some joining the Communists, others, convinced that getting rid of communism was the most important task, joining forces "with any and all 'enemies of communism.'" Neither group recognized that "authoritarianism is our worst enemy, wherever it springs up, even in our hearts." Lillian also criticized liberals for too often substituting paternalism for camaraderie.

"Liberals must confess that they themselves have not always accepted the rest of mankind," she wrote. "They . . . have been confused by the word *equality*. Secretly knowing men are not equal, puzzled by this knowledge which seemed in a sense to conflict with their belief in the worth of the human being and his freedom, they retreated to a position of *noblesse oblige*. Even today, they too often substitute paternalism for camaraderie. . . . too many have failed and are failing now to identify themselves with all men as human beings." Because of this, Lillian continued, the Communists were "winning the race for the hearts of men. While the white man in America withholds from colored fellow-citizens the courtesy title of *Mister*, Communists the world over are saying, 'Comrade, just call me by my first name.'"[39]

The story Lillian told in *Killers* was largely one of "failure and frustration and anxiety, a tale of shattered lives and a shattered culture" broken only by rare assertions of the dream of freedom and dignity. How was the South to turn from its "journey towards destruction"? The answer Lillian gave in *Killers* was essentially the one she had long insisted upon. Revitalizing the dream depended on an act of individual will. "Man . . . with feet tied to the past and hands clutching at the stars! Only by an agonizing pull of his dream can he wrench himself out of such fixating stuff and climb thin air into the unknown." It had been done before and now for the first time in history, Lillian declared, man had "the means, the technics, . . . the knowledge and insight and courage" to do it again. The question was, "Does he have the desire? That is a question that each human being must answer alone. It is a secret ballot that one by one we shall cast, and only those votes will be counted that are cast in time."[40]

Lillian's sense of urgency derived from her conviction regarding the symbolic importance of segregation in the United States. "The Negro deprived of his human rights in the United States is a broken promise clattering loudly across the earth, echoing and re-echoing in man's minds everywhere and profoundly shaking their faith in our way of life," she explained in the *Herald Tribune Weekly Book Review*. Much of the world refused to believe that democracy could be better than it was practiced in Dixie. "Democracy's crime" was that "it has not let its dream live where it has had the power to do so."[41] As a result, she believed, the appeal of communism was growing, not so much in the

United States as in the rest of the world. Just as during World War II she had called for an end to segregation to demonstrate the United States' commitment to democratic principles, now in the midst of the Cold War she saw the elimination of segregation as a way of indicating to its own citizens and the rest of the world the United States' commitment to the dream of freedom and human dignity.

Lillian offered the manuscript of *Killers* to Eugene Reynal, who had published *Strange Fruit*, but according to her recollection he did not like it. She then had her agents offer it to W. W. Norton who, she said, "snapped it up immediately." As with her novel, she was disappointed with the reaction to *Killers*. She contended that the reviewers misunderstood it. They reviewed it as a book about race relations, whereas she considered it broader in scope. It was "a criticism . . . of all western culture but especially that part of it we can call 'white culture,'" she argued. What Lillian stated only briefly and rather imprecisely, Daniel Singal has recently confirmed, arguing that she was an important figure in the assault on Victorianism and the development of Modernism that began in the South in the 1920s. Indeed, Singal contends that her writings provide "the clearest articulation" of the anti-Victorian ethos in the 1940s. More than anyone else at the time, he writes, she brought the issues of race and segregation into the open. "With her, the assault against the Victorian ethos reached maturity." In describing the psychic forces sustaining segregation, she "identified the Victorian dichotomy, with its separation of mind and body, as the chief culprit." She challenged the compartmentalization that the inherited southern culture depended upon and sought to "establish a new culture based upon the opening of 'doors' and the recapture of previously forbidden human energies. For her, 'integration' meant more than a racial strategy; it meant the effort to restore man's 'wholeness' in the deepest Modernist sense."[42]

None of the reviewers of *Killers* in the late 1940s discovered in Lillian's work what Singal did. Those who liked it praised it as honest, hard-hitting, blunt, and passionate. The most favorable reviews were by Vincent Sheean on the front page of the *Herald Tribune Weekly Book Review* and Homer Rainey in the *Saturday Review of Literature*. Rainey wrote that the many arguments and apologies previously offered to explain the South had "always left us feeling that the real problem was being dodged." By contrast, *Killers* went to the heart of the matter by dealing with the real trouble with the South—"the terrible curse of segregation." When one had finished reading Lillian's book, he would say, "This is it—this is what I have been waiting to hear," Rainey wrote.[43]

A number of reviewers, even some who liked the book, faulted what they variously described as Lillian's eloquent, impassioned, even tempestuous style. Sheean, for example, suggested that "a greater variety in mood and pace" would have strengthened the book. *Time,* which criticized her advocacy of an end to segregation as "extreme and impractical," was less gentle. *Killers* was written with "more moral power than analytical precision," the newsmagazine declared. It was "badly organized, excessively repetitious and too persistently eloquent," and reading it was "somewhat like eating seven courses of soufflé."[44]

Whether they liked the book or not, reviewers generally agreed that it offered a psychoanalytic analysis of the South. Those who liked the book withheld comment on the validity of the Freudian approach; those who did not like it complained that Lillian either oversimplified or exaggerated Freud's theories in applying them to the South. Nina Ridenour, reviewing the book as a member of the National Committee for Mental Hygiene, observed that Lillian seemed "to have taken her psychiatry in great raw hunks which have remained as yet undigested" and also objected to the overemphasis on sex and the "plethora of sex words" in the book. Ellsworth Faris, writing in the *Christian Century,* agreed that "the prime obsession is with sex" and contended that Lillian's use of Freudian theory resulted in a "confused and ambivalent utterance." He questioned whether her distorted view of the South might not be "only Freudian 'projection,'" a result of the psychic trauma she had suffered in childhood (referring to the story of her friend Julie) and her ambivalent feelings of love and hate for the South.[45]

The most hostile reviewer of *Killers* was Ralph McGill, editor of the Atlanta *Constitution.* The *Constitution* had ignored Lillian since the publication of *Strange Fruit,* which it had not deigned to review, but now it took notice of her and her new book with a vengeance. Jack Tarver, the associate editor, described *Killers* as "very badly done claptrap." McGill echoed the criticisms of other reviewers, but with a venom they had not displayed. Where Ridenour criticized Lillian's approach as too emotional, McGill described it as strident, and where other reviewers charged that her use of Freud resulted in oversimplification and exaggeration, McGill contended that it resulted in a fantastic and warped interpretation of the South. Like Faris, who suggested that *Killers* revealed more of Lillian's own psyche than that of the South, McGill viewed the book almost entirely as a revelation of Lillian's psychological agony. "Miss Smith is a prisoner in the monastery of her own mind," McGill wrote. "But rarely does she come out of its gates, and then, apparently, seeing only wicked things to send her back to her hair shirt and the pouring of ashes on her head and salt in her own psychiatric wounds." Although he credited *Killers* with honesty, eloquence, and even a measure of truth, he concluded that it was basically unsound and "too crowded with her own Freudian interpretations and emotions to be of real value."[46]

What repulsed McGill and discomforted other reviewers, even some who liked the book, was Lillian's fervor and passion, what McGill described as stridency. Those who criticized the Freudian approach of *Killers*, and turned it back on its author, were able to explain, and then dismiss, what they regarded as an overly emotional, wholly subjective, and extreme reaction to the South and segregation. That *Killers* met with this sort of reaction is not surprising. In 1949 few whites in the United States regarded segregation the way Lillian did—as the most important problem of race relations in the country. Moreover, Lillian published *Killers* at a time when, as Harold Rosenberg later observed, analysts of society were adopting the pose of scientific objectivity. In the decade and a half following World War II, Rosenberg pointed out, social critics no longer aimed to incite action; "a passion for social correction" no longer inspired them. "The bland deadpan of the Objective Observer [had] definitely replaced the scowl of the radical observer."[47] *Killers* revealed Lillian to be as much out of step with most liberals and social critics in 1949 as she had been in the early 1940s. Both her commitment to a psychological, and often highly emotional and subjective analysis of the South and segregation, and her stress on the debilitating effects of segregation and the need to abolish it immediately continued to set her apart from the mainstream of white opinion in the United States.

In December, 1949, Lillian was named to the honor roll of the Chicago *Defender* and cited for her "outstanding contribution in advancing the frontier of American democracy." The following year she won the Southern Authors' Award and a special citation from the National Book Award Committee. She was also awarded two honorary doctorates, the Doctor of Humane Letters at Howard University and the Doctor of Letters at Oberlin.[48]

*Killers* was less controversial than *Strange Fruit* had been. The first year of publication it sold about twenty-eight thousand copies. It was never banned, but Lillian said later that "it was quietly smothered to death in numerous places, including a few libraries and many bookstores." She was unable to prove this, however, and so she "swallowed hard and took it." Although she was unhappy with the reception of the book, neither was she particularly surprised by it. She explained in her *Defender* column that she had tried to say in *Killers* "what I feel about our South," and added, "I have tried to say it with love but because I have tried to say it honestly, I know that many will receive it with hate." She had written the book out of a kind of compulsion. "'I had to write this book,'" she told John Hutchens of the *Herald Tribune Weekly Book Review*. "It was like a ghost flitting in and out of my mind until I did." Now that it had been published she would continue to think and talk about segregation in an effort to make people understand its psychological roots. "I'm essentially optimistic about it," she said. "I wouldn't bother about it if I weren't, even though 75 per cent of the 'liberals' in the South seem to favor segregation. But I think some of them are wavering." But she thought she would not write about the race problem again. She told Hutchens she was going to resume work on "Julia," and, she said, it had "nothing at all to do with race."[49]

# VI Mastering Ordeal

I used the Negro-white situation . . . as symptom and symbol of
a broken, fragmented world, and too, as a symbol of a dehumanized
culture. Man is not solid . . . but in his essence is broken and fragmented; all of human growth is an attempt to bridge over the segregated parts of his nature and his culture. And that in a big sense is my
theme in writing.

After the publication of *Killers of the Dream*, Lillian resumed work on "Julia." Then, once again, she gave it up to do a nonfiction work, *The Journey*, which was published in 1954. It was a book
she said she "felt strangely compelled to write." Suddenly, she explained in a letter to Eleanor Roosevelt, "I felt I must drop my other
book and write it. I must find for myself, I said, something more real,
more deeply felt, more widely imagined than ever before; I felt as if I
would soon need what I searched for, to help me out of ordeal." *The
Journey* was a record of Lillian's search, at age fifty-five, for the meaning
and purpose of life. She confessed in the prologue that she was looking
for "something to believe in; something that intelligence and heart can
accept."[1] By the end of her journey she had renewed her belief in the
dignity of man and had discovered a new basis for religious faith.

*The Journey* was typical of the many works of introspection and in-
spiration published in the 1950s, something of a cross between Joseph
Wood Krutch's *The Measure of Man* and Anne Morrow Lindbergh's *Gift
from the Sea*. One critic called it "an inspirational book for the liter-
ate."[2] But it was also a personal, even autobiographical, work, as much
an outgrowth of Lillian's own search for meaning in and for her own life
as a response to questions raised during the so-called Age of Anxiety.

*The Journey* was an inquiry into the nature and destiny of man. "I

106

went on this journey to find an image of the human being that I could feel proud of," Lillian explained in the prologue. Through character sketches of people she had known in the past or met on a recent automobile trip through eastern Georgia, she revealed her belief in the dignity and worth of man. Virtually all the people she described had been through some sort of ordeal. Some had failed to master it, like Cephas who had traded poverty for a dehumanizing materialism, or his wife who (like Nonnie in *Strange Fruit*) had fled from reality into a make-believe world. But the majority of people Lillian described had mastered their ordeal through a combination of courage, love, intelligence, and faith, and in mastering it had become more fully human. Lillian believed that all men were broken or crippled in some way, physically or psychologically, and that they tried to overcome their "brokenness" by "reaching for wholeness." Here was the source of man's integrity, and one of the things that differentiated him from other animals. "He is forever laying a plank across the chasm, relating himself to time, to people, to knowledge, to God, narrowing the gap between dream and reality, creating more and more ties." Man's desire for wholeness would never be completely satisfied, but his effort to achieve it was what made him fully human. It was what persuaded Lillian of his "mortal strength, of man's power not only to survive on this earth but to continue growing in stature." She ended her journey convinced that "we can fulfill our role in this evolving universe of which we have been given such awesome glimpses."[3]

As a statement of Lillian's belief in the dignity and worth of man, *The Journey* is not particularly remarkable. After all, it did little more than reaffirm long-held beliefs, albeit in a larger context and in more philosophical language than her previous writings. The significance of the book is to be found in Lillian's description of her new-found religious faith. As a young woman she had rejected religion—or at least the Bible-thumping, hell-fire-and-damnation revivalism of the southern church—and had become an agnostic. In *The Journey* she recalled that she had embraced science as an alternative to religion. "I felt, as did so many of my generation, that we were at last stepping out of a dark tangled swamp of medieval superstitions and beliefs where mankind had been lost so long, where many were still lost, into a sunny open plain where facts could be clearly seen." There had been "too

much mystery in childhood, too many unanswered questions. . . .
Now we wanted only to get quickly to that open place cleared by science and lighted up with statistics and 'proofs' that no one could question, with 'laws' that could not be broken for anyone . . . , laws that
worked as impersonally, as mechanically, for man as for a machine."
Embracing science meant giving up every belief that could not be
proved. "It meant giving up the deeper presence, faith; it meant giving
up so much that our fathers had cherished." But science provided a
security that her generation desired. It enabled them to escape the unknown by insisting that "the unknown is only a dark closet where there
is a switch (if you are smart enough to find it) that will turn on the
lights 'science' has wired the whole universe with!" Science also seemed
to promise solutions to human problems here on earth, whereas religion, with its emphasis on individual salvation and resignation to the
will of God, seemed to offer none. The other-worldliness of southern
Protestantism had bothered Lillian since the 1930s and 1940s. In the
*North Georgia Review* she characterized it as "at its worst a strong support of an exploitative status quo with no spiritual content; at its best a
means of achieving various ameliorations of society's surface ills and of
giving mystical comfort to those who can take it." In *Killers of the
Dream* she criticized southern preachers' preoccupation with personal
sins to the exclusion of social evils. "Their religion was too narcistic to
be concerned with anything but a man's body and a man's soul," she
wrote. It provided no answers to "the problems of poverty, of race segregation, unions, wages, illness and ignorance, war, and waste of forest
and soil and human relations." In *The Journey* she admitted that religion had provided badly needed emotional support to believers like
Mrs. Timberlake, but she reiterated her charge that "faith in God's
Will was not enough. It had survival value for Mrs. Timberlake. . . .
But it did not keep her children alive; it did not ask the new questions
that led to the flies and mosquitoes and outdoor toilets that had caused
their deaths; it did not fight typhoid and dysentery, and build laborato-
ries and X-ray machines and train scientists and discover penicillin.
Alone, it was a breeding place for disease and ignorance. Alone, it can
only dream of heaven, it can create no future on earth for the children
of men."[4]

By the time she wrote *The Journey*, however, Lillian had decided that science alone was also insufficient. She did not reject science, only the tendency to overvalue it to the exclusion of religious faith. Religion as well as science was necessary to man's well-being and growth—not the "false notions" of southern religion, but some other sort of faith toward which she was now moving. She had begun a search, she later explained to her friend and attorney Donald Seawell, to find "what God is by discovering what He IS NOT; then religion, what it was not; and finally I began to see what it *is*." In *The Journey* she wrote that she and her generation were returning, one by one, from their "flight from the unknown." However, she did not spell out the principles of her new religious faith except to write: "We begin to understand that we can never have absolute knowledge of God and yet He is not 'relative.' It is simply that our knowledge is incomplete and while it will increase as we grow, always there will be the impenetrable between man and God." For Lillian believing in God and being religious meant "believing in something not yet proved and underwriting it with our lives." At this point Lillian was able to declare her belief in God, but that was as far as she had come in her religious quest. Her newfound religious belief was perhaps not as superficial as the "religion-in-general" that was so popular in the 1950s, but neither was it well thought out. Anthony West, reviewing *The Journey* for the *New Yorker*, complained that it "shares with many other inspirational books an irritating fuzziness—not, in this case, of expression, for the author is a graceful and disciplined writer, but of mind." West thought that Lillian was not "quite sure what she [was] driving at."[5]

*The Journey* was an optimistic book. Lillian stressed the dignity and worth of man, his "infinite possibilities," and the bright future that awaited him. She was confident of man's ability to master the ordeal of the modern age, sure that he had found a way of building a new and better life by "building firmly, steadily, swiftly on scientific facts and technics and on men's newly discovered humility and dignity and on their concern for each other." She retained her old faith in science as a means of making a better life in the future, but she now derived new hope from what seemed to be the beginning of a new era in human relationships. She thought that never before in the history of the world had there been so much tenderness and understanding shown toward children, never before "so much concern for the welfare of the stranger and for those who are different." Having concluded her search for meaning and purpose in life, Lillian predicted that the postwar age would not go down in history as the age of anxiety or even as the atomic age. "It will be stamped with the mark of a mastered ordeal," she wrote.

> I believe future generations will think of our times as the age of whole-ness: when the walls began to fall; when the fragments began to be re-lated to each other; when man learned finally to esteem tenderness and reason and awareness and the word which set him apart forever from other living creatures; when he learned to realize his brokenness and his great talent for creating ties that bind him together again; . . . when he learned to accept his need of God and the law that he cannot use Him, to accept his need of his fellow men and the law that he cannot use them, either; when he learned that "what is impenetrable to us really exists," and always there will be the need of the dream, the belief, the wonder, the faith.[6]

Lillian did not discuss the race question in *The Journey*, and in that regard the book represents a sharp break with much of her previous work. On the other hand, it reveals her continuing concern with segregation in the larger, more comprehensive sense in which she defined it—as a psychological mechanism used by men to shut out alien or frightening ideas, people, or events. Whereas previously Lillian had emphasized man's tendency to raise barriers between himself and his problems, now in *The Journey* she struck a more optimistic note in arguing that his innate desire for wholeness had begun to overcome that tendency.

On the basis of the many letters she received from readers of *The Journey*, Lillian claimed that the book had a "tremendous impact" on all kinds of people: "those in small towns and in cities; the sophisticated and the naive; men and women; southerner and northerner." Eleanor Roosevelt's enthusiastic response to the book especially delighted her. She was less happy about the reviews the book received. Before it was released, she had wondered what the eastern literary establishment would do to it and, remembering the reaction to *Strange Fruit* and *Killers of the Dream*, expected the worst. She wrote the philosopher

Horace Kallen that in New York "'the boys' are a bit hostile to me." She thought it was because for some she was too anti-Communist, for others too anti-McCarthy, because she refused to hate her own southern people, and because she refused to glamorize Negroes. Later, after the book had been published, she contended that too many reviewers, and many booksellers as well, had "failed to see its possibilities because they are blinded by their own personal view of me as 'controversial.'" She complained that many reviewers thought of her as a "tough, hard, dominating female." It was an image they had created in their own minds, she insisted. The real Lillian, she wrote Kallen, was "a woman who is trying to think through her human experiences and find something, some little something that is sweet and good and tough enough to cling to."[7]

In fact, few reviewers mentioned Lillian's earlier works, and then only in passing. Most reacted positively to *The Journey*, praising it as thoughtful, sensitive, and—the now familiar adjective—sincere. Their reviews were rather cursory, however, which may be what embittered Lillian. Few reviewers grappled with her notions of the nature of man, God, and the universe. They were more impressed with her character sketches than her metaphysics, with her poetic style of writing than with her philosophical analysis. They probably recognized, though they did not say it outright, that *The Journey* was not a particularly profound work. Still, they professed gratitude for its optimism. Gerold Frank called it "an inspiring, tonic book" and "a tribute to the human spirit, a reaffirmation of the Godhead that is in all of us, even in a day when the frightful shadow of our own destruction lurks in the atom which our own genius has so irrevocably unlocked."[8]

Receiving the Georgia Writers Association award for a book of "non-fiction of the highest literary value," which one might expect to reassure Lillian, merely exacerbated her bitterness about the response to *The Journey* and her other works. The award was made during a two-day meeting of the association in Atlanta in December, 1955. When she was invited to it, she was not asked to give a speech, only to appear and accept the award. She described the event in a letter to Denver Lindley, her editor at Viking Press. Upon arriving at the meeting, she said, she was given "a furtive once-over by everybody. And do you know what the decision was? 'She's a real lady,' they said to each other and to me, and then they said (to each other and to me) 'she is dressed like Park Avenue. Let's ask her to speak to us tonight.' Just like that. So they asked me." Lillian said she decided that if she refused, "their feelings would be hurt for they were feeling the dimensions of their generosity." So she agreed to speak extemporaneously.

> It wasn't much of a speech about the art of writing, it was instead a kind of profound ceremonial in which I, by my verbal gestures, communicated with them as a fellow-Georgian. They heard and their response was amusing but touching, too, as they rushed up afterward to tell me that "now they were going to read my books." One handsome old queen told me "My dear, no matter what you write I know now that your intentions are good." A young doctor told me "I have never read one word you have written; now I intend to read every book of yours." An elderly Baptist minister (of one of the fashionable churches in Atlanta) told me that he was going to preach a sermon on my phrase "security from hope." And so on. After it was over I went to a friend's house (there are only three houses that I now feel free to go to in Atlanta) and asked for as big a drink as she could give me. I was weak as a rag but it was good for me.[9]

Lillian interpreted the Georgia Writers Association award to mean that Atlanta had finally recognized her as a writer, something she had wanted for a long time. But the recognition came so late that she could not help but be resentful. She appreciated the remarks of the people at the meeting, but she felt they had not really responded to her as a writer or social critic. Like the New York reviewers, they had simply created their own image of Lillian Smith—the well dressed southern lady. Perhaps, too, Lillian regretted having allowed herself to be drawn into a "ceremonial" rather than using the occasion for talking about writing or social issues. Lillian praised Flannery O'Connor's speech on contemporary writing at the meeting, describing it as "witty, here and there; sardonic, now and then plain nasty about Georgia and full of good sense and sensitive understanding of the role of the writer." She told Lindley that she sat there "thinking how these young writers can now say things out loud without any realization, actually, of how one or two of us down in the South opened the way for them."[10]

Why she had not spoken as forthrightly as Flannery O'Connor she did not say. Apparently she wanted so desperately to be recognized and accepted in Atlanta that she was willing to tailor her remarks to Atlanta's standards rather than her own. Probably, too, her notion of good manners dictated that she thank the members of the association for the award rather than confront them over their social or racial views.

If *The Journey* did not bring Lillian the sort of public recognition she desired, it did help her through her own ordeal. In 1953 when she was halfway through the book, she learned that she had breast cancer. She wrote Eleanor Roosevelt that she "left the chapter on death half-written and went to the operating room; just before I went under anesthesia, the surgeon leaned down and said 'It is going to help the chapter, and the book; and you will finish both.' And it did; and I did finish it." By July of 1954, though her future health remained in doubt, the prognosis was favorable, and she had regained her old strength and was "looking life square in the face again."[11]

Although Lillian did not discuss the race question in *The Journey*, the Martha side of her nature would not let her neglect what she once referred to as her "racial chores." While working on *The Journey* she wrote several articles on the subject. She had grown increasingly optimistic in the late 1940s about the progress being made on civil rights in the United States, and now, in the early 1950s, she became even more hopeful. She cited the mounting evidence that the walls of segregation had begun to crumble: hundreds of Negroes in white colleges and universities in the South; public libraries in many southern cities open to all regardless of race; desegregated dining cars on southern railroads; Negro members on a number of civic boards in various southern cities; Negro policemen on nearly every southern city police force; more than 750,000 votes cast by Negroes in the last national elections and predictions of twice that in the 1952 elections. She admitted that such changes might seem small, and she agreed that much more needed to be done. But each small change paved the way for another. "Each change is like a hole in a dam; the hole is getting larger and larger; there is no way to plug it now, and soon the old dam will topple." In an article published in the *New York Times Magazine*, July 15, 1951, she predicted that "ten years from today racial segregation as a legal way of life will be gone from Dixie."[12]

Because she saw the South moving against segregation, Lillian was surprised when southern liberals continued to deny that it would or could be abolished. Reviewing Hodding Carter's *Southern Legacy*, she

found it "somewhat surprising that . . . a forward-looking Mississippi
editor and Pulitzer Prize winner should write a book in 1950 based on
the assumption that segregation cannot be questioned in Dixie." Not
only was segregation being questioned "by all of the South's serious
thinkers," it was already crumbling, she asserted. Southerners were beginning to make civil rights a reality, "at least here and there." Progress
was "spotty, much too slow for the stern necessities of our time, but it
is happening."[13]

Lillian also faulted Carter, and by implication other southern liberals, for counseling resistance and delay on the grounds that if desegregation were attempted, there would be racial violence. Such an argument rested on a derogatory and inaccurate judgment of the southern
people. In particular, Lillian disagreed with Carter's portrait of middle-
class southerners as "pompous, self-satisfied, stupidly blind to human
need, unaware of the intellectual currents sweeping across the earth."
She insisted that many of them were "profoundly troubled by the split
between their ideals and their acts, burdened by the authoritarian
pressures of white supremacy, fearful of what the practice of segregation is doing to their own children's growth as human beings." She
also criticized southern liberals' denigration of rural whites. She admitted that they were "frustrated, crippled, impoverished [and] guilt-
burdened" and therefore easy prey for demagogues. But there was another side to the rural white that should be taken into account. "The
rural Southerner cherishes some pretty evil beliefs," she wrote, "but he
holds stubbornly to some fine ones." He had been taught to take the
Bible seriously. If he had heard and absorbed "some vile and sadistic
talk of white supremacy," he had also heard and absorbed the Sermon
on the Mount. "The loudest demagogue cannot blot out with all his
talk of the white man . . . memories of the Man of Galilee who said
'Suffer little children' and who went about gentling the lives of the rejected." Lillian also argued that because of their evangelical background, southerners wanted to be good. "However vague [the] concept
of goodness, however narcissistic its over-concern with body morality,
the *desire to be good* exists, and plays a dynamic role in Southern psychology," she wrote. She cited family love as another positive attribute
of rural whites. "People on Tobacco Road know tenderness and can be
appealed to on its terms," she insisted. "Erskine Caldwell did not

understand this, but those who live close to the poor and esteem them as neighbors know well their concern for children, and the high value they give to kindness." Finally, Lillian noted, the young rural white was different from his father because of his more fortunate childhood and youth. The New Deal had brought him and his family "better health, better jobs, new ways of farming, new outlooks," and World War II had given him "a new world orientation, and sometimes new values and new purposes." She believed that he was "ready for drastic change and can accept it with grace if given help and encouragement from the South's leaders."[14]

Lillian differed from southern liberals in the early 1950s who, like Carter, claimed that desegregation could not occur because the majority of southern whites, especially rural whites, would oppose it even to the point of using violence. Lillian contended that the white leadership of the South, not the people, constituted the main obstacle to desegregation. She was thinking partly of the politicians who manipulated racial tensions to gain and maintain power and the white businessmen who made money from the Jim Crow system, but mainly of the public opinion leaders of the South. If preachers and editors, teachers and writers would stop being passive and start playing a "creative, positive role" in the desegregation process, Lillian was confident that the majority of southern whites, including rural whites, would accept it.[15]

In Lillian's view, in order to play a creative, positive role in the desegregation process, one must understand its psychological dimension. She argued that many southerners, both black and white, did not want to give up segregation because they had deep, psychological reasons for holding onto it. Segregation had become "a part of their personal defense system against the world," a "strong wall behind which weak egos have hidden for a long time." The white man who felt inferior or unsuccessful in his private or public life craved the feeling of superiority that his white skin conferred. The Negro who was frustrated and hurt by discrimination and segregation found a perverse satisfaction in hating white people and in the withdrawal that segregation enforced. "Whom is the Negro going to hate when the white man is no longer his enemy? On whom can he blame his frustrations? Whom is the white man going to feel 'superior to' when Negroes are fully accepted as citizens and human beings? . . . This loss of one's old psychic defense, one's old image of the self, is the price that mankind pays for profound cultural change. And this loss is often the cause of the insane violence that change sometimes brings forth." Violence could be prevented, however, if white leaders helped the southern people to build up new defenses to replace the lost ones.

> We must give back to our people, white and colored, in this time of severe change, *something equal to or better than* that which has been taken away from them. We must not let people feel cheated, if it can possibly be helped, when great change takes place. . . . we must give our people new beliefs, new images of themselves to substitute for the old "Superior white" and the old "Heart frustrated Negro," new outlets for their frustrations, new and creative outlets. . . . It is a tremendous responsibility, an awesome and fascinating job for our writers and speakers and teachers and leaders: to find new words for old, to create new images of ourselves without which we cannot live sane lives, to help men fall in love with new ideals, to find new outlets for the old hates and humiliations.[16]

The more wide-ranging the impact of desegregation, the more important it was to take into account its psychological dimension. Writing in the *New Leader* in September, 1951, Lillian noted that the desegregation of libraries, colleges and universities, and railroad dining cars, though significant, had had a limited impact. "The walls which have come down quickly are those that affect directly only the life of the educated and the socially and economically secure groups in the South," she pointed out. "The next walls are coming down, however, in a different part of town: segregation on buses and streetcars, segregation in movie houses, in railroad and bus stations, in public schools." When those walls began to crumble, there were few families in the South who would not be directly affected. What their reaction would be would depend on how well they were prepared for desegregation by their leaders. Change was inevitable, Lillian declared. *"But how this change is to be met is still in our hands. . . .* It is entirely within our resources to prepare the rural white and his brother in the city slums (North and South) and the Negro and ourselves to meet change harmoniously. We have the means, the psychological insight, the techniques, the communication facilities to see to it that the new psychic deprivations which change brings are met by psychic and physical compensations."[17]

Because it was in the schools that "the ritual of shame and arrogance does its profound harm to the personality," Lillian considered desegregation of the public schools the most important of all the desegregation efforts and the one that would constitute the greatest social change in the South since Reconstruction. Writing on the eve of the Supreme Court decision in *Brown* v. *the Board of Education of Topeka, Kansas,* when she, like most southerners, expected a ruling against public school segregation, Lillian was optimistic about the way the South would react. She admitted the possibility that under stress southerners would act irresponsibly, as she thought their fathers and grandfathers had during and after Reconstruction. But she did not think they would. She thought that many of the old pressures had been lifted from the South. The region was now prosperous and "in close touch with the world." The "old silence" on the race question had vanished, and the South now had "excellent reserves of intelligence, moral beliefs and scientific knowledge to fall back upon." She reiterated her faith in the rural whites' belief in Christian brotherhood. She also suggested, though she admitted that she had no concrete evidence, that television and the experience of the rural whites in the armed services had changed their views so as to make them more willing to accept integration. Finally, Lillian noted the prospect of "strong leadership among the young in the universities and schools." With the help of the younger generation, she was confident the South would be able to meet the ordeal of public school integration in a creative way. The young were not like the tired old southern liberals Lillian had been criticizing for so long. They were "not worried by the old ghost stories," they rarely stopped "to worry about what 'might happen,'" and they didn't "'scare easy.'" More than any other group in the South they could bring about "a richer, more human life for our region."[18]

Two weeks after the Supreme Court promulgated the *Brown* decision of May 17, 1954, Lillian sent a letter to the editors of the Atlanta *Constitution* hailing the decision as "a great historic document—not only because its timing turns it into the most powerful political instrument against communism that the United States has, as yet, devised, but because of its profound meaning for children." She described the decision as "every child's Magna Carta," pointing out that it affected not only the black children who suffered discrimination because of their color, not only the white children who were "injured spiritually" by segregation, but (thinking of segregation in the larger sense) the many children with physical or mental disabilities who were segregated in or prohibited from attending public schools. All of these children were now "protected by the magnificent statement that no artificial barriers, such as laws, can be set up in our land against a child's right to learn and to mature as a human being." Millions of southerners were as glad as she was about the decision, she wrote. She believed that they "will accept wholeheartedly the challenge of making a harmonious, tactful change-over from one kind of school to another."[19]

The *Constitution* did not publish the letter, so Lillian sent it to the New York *Times*, which printed it in full. She saw the *Constitution's* refusal to publish her letter as one more example of the smothering technique that the South had begun to use against her since the publication of *Killers of the Dream*. Not violence, but denigration, ostracism, and silence were the weapons used by those who opposed her views. The Atlanta papers, in particular, had systematically worked to "kill out" her usefulness in Georgia, she charged. They printed "only the 'bad' and 'sensational' news items" about her; they pictured her as "a maniac, a 'wild woman.'" As evidence she cited Ralph McGill's review of *Killers*, in which she said he had pictured her as "a zealot, a twisted person who lived up on a mountain and did not know what was happening," and a syndicated column by Hodding Carter "in which he called me a sex obsessed old spinster whose mind was inflamed etc. etc. by sex fantasies." The papers claimed that anything she said would inflame the people, even though her letters, she thought, were "quiet and sensible." On the other hand, the papers printed "every word the demagogues say about rivers of blood running, about 'intermarriage' etc. etc. etc." McGill and the Atlanta *Journal* would not let her be heard. "How, how in the name of all that is good and decent can I be heard by my southern people?" she asked. "It hurts like the very devil . . . because I really think I love the South in a way that Carter and McGill do not feel at all. You love it very much, you know, if you can accept its profound faults and failings and still want for it and hope for it something good and healthy and alive."[20]

Despite her hurt and bitterness at being smothered, on at least one occasion Lillian was herself guilty of advocating the same technique against a writer who espoused a view at odds with hers. In September, 1954, Paul Bixler, the chairman of the editorial board of the *Antioch Review,* wrote to her asking for a comment on an article by a professor at Alabama Polytechnic Institute advocating gradual desegregation of southern schools so as not to lower their quality. The *Review* wanted to publish the professor's article, along with others giving other points of view. After reading Bixler's letter and the galleys of the professor's article, Lillian replied that she was shocked that the *Review* was "taking seriously such spurious arguments" and was planning to give so much space to "a point of view that is aired by every demagogue, every illiberal newspaper." There was nothing constructive in the article, she declared. "Why publish such a thing? Segregation is no longer controversial. Our highest court in the land has ruled that it is illegal and must be changed. It will be changed." The problem now was how to bring about the change, quickly and "in such a good, creative spirit that it will lift the level of education itself." She concluded her letter by remarking that it was "a pity to encourage this kind of thing anywhere," but for Antioch to do so was truly disturbing. "What has happened to the intellectual life of Antioch?" she asked.[21]

Following the *Brown* decision, Lillian engaged in a variety of efforts to persuade southerners to comply with it. In the summer she began an extensive correspondence with other southerners and started inviting small groups of blacks and whites to the mountain "just to talk with each other, to lay our anxieties and our hopes out for all to examine." In a letter inviting her friend Frank Spencer of Savannah to one such meeting, Lillian explained her strategy. "I feel that if a hundred Georgians could realize that others are ready to act, ready to begin to get things going, that courage would grow in this pitiful old state of ours. Simply yeast: this is what these little meetings can be. . . . We want to bring together people who will scratch up some ideas; suggest what the basic problems are now; how to start things moving on a number of levels simultaneously." She did not plan to publicize the meetings. They were to be "grapevine stuff; the beginning of something that might, just might go far."[22]

In the fall of 1954 she helped Grace Thomas in her campaign for the governorship of Georgia. Mrs. Thomas was the only one of the nine candidates who, according to Lillian, came out "for the Constitution and obedience to the Supreme Court's decision." Lillian wrote one of her speeches, introduced her when she spoke in Clayton, placed ads in the local newspaper for her, contributed to her campaign fund, and even persuaded Eleanor Roosevelt to make a contribution. The outcome of the election disappointed Lillian. She and Mrs. Thomas' other workers failed to swing the liberal vote, which Lillian thought would have insured a victory. It was "the same old story of the liberals—at least, in the South," she reported to Mrs. Roosevelt. Initially they planned to vote for Mrs. Thomas, if only to make "a moral gesture." Then they began to "wobble" and ended up voting for two moderate candidates, both of whom supported segregation but who the liberals believed would not oppose integration. Mrs. Thomas received only 6,200 votes out of about 200,000, and "the liberals lost both ways, both politically and morally," according to Lillian. The election "made it possible for Talmadge to say over nation-wide television the following Sunday that only 6200 people in Georgia wanted integration of the schools." That was a lie, Lillian declared, "but the liberals helped make it sound like the truth." Although disappointed by the defeat, Lillian still thought the Thomas campaign had been of major significance. For the first time since the Civil War a statewide politician had spoken in favor of democracy and human rights, Lillian observed. Mrs. Thomas had been treated with respect; people had listened to her; she had made an impact on the conscience of the state. Lillian was sure she would not be forgotten, particularly by the many young voters who had worked in her campaign.[23]

Lillian believed that school desegregation was something southerners must work out largely by themselves, "each community in its own way." That was one of the reasons she declined to attend a conference on integration in education to be held at Atlanta University. It was sponsored by the Unitarian Service Committee, whose headquarters were in Boston. In replying to the invitation, Lillian said she believed it would be best if groups based in the North concentrated on northern areas and on Washington, D.C., rather than on the South. "There are tensions that must find outlets down here, and they are likely to be projected on to northern groups [who] come down 'to help us,'" she explained. Moreover, she said she did not see "how committees from the North can help us, down here." Southerners faced "subtle, complex problems" which not only varied from county to county but which, she implied, were different from those in the North. What northerners might do is provide an example to the South. "If we saw things working out well in Washington, that would give southerners great hope," she wrote; "if they saw big things actually begin to happen in New York City and Boston and other northern cities, this, too would give hope and encouragement." In the aftermath of the *Brown* decision, that would be the "strategic thing" for northerners to do.[24]

Lillian's main effort in support of desegregation was a book, *Now Is the Time*, which she began writing less than a month after the *Brown* decision and which was published in February, 1955. She referred to the book as "a tract, deliberately written as one," for the purpose of persuading Americans, and especially white southerners, that the time had come "to give up segregation, quickly and completely." She mainly sought to induce southerners to comply with the Supreme Court ruling against public school segregation, but she also hoped to persuade them to eliminate other forms of Jim Crow as well. She believed that with the *Brown* decision, the time was right for a book about segregation and, she told Keith Jennison of Viking Press, "I want, very much, to be the one who writes it."[25]

In Lillian's view, *Now Is the Time* differed significantly from her earlier books. Although some reviewers had regarded *Strange Fruit* and *Killers of the Dream* as social problem books written for the purpose of improving race relations, Lillian had never considered them as such. She viewed them as creative writing, as artistic works that she had written mainly for herself and in order to set down her own "private view of life." She said she wrote *Killers of the Dream* to give herself insight, *The Journey* "to find courage for myself," and *Strange Fruit* to tell a story that was "in its deepest sense my own story . . . the legend of my life." *Now Is the Time* she wrote for other people, "a lot of people—and all of them different," and "to 'do a job,'" to change minds and behavior. "My other books were written not to change anybody else's mind but to help me search for the meaning in my own experience of life," she observed.[26]

*Now Is the Time* had three sections. In the first, Lillian discussed the origins and development of segregation, as well as opposition to it, why it was wrong, and the obstacles in the way of abolishing it. She defined it broadly as man's oldest defense, a means of hiding "a part of the world from us because we want to make our own lives more secure." In this sense, she pointed out, segregation was synonymous with isolation, censorship, restriction, withdrawal, Jim Crow, caste, imprisonment, quarantine, and repression. Whatever its special meaning or purpose, it was a "profoundly immoral" and "anti-human act" because it cut men off from the human relationships that they needed to survive and grow. Lillian criticized racial segregation on this broad ground, but also because it contradicted the democratic ideals of the United States. In particular, public school segregation violated the right of children to learn and to have the esteem, the belief in their own worth and the worth of others, that would enable them to grow as human beings.[27]

Lillian contended that racial segregation in the United States alienated Asians and Africans from democracy and rendered communism attractive by comparison. "As long as we have legal segregation inside the United States we are a 'white democracy' to the Asians and Africans," she wrote; "*as long as we practice segregation against colored people, as long as there are signs over doors in this land, as long as there are laws in any of the states making race segregation compulsory, as long as our officials (whom we, the people, have chosen) make insulting public statements about the darker people,* Asians and Africans will not trust us." If the United States would give up segregation, she declared, many of the difficulties between East and West would be solved. "Suspicion of the United States will diminish. Trust in American integrity will increase. Faith in our moral strength will return to us, too. As the old guilts grow small, hope will grow large. We shall not fear the Communist conspiracy so desperately because we shall be in a stronger moral position to combat it. It will become for us a rational danger—not the terror it now is in many minds."[28]

Lillian's argument that the elimination of segregation was vital in the struggle against communism was not new. She had used it in 1949 in a Chicago *Defender* column discussing the loss of China and in *Killers of the Dream.* The number of pages she devoted to it in *Now Is the Time*— many more than to the criticism of segregation as a defense mechanism or, in the case of school segregation, as a violation of a child's right to learn and grow—shows the influence of the Cold War on her thinking. Certainly she employed the argument because she was convinced of the danger of communism and believed that the Third World would be better off adopting democratic rather than communist forms of government. Perhaps she also thought it would be an effective means of persuading white southerners to give up segregation. *Now Is the Time* was, after all, a tract; she sought to persuade; and therefore she believed she should stress reasons that the public could accept.[29] Still, her emphasis on desegregation as a weapon in the Cold War seems inconsistent with the position she had taken in the 1940s. Then she had criticized the Southern Conference for Human Welfare for urging the abolition of racial discrimination, not as an end in itself or because it was a "cancer in human culture," but as a means of winning the war.

Perhaps, too, Lillian argued that the elimination of segregation was vital to winning the Cold War in order to counteract the segregationists' charge that advocates of desegregation were Communists. She may have been thinking, in particular, of the investigation conducted by Senator James Eastland of the Senate Subcommittee on Internal Security in New Orleans in March of 1954, involving Aubrey Williams, James Dombrowski, and Virginia Durr, her former associates in the Southern Conference for Human Welfare and the Southern Conference Educational Fund. She addressed the question of communist influence in the civil rights movement directly, recalling that when the first meeting of the SCHW was held, demagogues shrieked, "The Communists are coming." Two or three did go, she noted, but added, "There were a thousand white Southerners at that meeting, and they knew they were not Communists." As for the demagogues' practice of labeling liberal, democratic southerners as Communists, she remarked that "it is strange how many Americans will not give democracy or Christianity the least credit for the good things done in our country. Always they credit 'the Communists' with our nation's finest acts."[30]

Lillian contended that the main thing holding the South back from eliminating Jim Crow was the anxiety aroused in many minds when segregation was questioned. It was this anxiety that demagogues were able to exploit for their own political and economic advantage. To allay the anxiety of southerners, Lillian pointed out that giving up segregation was "a change that takes place in minds." She insisted it would have little effect on external life. "We are confronted with no loss of life, no rationing of food and fuel, as in war; no economic difficulties, as in

a depression; no risk of crippling effects, as in certain epidemics; no
loss of property or disruption of communication, as in storms." Whatever upheavals would happen would occur "*inside people's minds,*" as a
result of their giving up the old idea of white superiority. "Now this is a
good thing to realize," she wrote. "For each of us can keep his own
mind in order. . . . We can maintain serenity within ourselves. And we
can ease the strain for others. . . . The responsibility is ours to keep the
doors open by reminding one another of the good things which can
come out of this 'trouble.'" Instead of fearing or dreading the "trouble,"
Lillian urged her readers to value it as a catalyst enabling people to
bring about necessary and beneficial change. Echoing the ideas she
had expressed in *The Journey,* she encouraged them to see that "this
ordeal of school integration can become for the entire nation a magnificent opportunity for growth, for soul-searching, for rediscovery of important things." She wanted people to see "the creative possibilities in
this crisis" and to feel confident about their ability to master it. This
first section of *Now Is the Time* was "the real pamphlet," she told Keith
Jennison; it "stirs the imagination, and the mind, and the heart." She
hoped it would make people "WANT TO GET RID OF SEGREGATION
. . . WANT TO ACCEPT THIS GREAT CHALLENGE."[31]

The second section of the book Lillian referred to as "down-to-
earth stuff." It was practical information that she thought would appeal
to "many people who will want to be told 'what to do'"—a handbook
of race relations. It consisted of some fourteen pages describing things
to do and say to smooth the course of desegregation, many of which
Lillian had urged on "intelligent white Southerners" a decade earlier in
*South Today.* She suggested meeting and talking with Negroes about
common problems and interests, writing letters to newspapers proposing measures to bring about harmonious change, and urging stores
and hospitals to stop discriminatory racial policies. She also listed
some "don'ts": don't use words like *nigger* or *coon* or tell race jokes; don't
repeat rumors of violence; don't say, "It will take fifty years"; don't talk
about "undue hardship" for white people in giving up segregation.
Whereas in her other writings in the 1950s Lillian stressed the importance of intelligent leadership in bringing about peaceful desegregation, in *Now Is the Time* she devoted only a sentence or two to it. She
was primarily concerned with "the simple, undramatic things we all
can do" because, she insisted, the ordeal of desegregation "touches

every one of us." There could be no innocent bystanders. All were involved, and all could help.[32]

The third section of the book consisted of twenty-five questions often used as arguments against desegregation, with answers to each. For example, to the question "Would you want your sister to marry a Negro?" Lillian responded that it was natural to fear that a marriage between members of groups long separated would not work. On the other hand, such marriages were taking place all over the world between Japanese and Americans, Jews and Christians, Protestants and Catholics. If a young woman asked her advice she would point out that it would not be easy to do, but it might be worth it. That would be for the young woman to decide. Responding to the question "What right has the government to invade our homes and tell us we must socialize with each other?" she wrote, "Our government has no right to invade our homes or meddle in our personal friendships. . . . Every American citizen has two kinds of rights: public and private. . . . When the Supreme Court ruled legal segregation unconstitutional it was protecting the *public rights* of a minority against a majority, in certain states, that had taken those rights away. It was in no way infringing on any citizen's private rights. There is nothing in the decision that affects anyone's home, friends, private clubs, or social affairs." To the questions "You'll only stir up trouble by pushing too fast, won't you?" and "Is not gradualism the answer?" she replied:

> These questions are dead now. The Supreme Court has made its decision. We, as good citizens, must obey the law. The sooner we do so the more stable our community and country will be. The less we temporize, the easier it will be to accomplish the change-over in a harmonious manner. There is, however, need for preparation of the community. The time to begin this preparation is now. The place to begin is within one's own mind. Once we begin, numerous possibilities will open up. There are few Southern communities so bereft of leadership and resources that they cannot quickly and harmoniously solve the problems which this change-over will present—if they want to. They will want to, once the people realize the harm segregation inflicts on all the children of the community.[33]

*Now Is the Time* was published by Viking Press in a clothbound volume costing two dollars and in a twenty-five cent paperbound edition by Dell Books. Lillian thought that because it was "a special book for a special time," it was appropriate to bring it out simultaneously in hard and soft covers. Since she also thought it wasn't a book "to make a lot of money from," she accepted a 10 percent royalty from Viking.[34]

On the basis of the letters she received, Lillian decided that southerners liked the book better than northerners did. She felt southerners liked it because she understood the southern psychology well enough to know how to appeal to them. She was disappointed that some of her old friends in the North had criticized her for making things sound too easy and for stretching some facts in order to persuade. One of those friends was Dr. Lawrence Kubie, a prominent New York psychoanalyst. She had asked him for his opinion of the book, and he had responded with two criticisms. First, he questioned her pointing to large southern cities such as Baltimore and Washington, D.C., which had a high percentage of black pupils, as examples of successful school desegregation. "Is this not a slanted statement?" he asked. "Are there not many smaller Southern cities and towns and villages where the percentage is higher, and where because of the small size and the high ratio of Negro to White children the practical and psychological problems are basically different? If so, then to take these two cities alone, emphasizing their size without discussing the situation in the small towns with a higher percentage of Negro population distorts the picture." Kubie viewed Lillian's avoidance of difficult cases of school desegregation as symptomatic of a more general weakness in the first section of the book—her attempt "to overcome obstacles by exhortation and generalizations, instead of building from concrete realities." His second criticism was that she had failed to probe the psychological origins of racism and segregation, "those unconscious forces which are involved in fantasies of dirt and power." In response, Lillian pointed out that she had written *Now Is the Time* "deliberately to persuade" and therefore thought it necessary "to stress reasons that the public can accept and to play down a bit deeper interpretations that will only arouse more anxiety." She pointed out that she had explored the psychology of racism thoroughly in *Killers of the Dream,* treating "the symbolic significance of darkness . . . the effect of our bi-racial childhood . . . the ambivalence in white southern men who had had a nurse in childhood." But she had written *Now Is the Time* "for the purpose of reassurance; giving reasons for our trouble but exploring not [*sic*] further

below the surface than was necessary." As for her exhortative, optimistic approach, she insisted, "We cannot come through this ordeal,
Larry, without optimism." She knew the difficulties better, she thought,
than "the Hodding Carters and Ralph McGills whose fears have always
kept them from speaking out until it is safe to speak out." She thought
that a southerner was the only person who could encourage other
southerners. "We want other people not to be afraid," she wrote; "we
want them to see it as a challenge; as something worth doing, that can
be done rather quickly if we believe it can be done."[35]

    In general, northern reviewers praised *Now Is the Time* for its elo-
quence and Lillian for advocating a moderate approach to desegregation. By contrast, southern reviewers such as Hodding Carter and
Ralph McGill resented the book's accusing tone and thought that she
spent "overmuch time scolding people for their prejudices—almost always white people." Carter made it quite clear that he disagreed with
her conviction that the South was not moving fast enough in the matter
of desegregation. Still, although he thought that few southerners would
be soothed by what she had to say—or would even read the book—he
pronounced it hopeful and generally helpful. McGill, who reviewed
the book in the *New York Times Book Review* and in the Atlanta *Journal
and Constitution*, took away with one hand what he gave with the other.
He praised Lillian as "honest and sincere," neither a Communist nor a
radical left-winger, "a Christian of conviction" whose moral position
was unimpeachable, but at the same time dogmatic and naive. She "in-
variably simplifies grave problems for the good reason that they seem
simple to her," McGill wrote. He paraphrased her argument as follows: "now is the time to end the problem of race and segregation by
all people everywhere doing what morally is right about it and making
the commandment of brotherhood come true on earth." It was "all
very simple," McGill noted. "All we have to do is to do it." But, he
argued, "troublesome mores" could not be "willed, or wished, away,"
and "attitudes don't really 'change.'" They only were watered down,
worn away, or lost strength and meaning with the passage of time.
"Also," McGill insisted, "human problems are never solved with a for-
mula. . . . They are, in a sense, ameliorated, and reameliorated, until
there isn't any real problem left." This, he said, was what the South was
experiencing at the moment, and there would have to be a great deal

more of it—of what he referred to as "a process of erosion"—before
there would be a solution. "It's too bad Miss Smith isn't right about it,"
he added.[36]

Lillian was incensed by Carter's and McGill's reactions to her book
and especially by their patronizing attitude. We know the situation
better than you, we are being realistic whereas you are too idealistic,
we are rational whereas you are too emotional (too feminine?), they
seemed to be saying. Of course her feud with McGill dated back at
least as far as his review of *Killers of the Dream*. In the 1950s she continued to take his and Carter's criticisms personally. She went so far as
to accuse them of distorting *Now Is the Time* "(even to the point of
dishonesty) in order to belittle it." To a friend she wrote, "Even if they
do not agree with me that segregation must go and should go as quickly
as possible, they should have been wise enough to see that the little
book might restrain the hotheads by creating a better climate of opinion for all to work in."[37]

Lillian also resented the growing reputations of Carter and McGill
as southern moderates and as "the race relations experts of the South."
Neither man was willing to take a really positive and forthright stand in
support of desegregation. Before 1954 they had urged the South to
make separate facilities for blacks truly equal as a way of staving off
decisions like *Brown*. After the 1954 ruling they counseled obedience to
the law, but they also were satisfied with token and gradual desegregation on the grounds that change could not occur overnight in the
South. Lillian thought that "intelligent white Southerners" were in advance of Carter and McGill and could be persuaded to support immediate and widespread desegregation.[38]

By the summer of 1955, Lillian had become increasingly alarmed
by the undue and harmful influence she thought Carter and McGill
and others like them were exerting on northern liberals. "There is an
increasing group of appeasers [in the North] who have been won over
by our Hodding Carters and Ralph McGills and who now say 'The
South must be let alone; they must take their own time about this,'"
she complained to a friend. Northern liberals were particularly influenced by McGill's notion that change was brought about by "'erosion'
. . . and not by writings and acts and words," she wrote sociologist
Charles S. Johnson. Also, they did not want to antagonize the white

South. She lamented their "sudden gush of sympathy for the poor white southerners who are having to go through the 'ordeal' of change." What about "the poor colored southerners" who had been "held down for decades and decades?" she asked. The appeasers thought the Negro should be "satisfied for a while," she wrote, and "give the South at least 30 or 40 more years to change itself in." But Lillian thought the South did not have the time. "The international situation presses so hard," she noted, and besides, "the Negroes are not going to take it passively; they are already taking new cases to court; and we must meet their quiet, legal determination with a receptive and constructive spirit."[39]

The year 1955 ended on a sour note. In the summer Lillian returned from a six-month visit to India, where she had been doing research for a book, to find that the cancer had returned. She recovered sufficiently from a second operation and x-ray treatment to spend a month at Vassar College as writer on campus. Then, in November, three days before she was to leave Vassar, she received word that a fire on Old Screamer had destroyed her bedroom and study. It was the second such fire, the first having occurred eleven years before when the camp dining room burned. The first fire, caused by an overheated stove, had destroyed many of Lillian's papers, including hundreds of letters, as well as things she had brought from China. The second fire resulted in a much greater loss: some thirteen thousand letters, the manuscripts of three novellas and both copies of the novel about China, sketches and plans for future writing, all the books and notes she had collected in India, as well as family mementos, pictures, and the like. Two white boys had set the fire. There was no publicity, no trial; the boys and their families were "whisked out of town" and taken to another state. Lillian was inclined to see the incident as a simple case of juvenile delinquency, but on at least one occasion she admitted thinking that it was "mixed . . . with feelings about me and my work." In the summer of 1954 the black and white Baptists of Clayton (thirty-two blacks, thirty-six whites) had held a "sing" in the gymnasium on Old Screamer, and on the Fourth of July Lillian had invited a group of forty-five children, black and white, "all poor, all rural," for a hot dog and ice cream supper. These were not the first biracial meetings on the mountain, of course, but before the participants had not been from the neighborhood but had been "city people." At the time Lillian thought the get-togethers were "accepted nicely." But she later learned from her cook that while she was in India there was a good deal of talk about them. She was now seen as infiltrating the home territory. "The colored folks were warned never to do that again," she wrote her friend Anna Hedgeman; "the white (poor whites) were warned that if they did, certain jobs would no longer be available to them."[40]

Stunned by the fire and the loss it entailed, Lillian decided to spend some time at her brother's fishing camp in Florida to recuperate from her latest ordeal. "The family insist that I leave the ashes to themselves for a while," she wrote Denver Lindley, "and I think it is well to do so." Despite the fire, she was determined to do the book on India. She had already decided, after the publication of *Now Is the Time,* that she was "about finished with 'the South.'" She did not want to be "stereotyped as a 'southern writer'" and was going to "browse in other fields."[41]

# VII The Conspiracy of Silence

I am really a shy quiet person who loves poetry, painting, music and good writing and wants above everything else to be a good writer, herself. But I feel that as a southerner and a human being I have a few chores to do in addition to my dreaming and writing and so I roll up my sleeves, wipe the fantasy off my face, and light in like the old Methodist parsons used to do.

Lillian spent the winter and spring of 1956 at Neptune Beach, Florida, walking the beach every morning, staring at the ocean, trying to get over the hurt, shock, and anger she was feeling as a result of the fire on Old Screamer. In the summer she returned to Clayton and resumed work on a novel, *One Hour*, which she had begun writing the year before. Working on it for the next three years, she also continued to do her racial chores.

Late in December, 1955, she had heard from a professor at Florida State University that Dell Books had refused to fill an order for copies of *Now Is the Time*, saying that the book was out of stock and there were no plans to reprint it. Subsequently Lillian discovered that the publisher had quietly withdrawn all copies of the book from stores in Atlanta and other parts of Georgia. When she asked her friend and editor at Dell, Frank Taylor, about the matter, he claimed that the publisher was routinely calling in copies of the book to count them, insisted that Dell was filling orders for it, and hinted that another edition might be published. Lillian was not satisfied. She noted that people did not often order paperback books because they expected to be able to buy them at newsstands, drugstores, and dime stores. She began to suspect that Dell had withdrawn the book in response to pressure. (Taylor on one occasion had referred vaguely to pressure from stores that did not

131

want the book.) Remembering that he had been enthusiastic when he offered her the contract to publish the book, Lillian tried to persuade him of the importance of making it available. It had been hailed by blacks and whites alike, including Charles S. Johnson and Mrs. Dorothy Tilly, as the best book for furthering the cause of integration and the one most likely to appeal to the middle and lower classes—because it "talks their language," Lillian pointed out. The Baptists, Methodists, Episcopalians, and Unitarians were using it. The southern colleges were ready for it (and college students could not afford the higher-priced clothbound book). Citing the student riot that had recently erupted when Autherine Lucy was admitted to the University of Alabama, she declared that southerners were outraged and ashamed. It was "a wonderful mood to catch them in" and she was sorry that her book was not "here ready for them to use, right this moment." If Dell was being pressured, she continued, why not take advantage of the publicity to be gained from "a little banning fight." She suggested Taylor contact the American Civil Liberties Union (ACLU) and get a few columnists to write about efforts to suppress the book. Here was a "readymade fight" that would get the book back into the news. "You've got a big chance, here, Frank; have you seen it?" she wrote.[1] Perhaps she thought that Taylor, having handled *Strange Fruit* for Reynal and Hitchcock, would respond positively to the idea of a second banning controversy. He did not.

Lillian had written to the ACLU herself in January. A member of the organization's national committee since 1944, in 1956 she served as one of its eight vice-chairmen. In the several letters she wrote to the executive and assistant directors, Patrick Murphy Malin and Alan Reitman, she recounted her discussions with Taylor (noting that he had been unwilling to put anything in writing and had talked with her only by phone), asked for advice, and wondered if the ACLU would be interested in airing the matter or talking with Dell officials. She thought that publicizing the withdrawal would embarrass Dell and force the company to put the book back on the market.

In her letters to Malin and Reitman, Lillian wondered what powers had put pressure on Dell. She thought they included southern book distributors and store managers who opposed desegregation, but she was also convinced that officials within the firm were involved—

people who either disapproved her view of race relations or feared *Now Is the Time* would hurt the sale of Dell's other books. (In a letter to a friend Lillian suggested another motive, self-protection. There were, she explained, "among book publishers, many especially among the Jewish group who are not interested in working on the color problem. They, somehow, fear it will boomerang against the Jewish group. They are shortsighted, of course; but they are successful men in 'grey flannel suits' who don't want to risk much for anybody.") Lillian also thought it likely that powerful businessmen in the South, along with "big-time politicians like Herman Talmadge" and officials in various southern cities, had persuaded Dell to withdraw the book. It was the latest instance of a long-standing practice she had noted in "Two Men and a Bargain"—northern businessmen conniving with southern businessmen and politicians to maintain segregation. It also constituted a new type of censorship. *Strange Fruit* had been banned by the police. *Now Is the Time* was being banned by a gentleman's agreement. She compared it to the blacklisting of one-time Communists and fellow travelers and contended that the new kind of censorship was "more malignant . . . than . . . banning by the police force of a city because of statute infringement."[2]

Malin and Reitman promised to discuss the matter with some of the ACLU board members who worked in publishing. Early in April, Reitman reported that Charles Bolté, executive secretary of the American Book Publishers Council, had investigated and found that the reply Dell had sent Florida State was in error and that *Now Is the Time* had not been taken out of circulation. Indeed, according to Bolté, the publisher was planning a special promotion in Mobile, Alabama, in connection with the National Conference of Christians and Jews, which had recently given an award to the book. Reitman went on to concede the likelihood that some booksellers and drugstore managers had bowed to pressure and removed the book from their racks or decided not to stock it. He insisted that the ACLU was interested in fighting such pressure-group censorship as well as police censorship. But he admitted that so far the ACLU had not been able to decide what type of legal action might be successfully employed against it. He hoped that in the future strong ACLU groups would be established in the South that would be able to combat such censorship.[3]

Lillian characterized Reitman's letter as "the kind . . . a young brash sophomore might write to an old fretful lady." It was "patronizing, full of veiled sneers, telling me I had made a mistake and Dell had done nothing wrong." She contended that the situation in April was the same as it had been in December and January: there were no paperbacks available in the stores, and organizations were having difficulty obtaining large quantities from Dell. She was equally contemptuous of Bolté's report, which she dismissed as the result of two publishers (Bolté and Dell) talking the matter over and "stand[ing] together regardless of the author and civil liberties."[4]

Hurt by what she regarded as shabby treatment by the ACLU, unable to do anything about the banning (she admitted she had no real proof of it), Lillian gave up the fight. She consoled herself with the thought that about 100,000 copies of the paperback had sold before it was withdrawn and the hardcover edition was still selling. For a time she considered resigning from the ACLU, having decided that "the best way to work for civil liberties is to live it in one's life." But she soon changed her mind. She decided that the cause of civil liberties was too grave for her to withhold support from the ACLU. The organization might not be able to deal with the new types of censorship, but at least it could combat the grosser infringements of civil liberties that were appearing in the South, and that was important.[5]

Lillian's friendship with Frank Taylor did not survive the Dell affair. Initially, giving him the benefit of the doubt, she speculated that, having persuaded Dell to publish *Now Is the Time,* he had come under pressure from people in the firm who wanted to withdraw it. If he fought too hard for the book, he might lose his job. It was "the usual sad old story." With a wife and four sons to support, he had to "watch his step." By April, however, Lillian had become completely disillusioned—and angry. In a long letter to her close friend, Dorothy Norman, she poured out her feelings. She now blamed Taylor for "convincing the ACLU that I was all wrong and he and Dell were right." After the Bolté investigation and before she had heard the results from Reitman, Taylor had sent her a present of a book, along with "a most cozy, affectionate note. . . . I knew the moment I received it that the cat had eaten the canary," she wrote. "Frank perhaps could not help Dell doing this to my book," she continued, "but he could have played it straight and with honesty. He could have told me the truth about it; told me he was helpless to do anything if he is helpless. . . . he could have handled it with integrity and clean honesty." She admitted that he had been "so sweet to me in dozens of ways over the years" (though he had also done some questionable things regarding *Strange Fruit*), and so it was difficult to know what was the right thing to do. She had decided, however, that she could not understand and forgive him this time, as she had in the past. So she was not going to see or communicate with him any more.[6]

Lillian saw the Dell banning as one more instance of the smothering technique, or conspiracy of silence, that had been used against her in the South and parts of the North since *Killers of the Dream*. Previously she had been able for the most part to disregard it, but in the late 1950s it became a preoccupation. She also became concerned, for the first time, about the possibility of physical violence against her and Paula, living alone on Old Screamer two miles from town. She did not often betray such fears, thinking that people would say she was making a martyr of herself or that it would "scare other southerners and keep them from taking a brave stand." But in March, 1957, she confided to Mozell Hill, editor of *Phylon*, that strangers driving up the mountain very late at night had prompted her to install an outdoor lighting system. "I switch the lights on all over the hill and down go the cars," she wrote. "But a time may come when they won't go down." The following year the woods on the mountain were twice set on fire, and it took the fire departments of both Clayton and the United States Forestry Service to put them out.[7]

Against the conspiracy of silence she employed other weapons. She continued to view it as a joint effort of southerners and northerners, started by Ralph McGill and Hodding Carter, among southern whites, and Walter White, among blacks. "You see," she explained to a friend, "Carter and McGill don't want anybody in the South to be more liberal than they are; and Walter White wanted the Negroes to get all the credit for whatever change took place." She believed that McGill and Carter used their influence over the editors of northern magazines and newspapers to persuade them not to publicize the views of white southerners, including herself, opposed to segregation. She also believed that northern editors were easily persuaded because, as she wrote Wilma

Dykeman Stokely, many of them were Jews and were "for the most part ambivalent about this situation." There were some "real liberals" among them, but "most want to tone down the conflict because they fear the hate feelings may swing over into a wave of anti-Semitism." The editors of the New York *Times* occasionally wrote good editorials on the race question, but, she declared, "the line is DONT [*sic*] LET THE WHITE SOUTHERNERS SPEAK UP AGAINST SEGREGATION." *The Reporter, Harper's,* and *Atlantic Monthly* took the same position, she contended, as such mass circulation magazines as *Life, Look, Time, Newsweek,* and *Colliers.* The only magazines she thought would allow white southerners opposed to segregation to speak out were the *Progressive,* the *New Leader,* the *New Republic,* and the *Nation.*[8]

Lillian wanted to break the conspiracy of silence so that the voice of "the good, creative South" would be heard, either through her or other white southerners. Northern magazines and newspapers reported only the resistance to integration. She wanted to see coverage of "the good work going on" because it would give Negroes hope and make white southerners aware that they were not alone in opposing segregation.[9]

Early in 1956, therefore, Lillian launched a two-pronged attack on the conspiracy of silence. She urged friends to write, telegraph, or phone editors of the mass circulation magazines and newspapers asking them to open their columns to her. At the same time she herself wrote to some of the magazines, offering opinions on the racial situation in the South and making suggestions for improving coverage of it.[10]

When *Life* published "A Letter to the North" by William Faulkner early in March, Lillian wired the magazine, asking for an opportunity to reply to it. In the letter Faulkner said that though he had long opposed compulsory segregation, now, disturbed by the violence arising out of southern resistance to school integration, most recently at the University of Alabama, he felt he "must go on record as opposing the forces outside the South which would use legal or police compulsion to eradicate that evil overnight." He urged the NAACP and all organizations that "would compel immediate and unconditional integration" to "'Go slow now.'" If they did not, he predicted, the white minority in the South opposed to segregation would feel compelled, out of sympathy for those being forced to integrate, to join the segregationist majority. Lillian had been somewhat skeptical of Faulkner since the 1930s, when *South Today* had published several less than enthusiastic reviews of his novels, and his 1956 pronouncements on the racial situation in the South confirmed her skepticism. She regarded him as a talented writer of fiction, but, she declared, he was "not an intellectual . . . not a thinker . . . not mature psychologically and socially." He had not thought much or deeply on the subject of race. She admitted that he had said some good things on the race problem "when he wasn't under pressure," but he was at best, and only since receiving the Nobel Prize, "a mighty lukewarm liberal." Now, in a time of stress, he was backsliding. The "Letter to the North" showed that he was "still a mighty white man; and more southern than he is an integrationist."[11]

*Life* did not accept her offer to reply to Faulkner, but Lillian had better luck with *Time*, which published a letter criticizing a speech by Mark Ethridge, editor-publisher of the Louisville *Courier-Journal*, because he equated the NAACP and Senator James Eastland by labeling both "radical." She asked, "Are those who insist on obedience to the highest law of our land to be classed ethically with those who encourage disesteem for law?" She also wrote a letter to the editor of *Look* magazine in which she criticized the article "The South vs the Supreme Court" for minimizing the efforts of southerners opposed to segregation. At the time of the Little Rock school desegregation crisis in the fall of 1957, Lillian sent a telegram to television commentator Eric Sevareid praising his coverage of the crisis but asking why the opinions of enlightened southerners were not being heard alongside those of the mobs and demagogues. She also wrote a seven-page letter to the editor of the New York *Times*. The letters editor replied that it was too long to print, but offered to use it if it were condensed to about six hundred words. Irritated by what she regarded as a "polite brush-off," Lillian remembered that in 1948 publisher Arthur Hays Sulzberger had not only printed a long letter of hers but had written to congratulate her for writing it. But now, she noted, the editor of the daily *Times* was a southerner. Indeed, she observed to Lawrence Kubie, "southerners have infiltrated every paper in New York; and while a few are truly liberal men, most are barnacled with prejudice and body anxiety."[12]

The New York *Times*'s rejection was minor compared to the treatment Lillian received on Dave Garroway's "Today" show on October 2,

1957. The network, NBC, had planned an hour-long program on integration and hoped to present a wide range of southern opinion, but of several southerners invited to appear, only Lillian and Senator James Eastland of Mississippi accepted. Originally, Lillian had agreed to present a four- or five-minute statement on why she thought segregation was harmful and then answer a few questions. However, when she arrived in New York the day before the show, she learned that she could not present the statement she had prepared. She then insisted on being asked her opinion of segregation, and the network officials promised that Garroway would ask her one question on segregation out of a total of four. However, on the show he asked her only two questions, neither on segregation, then quickly thanked her and ended the interview. Lillian believed the whole matter was the result of pressure put on the network. When network officials told her she could not give her prepared statement (without their even having read it), they explained that after the program had been announced in the newspapers, they had received numerous telephone calls from television stations and prominent businessmen and politicians in the South urging them to take her off the program or even to cancel the entire program. "It was not a spontaneous reaction from the people; it was a concerted intensive drive put on by an interested few," she wrote to Lawrence Kubie. She was shocked by the way the telephone callers were able to strike "fear and terror" in a giant television network. She was also shocked by "the curtness, the indignity" and the lack of consideration with which she had been treated. She felt she had wasted precious time preparing for and appearing on the show, when she was supposed to be working on *One Hour* to meet a November deadline. The phone calls she received after the show from friends who wanted to know why she had not "spoken out" added to her feeling of anxiety. She told Kubie and historian Wilma Dykeman Stokely that she felt cheated by the network officials and Garroway; she thought that she should have given her opinion on segregation even though Garroway did not question her about it. "I would have outwitted him had I believed he was going to cheat me," she wrote Kubie. "This is my weakness: my belief in the innate decency of people. I lean backward to try not to feel persecuted, not to let myself believe 'everybody is against me'—but I should have known. Of course I should have known."[13]

Lillian viewed what happened on the "Today" show as another application of the smothering technique. Paula sent out a letter to various friends describing the incident in detail and asking them to "do all in your power to see that white southerners of intelligence and with ability to speak are given an opportunity to make a stand against segregation so that the whole nation can hear." Specifically, she suggested they write Garroway asking why Lillian had been given so little time on the show and Senator Eastland so much, and urging a better program in the future. Lillian toyed with the idea of setting up another appearance on NBC or going on the Mike Wallace show, but she apparently did not follow up on either project.[14]

Lillian wanted to be heard, but on her own terms. Early in March, 1956, when she was complaining about the conspiracy of silence and urging friends to ask the mass circulation magazines and newspapers to publish her views, she had received a letter from the Vermont writer Dorothy Canfield Fisher. Fisher wrote on behalf of a small Quaker group in her hometown of Arlington. They had become alarmed about the racial crisis in the South and decided to write to Lillian to express their appreciation for her efforts and to ask how they might be helpful. Touched and encouraged by Fisher's letter, Lillian replied that one way Fisher might help would be by "persuading some of the mass-circulation papers to let me speak quietly to the South and the North." She said she wanted to write several brief articles that would clarify racial issues and publicize "the good, creative forces in the South." However, when Fisher said that she was writing several editors, including Norman Cousins of the *Saturday Review*, Lillian backed off. She had decided she should not have requested Fisher's help *"for me."* She had decided that as a writer she should work out her problems alone. "It seems to me that it comes so close to asking a favor for me—I have grown a bit embarrassed about it," she wrote. It would be good for the country to hear what she had to say about the South, and she would like to get "a wide hearing rather than the smaller hearing in the more progressive magazines." But she did not think others could do anything about that, so instead of trying to help her, she suggested Fisher and the Quakers support the work of the Reverend Martin Luther King, Jr., and the Montgomery Improvement Association. When Fisher, undaunted, wrote a month and a half later that not only Cousins but

DeWitt Wallace of the *Reader's Digest* was interested in publishing an
article by her, Lillian thanked her but went on to explain her position.

> The whole point is this: these [northern] editors know that I could give
> them a story that no one else in the South has had the experience and
> intellectual background to give them. They are aware of this but for
> some reason have chosen not to let me tell this story at this time. . . .
> I think the real reason they avoid asking me for a piece is just this: they
> do fear that they will alienate their southern readers. Actually, they
> wouldn't. But they fear that they would.
>
> Under these circumstances, despite their pleasant letters to you
> whom they admire and love, I do not think it either wise or appropriate
> for me to beg them to let me write a piece. They know me; they know
> my abilities; they know my experience and background and surely they
> know the interesting fact that my writings on segregation and race have
> sold more throughout the world than those of any other author in any
> country. They know this: still they avoid asking me. I think, under these
> circumstances, it would be rather humiliating for me to write them and
> ask them when, if they wanted a piece, they could and should be writing
> me and asking me for it. I would humiliate myself for the cause of segre-
> gation if I thought there was a reason to do so. But I don't think this is a
> good reason. I am working very hard down here in the South to help
> our people change; I have decided that this direct work *as a person* (not
> necessarily as a writer since I have already written three books on this
> subject and dozens of articles and given hundreds of speeches North
> and South) is what will now count the most. . . . This is the way I now
> feel I can contribute the most to this phase of human relations.[15]

Lillian was not really ungrateful for Fisher's help. However, she may
have been envious of her ability to evoke an affirmative response from
some of her editor friends, and she apparently felt some resentment,
too. In a letter to her Atlanta friend Helen Bullard, Lillian described
Fisher's initial letter as a "sweet letter, but ten years too late," adding
that "her Book Club [could have] helped spread the good tidgins [*sic*]
by publishing Strange Fruit, or Killers of the Dream or Journey . . . or
even Now is the Time."[16] Lillian was not enthusiastic about publishing
in the *Saturday Review* (or the *Yale Review*, which Fisher had mentioned as another possibility). She wanted the influence she thought
would result from appearing in a mass circulation magazine like *Life*
or *Look*. It is difficult to understand why she dismissed the *Reader's
Digest*, which had a circulation of over ten million. In explaining her

desire to avoid being humiliated, Lillian resorted to her Martha/Mary dichotomy. She insisted that her Martha side was willing to do whatever would help the cause of integration, but her Mary side was committed to maintaining her sense of pride and integrity as a writer. She felt she was satisfying both sides by not asking to be published and by working for integration "*as a person*" rather than a writer.

Concern for her integrity as a writer was the reason Lillian gave for turning down another opportunity to publish her opinions on the racial situation in the South. In December, 1957, Robert Evett, book editor of the *New Republic,* invited her to review Harry Ashmore's *An Epitaph for Dixie.* Lillian declined, explaining that she was totally engrossed in *One Hour* and would interrupt her work "only for something urgent," such as making a speech somewhere in the South. She went on to suggest that Ashmore's book was not really worth her effort. She was "a creative writer, not a propagandist nor a reformer nor a person primarily interested in public affairs," she told Evett. (Writing *One Hour,* she was indulging her Mary side, having decided after *Now Is the Time* that she was through writing about race and the South.) Moreover, she regarded Ashmore as a moderate, in the same category as Hodding Carter and Ralph McGill. "It would be fun to do a critical study of an important book," she wrote. "But to review what I know already to be a journalistic piece of writing of ephemeral worth seems a kind of waste of time. These people are not writing important books about the white people's attitude toward darkness and Negroes, etc. They are defending their public position."[17]

Of course Lillian was not completely smothered. Although she was not able to speak out in the mass circulation magazines as she desired, she did have other opportunities to express her opinions. By the middle 1950s she was sufficiently well known as an observer of the South and an advocate of desegregation to receive numerous requests for information or advice on helping the cause. In reply, she usually urged support of the NAACP and the Montgomery Improvement Association; she also recommended her book, *Now Is the Time.*[18]

The 1956 presidential campaign also offered her an opportunity to express her views. She supported the Democratic ticket mainly because she admired Estes Kefauver for speaking out—more frankly than Adlai Stevenson, she thought—against segregation, even in the Deep South.

She conceded that Stevenson was probably the better man for president because he was "more urbane, more brilliant intellectually, more erudie [*sic*] and suave," but, she insisted, Kefauver was "braver and more honest and more deeply liberal inside."[19]

When a worker for the Stevenson for President Committee wrote asking about an article Lillian had published, she replied with advice on how the Illinois Democrat should conduct his campaign. She began by commenting on a speech Stevenson had made to a black audience in Los Angeles in which he said that he would not withhold federal funds from segregated schools or use the army or navy to enforce the *Brown* decision. Regarding the use of federal troops, Stevenson said, "I think that would be a great mistake. That is exactly what brought on the Civil War. It can't be done by troops or bayonets. We must proceed gradually, not upsetting habits or traditions that are older than the Republic." Without mincing words, Lillian wrote that "he made the biggest mistake of his public life when he made that speech." She thought he had erred partly because of his lack of understanding of "the whole problem of color, or human differences," but also because he depended, as he had in his last campaign, on the wrong southerners for advice. "He depends on the men like David Cohn, Hodding Carter, Ralph McGill who are 'gradualists' and who are not deeply concerned themselves over the problem as it has injured white people's integrity." Lillian declared that they had favored segregation until about five years ago and even now did not think it would do great harm if the racial situation remained as it was for the next fifty years.

> At best, they think segregation is mildly bad; they would not mind seeing it go if it goes slowly enough not to inconvenience any white folks. . . . They are not real liberals nor are they even good at predicting what can or will happen in the South. Six years ago, everyone [*sic*] of them was saying "Never, never will segregation even be questioned in the South." They have blocked every step of the way by their doubts, spoken out loud always, by their negativism, their doleful shaking of the head, and their actual arousing, oftentimes, of anxiety in quite decent, well-meaning people. . . . These men have held the South back, have made it harder to change than it would have been had they spoken out bravely, hopefully and calmly.[20]

Lillian urged Stevenson to deal with what she called "the symbolic issue" in the 1956 election. Demagogues, she noted, never failed to grab hold of the symbolic issue, but good politicians sometimes tried to evade it and talk rationally about rational matters. The symbolic issue in 1956 was segregation, and Stevenson was not dealing with it by talking about gradualism. A symbolic issue was grounded in myth—in the case of segregation, in the myth of white supremacy. "You don't hush a myth up by talking rationally about something else," she declared. "To fight a myth you've got to fight with something that goes down just as deep inside a man. There is only one thing: religion. Or in modern times a fervid morality. Mr. Stevenson is capable of that kind of talk." Instead of talking about gradualism, he should say that "change must be brought about without violence and as quickly as possible." More important, "he should talk about the big things: the role of Constitutional law in our democracy; what it would mean to encourage lawlessness; what it means to the whole world for us to move over and make room for the little colored children in our schools. . . . He must appeal to people's love, their sense of justice, their compassion, their sportsmanship, their need and desire to be law-abiding, to be good, to be fair, to do what is right. Only by substituting good feelings for bad ones, good plans for bad ones, can he hope to lead this country to a higher level of human relations." Lillian believed "Mr. Stevenson could speak out like this and win hundreds of thousands of southerners to his side." Most southerners were decent and sane, she contended, but they were also frightened and unsure of the future. All they needed was leadership. "They need somebody who is quietly unafraid to do the right thing; and who, speaking as a friend, can give them the moral strength to do the right thing." She was sure Stevenson could be that person.[21]

Lillian was not shy about offering unsolicited advice or opinions. When the trustees of the University of Alabama rescinded the admission of Autherine Lucy following rioting by a mob of one thousand white students, she fired off a barrage of telegrams: to O. C. Carmichael, president of the university, and Governor Jim Folsom, protesting the dishonorable action of the trustees; to Thurgood Marshall of the NAACP, praising an interview he had given on the situation; to George Mitchell of the Southern Regional Council, urging the SRC to make a strong statement; and to the student body president, expressing the hope that the students would protest the trustees' action. She followed up the telegrams with a letter to President Carmichael in which she reiterated her opposition to Miss Lucy's dismissal but praised Carmichael and the trustees for expelling the alleged ringleader of the mob. "This will put a quietus on the professional haters and those slightly psychotic people who throw gasoline on a fire just to see the blaze. If they know they cannot get by with it, they will be more cautious next time," she wrote.[22]

She expressed similar concern about the danger of mob violence in a telegram commending President Eisenhower for sending federal troops to Little Rock to enforce school desegregation. "It is sad that it should be necessary but every thoughtful southerner knows in his heart that it was," she assured him. She said that his action "dramatized the importance of law and order, of the priority that all Americans must give to our Constitution and the Supreme Court's interpretations of it. Our great danger in America today is mob violence; our true subversives are the demagogues who whip up this violence."[23]

While working on *One Hour* and engaging in voluminous correspondence, Lillian occasionally took time out to talk in what she called "strategic places," where she thought her views would have an influence. Her audiences were usually rather small, but several of her speeches were published, giving them a wider impact. A speech read before the Institute on Non-Violence and Social Change sponsored by the Montgomery Improvement Association in December, 1956, was published in several journals; a commencement address at Atlanta University in June of the following year appeared in the *Progressive,* the *New Leader,* and *Phylon;* and another address in November, 1957, to the Arkansas Council on Human Relations was printed in the *New Republic.*[24]

In her speeches as well as in her private correspondence and published writings of the late 1950s, Lillian continued to emphasize the psychological dimension of the race problem. She believed that the same impulse that had prompted southern liberals in the 1940s to resist black demands to end segregation lay behind the massive resistance to desegregation following the *Brown* decision. Under the stress of the racial crisis, southerners were regressing to the point of allowing primitive fears, hatreds, anxieties, and guilt to shape their response. She thought this was what Faulkner had done in his "Letter to the North." Two years later she observed the same process at work in the Little Rock crisis.[25]

In the late 1950s Lillian also continued her long-standing quarrel with racial moderates in both the South and the North. The "AWFUL MODERATES" she called them in a letter to Harry Golden, editor of the *Carolina Israelite*. As in the past, she faulted them for obstructing good and necessary changes in southern race relations and for defending their position as the only way to prevent racial violence. She also resented the way they discounted the significance of those, including herself, who took a strong stand against segregation. She quoted Harold Fleming as saying that the difference between a moderate and a liberal was that a moderate had a wife and children. "That is a cynical remark if I ever heard one," she wrote Morris Rubin, editor of the *Progressive*, "for I don't know a single liberal who is speaking out in the South who does not have to support himself (or herself) and a family. It is a difference in conviction and courage—not in how many people have to be supported." In her own case, the moderates were wrong in thinking Lillian could afford to speak out because she had no family to support. She told Rubin:

> As a matter of actual fact, when I stood out (with Paula Snelling) almost alone, my income was $3000.00 a year, I had a heavy mortgage on my camp, many of my deceased father's debts still to pay, and a camp that depended on the goodwill and opinion of the families who chose to send their children to me. I also had a family to support. And always have had. At present, my income is less than $3000 a year; and Harold Fleming's is probably $12,000 a year as he is supported by the money from Ford. But—you see, this is the way it goes. Down here, in the South, all of us who speak out, who risk are suppressed and sneered at by the "moderates." [26]

Lillian's smothering experience prompted another criticism of the moderates. "My strongest objection to the self-named 'moderates' is their bigotry," she told the Arkansas Council on Human Relations. She admitted their right to be cautious. "But they refuse to let others move faster, or to speak more clearly and perhaps even more persuasively than they. They are almost fanatically religious in their view that their way is the only 'holy way.'" In the letter to Golden she named Hodding Carter, Jonathan Daniels, Virginius Dabney, and especially Ralph McGill as the chief villains. "Mr. McGill does not like to believe in the existence of anyone in the South who dares to speak out more plainly than he; he is God—but perhaps you did not know: and when God

*Clockwise from left,* Joe, DeWitt, Lillian, Frank, Annie Laurie
Smith, *ca.* 1899

Courtesy of Esther Smith

Annie and Calvin Smith, Lillian Smith's parents, *ca.* 1915
Courtesy of Esther Smith

Paula Snelling and Lillian Smith at Laurel Falls Camp, *ca.* 1933

Lillian Smith Collection, Special Collections, University of Georgia Libraries

First page, first issue of
*Pseudopodia*

Esther Smith, middle 1930s

Lillian Smith Collection, Special
Collections, University of Georgia
Libraries

Paula Snelling, middle
1940s

Lillian Smith Collection, Special
Collections, University of Georgia
Libraries

Paula Snelling, Lillian Smith, and secretary, Betty Tipton, in
Lillian's library, *ca.* 1945

Jane White as Nonnie and Mel Ferrer as Tracy in *Strange Fruit*,
Royale Theatre, New York City, December, 1945

Courtesy of Jane White Viazzi

Lillian Smith, late 1950s

Photograph by Hans Namuth, Lillian Smith
Collection, Special Collections, University
of Georgia Libraries

says 'This is not the time to speak out plainly,' He punishes those who seem deaf to His words."[27]

By the late 1950s Dabney could no longer be considered a moderate; he was calling himself a racial conservative and supporting massive resistance, at least implicitly. On the other hand McGill, Carter, and Daniels were urging compliance with the *Brown* decision. Why then did Lillian continue to regard them as "AWFUL MODERATES"? In the case of McGill and Carter, personal animosity was an important factor. Lillian also opposed the three because, even though they urged compliance with the Supreme Court ruling, they favored only gradual or merely token desegregation. Most important, though they opposed advocates of massive resistance, they regarded outspoken opponents of segregation as equally dangerous and wrong-minded. Mark Ethridge's labeling both the NAACP and Senator Eastland as radicals was a perfect illustration of such "fuzzy thinking," according to Lillian. He made no moral distinction between the two. "This kind of thinking," she declared in her letter to *Time*, "would place the hero and coward in the same category, also the extremely generous man and the miser. Indeed, such thinking would actually destroy all value and all discrimination in judging human acts. Everybody would be judged according to the amount of energy that goes into his actions, not by the quality of his acts." Such indiscriminate use of words like *extremists* not only unfairly denigrated Negroes, who were only asking for their constitutional rights, but also—and this was Lillian's chief complaint against the moderates—made it difficult for white southerners to speak out against segregation. They feared to be called extremists, she observed, and moderates like McGill, Carter, and Daniels were suggesting that anyone who spoke out against segregation was an extremist. The manner and tone of speaking, the choice of words, the moral quality of the statement were all irrelevant. It was the speaking out that made one an extremist.[28]

Whereas the moderates denounced all extremists indiscriminately, Lillian distinguished between good and bad ones. In her address to the Institute on Non-Violence and Social Change, she praised the blacks who had maintained the year-long Montgomery bus boycott for being "good, creative, loving extremists." They had shown all Americans "that in times of ordeal, in times of crisis, only the extremist can meet the challenge. . . . Moderation is the slogan of our times," she noted. "But moderation never made a man or a nation great. Moderation never mastered ordeal or met a crisis successfully." The moderates were avoiding the ordeal of integration. Most of them were doing nothing, thinking that if they closed their eyes to the problem, it would eventually go away. "That does not mean they are not worried," she continued. "It means they are suffering from temporary moral and psychic paralysis. They are working harder to be moderates than they are working to meet the crisis. They are driving straight down the middle of the road with their eyes shut and you know what happens in traffic when you do that. But they are trying to believe there is no traffic. They are telling themselves nobody is on the road but themselves. They are, you see, trying very hard not to be extremists: they are trying to be neither good nor evil." But they paid a tremendous price for their moderation. To maintain segregation they gave up their freedoms: to do right, to obey the law, to speak out or write or teach what one believes is true and just. Having lost those three freedoms, white people in the South were also losing their freedom from fear. "Today, they are afraid of each other and themselves," she declared. To those who said that the risk of opposing segregation was too great, she replied:

> The time has now come when it is dangerous not to risk. We must take calculated risks in order to save our integrity, our moral nature, our lives, and all that is rich and creative in our culture. We must do what we do with love and dignity, with non-violence and wisdom, but we must do something big and imaginative and keep doing it until we master our ordeal.

Lillian observed that many young white southerners she had talked to about the Montgomery bus boycott had been excited and inspired by it. In attempting to secure their own freedom, the Montgomery Negroes were helping young white southerners secure theirs, too, she concluded. "In dramatizing that the extreme way can be the good way, the creative way, and that in times of ordeal it is the only way, you are helping the white South find its way, too. . . . Thank you for dramatizing before the eyes of America that the question is not, 'Are you an extremist?' but 'What kind of extremist are you?'"[29]

Lillian's Montgomery address reveals two new emphases in her thinking about the race problem in the late 1950s. First she stressed the close connection between the race problem and freedom of speech. This new emphasis resulted partly from her own smothering, but also from her opposition to the McCarthyism of the early 1950s. She had first spoken out against Senator Joseph McCarthy and his tactics in an article for the *New York Times Magazine* in September, 1952. Lillian had mentioned McCarthy by name in the manuscript, but the *Times* deleted that part, without her knowledge, before publishing the article. Then late in 1954 in the Sidney Hillman Lectures delivered at Roosevelt University, Lillian again attacked McCarthy as a demagogue, mentioning his name several times. The immediate cause of Lillian's concern for freedom of speech was the escalation of efforts to prevent enforcement of the *Brown* decision. By the time of the Little Rock crisis Lillian had become convinced that the South's "Number One problem" was "how to regain the people's freedom to speak out." She had grown increasingly fearful of the power of the mob—not so much what she called "Mob No. 1," the mob that dynamited houses and churches. Its members were much less numerous and weaker in influence than "Mob No. 2," which was made up not of hoodlums and riffraff, but of business and professional men—bankers, doctors, lawyers, engineers, newspaper editors and publishers, preachers and industrial leaders. Mob No. 2 was "a quiet well-bred mob," but a mob nonetheless. "For they not only protect the rabble, and tolerate its violence, they *think in the same primitive mode,* they share the same irrational anxieties, they are just as lawless in their own quiet way, and they are dominated by the same 'holy idea' of white supremacy." They used different tactics from Mob No. 1. "They smother: By their use of boycott, by their quiet threats, and economic pressures, by suppression of news, they strip college professors, school teachers, preachers, writers, reporters, editors, students, their own employees, and many other white Southerners of their Constitutional rights to speak and write—and to be heard." They were law-breakers as much as the people who comprised Mob No. 1, and in Lillian's opinion "far more dangerous."[30]

The growing, insidious power of the mob frightened Lillian, not personally but, as she explained to a friend, imaginatively. "I find myself reacting with a kind of terror . . . an imaginative terror: as I see what is happening to our American souls and minds," she wrote. She thought the situation in the South was increasingly similar to the situation in Germany in the early 1930s. She was reading Karl Kraus's *Last Days* and said she felt "to a degree, at least, what he felt: that WE ARE CLOSE TO SELF DESTRUCTION."[31] For the first time in her life she was pessimistic about the direction in which race relations were moving. The "intelligent white Southerners" in whom she had always put so much faith seemed no match for the "AWFUL MODERATES," the citizens councils, and Mob No. 2 combined.

Balancing Lillian's fearfulness and pessimism was a feeling of hope inspired by the emergence of the black civil rights movement under the leadership of Martin Luther King, Jr. The effectiveness of nonviolence and passive resistance as a means of abolishing segregation became the second new emphasis in her thinking. As she observed the progress of the Montgomery, Alabama, bus boycott led by King, she was enabled to believe and hope that through such means southerners might yet master the ordeal of desegregation.

From its beginning in December, 1955, Lillian followed the Montgomery boycott with enormous interest. By the spring of 1956 she talked of going down to observe it firsthand and recommended that friends and correspondents support it. She responded positively to King's nonviolent protest methods partly because they were an outgrowth of the Gandhian philosophy she had long admired, but also because they now seemed to her the most effective means of solving the race problem in the South. "The situation down here has always been too involved, too tangled up with sin and sex and God and money to be unravelled by a Supreme Court decision," she wrote Morris Rubin. Of course she valued the *Brown* decision because until segregation was declared unconstitutional opponents were hampered in their efforts to eliminate it. But the Court decision had not changed people's minds and hearts the way King's philosophy and movement seemed likely to do. "It is the right way," she wrote King in March, 1956. "Only through persuasion, love, goodwill, and firm nonviolent resistance can the change take place in our South." She believed the black protest movement would stir the consciences of white southerners because it employed religious symbols that they shared with blacks and that they responded to "on a deep level of their hearts and minds." She told King that "being a Deep South white, reared in a religious home and the

Methodist church," she realized "the deep ties of common songs, common prayer, common symbols that bind our two races together on a religio-mystical level, even as another brutally mythic idea, the concept of White Supremacy, tears our two people apart." To Lillian it must have seemed that King was doing what she had urged Adlai Stevenson to do—confronting the symbolic issue of segregation. "To fight a myth," she had explained to one of the Stevenson for President Committee workers, "you've got to fight with something that goes down just as deep inside a man. There is only one thing: religion. Or in modern times a fervid morality." King's "moral and spiritual protest" seemed perfectly designed to deal with the psychological and mythic dimensions of the race problem. Lillian may also have responded positively to King's movement because it reminded her of her high hopes for the Southern Conference for Human Welfare. She described King's movement in much the same terms she had used to describe the SCHW in its early years, as "a spontaneous religio-social movement" that was having "a tremendous effect on the consciences of the people everywhere." Moreover, King seemed to be directing the movement so "wisely and well" that she was able to hope it would not fail to realize its potential as she thought the SCHW had.[32]

Lillian continued her membership in the NAACP in the late 1950s, but she believed King's philosophy and movement were better adapted than the NAACP to meet the ordeal of integration. While she did not underestimate the tremendous effort put forth by the NAACP in its legal battle against segregation, by 1956 she wondered whether the organization would be able to survive success. In a review of Walter White's *How Far the Promised Land?*, she criticized the former executive secretary of the NAACP for focusing exclusively on civil rights for Negroes instead of joining the larger struggle that engaged some of his contemporaries, including herself, "for an open society for all people everywhere." Such a society, she explained in the review, "requires that barriers in minds and imaginations and hearts be leveled as well as barriers in the external world." Its advocates were concerned with "the inner man, with the quality of human beings," and with the problem of "the individual versus mass-conformity" and the right of individuals to be different in ideas as well as in other ways. White, according to Lillian, was not concerned with such matters. "He wanted 'sensible things': he wanted for the Negro group the right to be 'normal Americans,' he wanted for them freedom to conform, and especially did he want for them a big role in the great American success story. The urgent question in Mr. White's mind was, 'How soon can we get every Negro into a gray flannel suit and traveling down the middle of the road shoulder to shoulder with all the other gray flannel suits?'" But "Traveling where?" Lillian asked. "To the Promised Land? Or to the point of no return?" She questioned whether the new leadership of the NAACP saw the need to enlarge the dimensions of its cause, and she seems to have sensed in King's philosophy a breadth of vision lacking in the NAACP.[33]

Lillian also thought King's movement more effective than the Southern Regional Council, though by the late 1950s she had become less critical of the SRC than formerly. In 1957 she still regarded it as "cautious, and on the side of 'moderation,'" but by 1959 her opinion of the council was more favorable. "I am all for the Southern Regional Council and I hope its work can continue," she wrote. "It was simply in the hands of cautious, unimaginative people too long. Now—well, things are different; and the leadership is different and I am sure history will show that the Council has exerted a creative, constructive effect on the region, certainly during the past five years."[34]

As in the 1930s and 1940s, Lillian remained distrustful of Communists and leftists. She wrote Irwin Ross of the New York *Post* in November, 1957, that after being undercover for about five years, the "commies are back at it again" and "working hard." However she did not think Communists were very numerous or influential in the civil rights movement, and she was incensed by Ku Klux Klan and White Citizens Council propaganda describing all who opposed segregation as Communists. (She herself was the subject of at least one such smear campaign, conducted by a Jacksonville, Florida, businessman.)[35]

Lillian's antipathy toward leftists was rekindled in December, 1956, when she received a letter from Aubrey Williams, formerly director of the National Youth Administration, now editor of the *Southern Farmer* and president of the Southern Conference Educational Fund (SCEF). He accused her of having done him "a grievous wrong" as well as harming the cause of civil rights by refusing to allow him to read her address before the Institute on Non-Violence and Social Change. Illness had prevented Lillian from appearing in person in Montgomery and so, according to Williams, she had asked the institute to find someone to read her address. He said she had initially agreed to the institute's choice of him but had later decided he would not be acceptable. "I have an idea why you did it," Williams wrote.

> I suspect it was because I was hailed by Sen. Eastland before his so-called Sub-Committee to Investigate the Administration of Internal Security Act and other Internal Laws, and accused of being a Communist by Paul Crouch, the same man who demanded that Att. Gen. Brownell be investigated, etc.
>
> By your action Wednesday you joined Sen. Eastland in his work of destroying any southern white person who dares to stand up unequivocally in behalf of Negroes. . . .
>
> You are too intelligent not to have long since understood fully Eastland's technique; to wit, hoist on the block any person who stands for across the board equality for Negroes and brand him with the name most hated and feared. Yet you have not the courage to follow this knowledge with personal acts designed to negate the diabolical scheming of Eastland, Talmadge, etc.
>
> Because of the sort of thing you did, Eastland and his cohorts, Jenner, McCarthy, Talmadge, etc., are succeeding, probably, beyond their fondest dreams. They are succeeding in making a new category in America—the untouchables who went too far in their fight for equality for the Negro people. Such people as you will write, but never join in an organized—out in the open fight. You even strike out at those who do.
>
> Your conduct is symptomatic of one of the great evils of our time which is that men are punished because they dare come out in the open and fight for what they believe. Few white people can be found any longer in the South who stand for a simple unequivocal equality and one reason is that they have had no support from so called liberals in either the North or South.[36]

Lillian's and Williams's paths had crossed briefly in the 1940s, though they had never met face to face. They had both worked with the Southern Conference for Human Welfare and then with the Southern Conference Educational Fund, created in 1946 to direct the educational activities of the conference. When the SCHW died in 1948, Williams became president of the SCEF and quickly made it into what his biographer calls "the most militantly antisegregationist force in southern life in the late 1940s and early 1950s." Like its parent organization, the SCEF was tagged a Communist group, and in March, 1954, Williams and several other officers were called before Senator James Eastland's Senate Internal Security Subcommittee investigation in New Orleans. In his testimony Williams' denied being a member of the Communist party but refused on First Amendment grounds to answer further questions from the subcommittee. Eastland later stated that he did not think Williams was a Communist, but the hearing succeeded in stigmatizing the SCEF as a "Communist-front group," and harassment of Williams and the SCEF continued. In the middle 1950s, Williams became increasingly hurt and resentful when civil rights groups, especially those with a predominantly Negro leadership, shied away from the SCEF because of the taint left by the Eastland investigation.[37]

Williams' outburst in his letter to Lillian reveals how embittered he had become as a result of his increasing isolation within the civil rights movement and his pessimism about the future of race relations in the United States. How familiar Lillian was with his recent difficulties is not known. Nevertheless, his letter, coming on the heels of the *Now Is the Time* banning and several years of smothering, elicited not sympathy but indignation. She claimed she had not known the institute was going to ask him to read her address. When the secretary called and told her that he had been asked and inquired whether he was acceptable and whether she would be willing to have him told that she had especially wanted him, "I immediately told her 'No, I would not be willing.' I said, 'I am sorry and I would not like for Mr. Williams to be embarrassed or hurt in any way' but I did not think I wanted to be as closely identified with Mr. Williams as his reading my speech would cause me to be identified. I went on to say, 'I have heard very fine things of Mr. Williams but he has in the past been identified with certain groups whose acts I have not always approved of. He is known mainly for his work in these organizations and as editor of his paper which I have never read even one copy of. Therefore I would not be willing to have a speech like mine read by a man who is a total stranger to me.' That was all there was to it."[38]

To Williams' charge that she had been influenced by the Eastland investigation, she replied:

> Your having been fought by Eastland did not even cross my mind when I made that decision. I have been fought so many years by not

only the Eastlands and Bilbos and Talmadges et cetera but also by the
Ralph McGills and Hodding Carters etc that who fights whom is to me
insignificant. As for Joe McCarthy, I wrote one of the first pieces written
in this country opposing him. It was so "hot" that the New York Times
cut most of the condemnation out before publishing the rest of the
speech. . . . But McCarthy fighting me, or my fighting him adds moral
grandeur to neither of us. I still insist we are not known "by our
enemies." Or "by our friends." We are known by what we are, ourselves. . . . You seem singularly ignorant of me and my life not to know
that I have endured as much opposition from these committees and
these bigots as you have; and other members of my family have, too. We
don't boast about our hard times, however; we think it is part of the
price any creative, decent person working for a good world has to pay.
There is no more use to talk about it than to talk about the weather. I
have also been hounded by the Communists in this country, so you see,
I know it both ways. The bigotry and cruelty and viciousness are
equally in the Communist–fellow traveling group as in the McCarthy
group; and is also in the "moderates." The bitter truth is this: any individual standing out in our world today for what is good and creative and
right has a lonely row to hoe. We accept that; and take it in our stride.[39]

Two embittered people, trading stories of persecution—although
Lillian chastised Williams for his "moral arrogance," she admitted that
hers was "a poor kind of letter at Christmas time" and observed that
"the one thing none of us down here can afford to do is to hold grudges
and get hurt and mad with each other." The exchange between the two
shows how Cold War issues could divide people in the civil rights
movement. Even if the Eastland investigation did not influence Lillian's
thinking about Williams, it is clear from her letter that his connection
with the SCEF was decisive. She referred to the SCEF as an organization "which I refused many years ago to have anything to do with."
Lillian was one of the early members of the fund, but like many white
southern liberals she left the organization in the late 1940s, probably
because she disapproved of its advocacy of popular front liberalism.
She shared Williams' antipathy toward moderation and gradualism,
but she wanted to distance herself from him and the SCEF because of
the connection with popular front liberalism. She believed that had
Williams read her address in Montgomery, she would have been con-
victed in the public mind of guilt by association with views she did not
approve.[40]

Lillian's Montgomery address facilitated a reconciliation with another leftist, Virginia Durr, who had been active in the SCHW and later the SCEF. Durr shared Williams' popular front liberalism, and, like Williams, had been called before the Eastland hearing. She attended the Montgomery meeting at which Lillian's address was read and wrote a letter describing the scene. "The church was packed and people standing on the outside and bulging in the doors and windows," she wrote. Hylan Lewis, a sociology professor from Atlanta University, read the speech "beautifully and feelingly and there was not a sound during the reading. It was a most wonderful speech and so full of love and truth and at the end when you thankd [*sic*] them for what they were doing to free the South and the white people of the South from their load of fear and prejudice, you could hear a deep sigh go all over the audience." Durr expressed concern over Lillian's illness and added: "I *am so sorry* and so regretful that we were divided and did not ever become friends. How silly it all seems now in the light of what has actually happened. We should have known that the Negroes in the end were going to find their own way and that what we did and thought could only come to fruition in what they did."[41]

Durr's letter touched Lillian deeply and she told her so. She said she had heard "indirectly, of the troubled, difficult, hearbreaking [*sic*] times you and your husband have had" (probably a reference to the Eastland investigation and its aftermath) and added that she was sorry about it.

> I am so sorry, too, that we never quite understood the other, although I think I liked you much more than you liked me! But never mind that. . . . the letter brought back, too, the old memories of our resurgence of hope and the feverish desire we had to "do something," to change things. We knew, in a way that the younger people will never know, the pain of it, the wrong of it. Our differences were that some of us felt it could be done in one way, and others of us felt it must be done in another. Because of my years in China when young and my coming under the influence of Gandhi in those years, I held on rather grimly to the importance of the means we used. I made big mistakes, too; we all did; but we shared something very real, together.[42]

One aspect of Lillian's thinking that received increasing emphasis in the late 1950s was her desire to bring young people into the civil rights movement. To this end she worked with the YWCA and visited a number of white and Negro college campuses to talk with students and urge them to join the movement. She believed many old-timers in the movement were too cautious or had become too doctrinaire about the best way to effect change in the South. A fresh approach was needed, she wrote Mozell Hill, editor of *Phylon*. "Something younger, more vital, more risky, full of fun and ardor. We need to get the youngsters involved; they haven't got sense enough to know there is danger, so they'll go ahead and do what even you and I would gulp over. But we've got to let them try. If the young white men and women and young colored men and women of Georgia can't do something, it just can't be done. The rest of us have broken down walls, filled up ditches, defined problems, put a sharp edge on dilemmas, we've shaken everybody's souls with the moral issue—now something more has to be done. And what we who are more experienced, more aware, can do is encourage the young ones to try, to take over, TO DO SOMETHING." In her talks with young people, she emphasized the need to take risks to bring about a new, better way of life. Describing the approach she planned to take at a YWCA conference, she wrote:

> I think we need to stress the point that all change involves risk; that a good way of life, a new way that encourages growth will come about only by our running risks for it. I want us to persuade our young people that life, if it is creative, is full of risks and nothing, truly nothing is worth talking about or believing in if it is not worth running risks for. . . . At the same time that we stress the necessity for risk we should also stress the necessity for non-violence, for love and goodwill, for thoughtful exploration of the problems, for self discipline. . . . I believe we have failed in the South for the past 20 years in our work in so-called "race relations" because we have been too cautious, too scared to speak out or to take a stand. We have confused caution with wisdom . . . and courage with hate.[43]

Lillian viewed the *Brown* decision as the climax of the old-timers' efforts to change the laws regarding race relations. The remaining task was the one she had long emphasized, changing "the psychology of the South, the spirit of things, the quality of human relationships."[44] By the late 1950s she had decided that only young southerners, using the methods of nonviolence and passive resistance, would be able to accomplish that task.

# VIII Nihilism

> Each book I write is for me an exploration: always a search for a
> deeper more authentic meaning; always a painful asking of new ques-
> tions. And afterward, I seem to grow suddenly in all parts of my being:
> my book acting on me, its author, as a powerful dose of vitamins and
> hormones!

Lillian said that the idea for *One Hour* was born in 1949 during a conversation in Irita Van Doren's apartment about innocence and guilt, false accusations, and McCarthyism. However, she did not begin working intensively on the novel until 1956. It gave her "something to live for" following the fire on Old Screamer and her second bout with cancer. Initially, she conceived it as the story of Mark Channing, a young cancer research scientist accused of molesting a little girl. Writing to friends, she described it as "a fable of our times" treating the "mob spirit" that had become endemic in the United States. She hoped it would remind people of the Alger Hiss and J. Robert Oppenheimer cases and "the Joe McCarthy mess."[1]

In some respects, *One Hour* was a rephrasing of *Strange Fruit*. The setting is the upper rather than the deep South, but the bittersweet love affair between Dave Landrum and Grace Channing is reminiscent of the one between Tracy Deen and Nonnie Anderson. Dave, like Tracy, is crippled, having lost a leg in World War II. *One Hour* ends with a cross burning rather than a lynching, but as in the earlier novel, an innocent man dies as a result. In *One Hour,* however, responsibility for the mob action rests not only on the teenage hoodlums who instigate it, but on the middle- and upper-class members of the community who contribute to the climate of suspicion, fear, and anger. Lillian did not deal explicitly with the race question in *One Hour,* but treated what she saw

as the more inclusive issue confronting Americans in the 1950s. "It isn't
only race . . . it is anybody who is different from the crowd, different
in belief, different in looks, different in interests," she explained to
Richard V. Moore, president of Bethune-Cookman College. "The great
scareword today, is DIFFERENT, not color."[2]

Lillian decided that the story of *One Hour* would be told in the first
person, by Dave Landrum, the rector of All Saints Church in Windsor
Hills, Virginia. "Nothing wrong about a woman writing in first person
male; she just has to prove she can do it," she declared. Landrum tells
the story of Mark and Grace Channing in order to try to discover some
meaning in the "insane chaos" that had enveloped their lives two years
earlier. In the midst of the chaos he had come close to despair. He no
longer understood his relationship with God or the relevance of the
Church, no longer trusted in the goodness and rationality of human
nature. "Good and evil had canceled each other out, . . . the tender the
brutal the truth and the lie, death and life, had merged into nothing.
Nothing. Nothing." He is saved by Grace and her love for him and
then, apparently, by the grace of God. He is reading a passage from
Rilke's *Duino Elegies.*

> Slowly, as I read Rilke's words, something opened . . . something shut.
> All was as it had been, months ago. My mind had not answered one
> question; had not solved one problem; had not found new facts; nor
> reached new depths; nor climbed one step toward new insight—and
> yet, I felt at peace. I had not earned this quietude but it was given me. I
> could feel the afternoon falling away, light dimming . . . traffic on Ar-
> lington growing heavier . . . all of it I was aware of and not aware of.
> Slowly I was flooded with unwarranted certainty: some day it would
> come clear, not in answers but in a new feeling among men; some day
> there'd be understanding, and forgiveness. Some day this mad, obscene,
> ambiguous, anonymous hour in which we live will find its name and its
> place in time, will slip into its small crevice and lie there diminished
> and tamed by love, and compassion, and the slow-growing knowledge
> of a truth beyond facts, an intelligence beyond our small logic, a love
> beyond the anguish.

Dave has come to recognize and accept the "fragmented quality of human awareness." He also admits "the unconquerable evil in man." But
he no longer despairs because he is able to see, because God gives him
the power to see, "the good that is so close to the evil, and that we must

see and acknowledge or perish." Whereas other characters in the book view the death of Andy, the Channings' son, and Charlie, the church organist, as senseless, Dave is able to see them as moral triumphs. Andy, he tells Grace, died with dignity, for something good; "he died *because* of human evil but he died *for* the best thing a human can die for: a good relationship." And Charlie's moral triumph, Dave realizes, came when he was fighting the mob and realized that he had mustered the courage he had always felt guilty for lacking. Thus *One Hour* closes on an affirmative note similar to the one Lillian had sounded in *The Journey*. Dave has attained, or been given, the certainty that life is not meaningless and that man can discover its meaning and indeed shares in the making of it. In the epilogue to the book he says:

> For days, I have read again and again what I have written down here, pondering it. . . . I said when I began that I wanted to find its meaning, its form. I see now that its meaning is still in the making, its form is still being shaped by the living: For the rest of us are still here and this experience lies, even now, only half formed in the hard rock of our awareness.
>
> I am not sure what will come next for we are still changing it: each time we feel one small movement of compassion or mercy or fear or hate, each time we glimpse a deeper level or turn away from the new vision, each time we find our courage or lose it, we are forming this hour. . . . I am not sure what is ahead: or where the next hour lies: except I know it is hidden somewhere in this one, among quiet and noisy and uncounted possibilities. And we, the living, will find it or fail to, as we continue to shape this small piece of time we call our own.[3]

*One Hour* elicited praise from reviewers for its earnestness, sincerity, and high purpose. Most of the criticism focused on the philosophical thinking in the novel. Carter Brooke Jones of the Washington *Sunday Star* wished Dave's "cerebral wanderings" had been shortened. Edmund Fuller of the *Saturday Review* characterized him as "a self-conscious literary-theological name-dropper," while Harold C. Gardiner, writing in *America*, described him as "a prime prig and a would-be deep-browed intellectual [who] engages in lots of obviously spurious philosophizing." They were not primarily concerned with the content of the philosophizing; they criticized it for spoiling the narrative and robbing an exciting story of vitality.[4]

Leslie Fiedler also criticized the philosophizing, but for a different reason. In a review in the *New Republic* entitled "Decency Is Not Enough," he declared *One Hour* an exemplary book, "the embodiment of all that is socially, even ethically admirable in latter-day liberal humanism—and of all in that movement which is, from the point of view of art, inert, smug, false and hopelessly dull." He seemed to be saying that, while admirable, Lillian's political and social beliefs did not translate into great literature. According to Fiedler, Lillian had stripped the Modernist point of view of its antisocial, subversive tendencies and made it into a "code of genteel sentimentality." In *One Hour* she paraded all "the standard problems of our era," trivialized versions of the terrors and ambiguities revealed in the great Modernist works.

> In return she asks only the price sentimentality demands of truth: the right to assert, at the last possible minute, what the jacket blurb calls "a passionate affirmation." In her conclusion, not only does the book's most cowardly protagonist [Charlie] improbably find his courage, but the book's conscience [Dave], the holy adulterer, earlier freed in bed from guilt and terror, finds the strength to pray that he may "look at the good that is so close to the evil, that we must see and acknowledge or perish."
>
> Everything is there finally, everything but the ultimate truth and the ultimate courage, which have no need to assert courage as a fact or truth as a moral tag. The lessons of Freud and Kierkegaard and of the tortured makers of modern art, the ambiguities of the apostles of a terrible freedom and the uses of *angst*, all is reduced to the level of middlebrow piety, of the sophisticated philistinism just now replacing the older, more naive model. And who could ask more than the warmth, the decency, the compassion, the love of justice, even the comfortable dullness which inform this book—except one who has known the outrage, the scandal, the offense of great art.[5]

Before Fiedler's review appeared, Lillian had received a letter from her friend Lawrence Kubie, the psychoanalyst, giving his opinion of *One Hour*. He wrote that he had been deeply moved by the book and declared that it had "depth and power and greatness of spirit, conception and movement, . . . a Tolstoian sweep and grandeur." Nevertheless, he offered two significant criticisms, one of them similar to Fiedler's but without his contemptuous tone. The first had to do with the character of Dave, whom Kubie found convincing as a man but not as a clergyman. "One never really hears him preach or sees him pray or feels him in his experience of any transcendent moment. He could as well has [*sic*] been a lawyer, a doctor, a teacher, or a newspaper editor. Indeed everything fruitful and creative and positive which he did, he did not in his clerical role." To Kubie, Dave's clerical role seemed "almost adventitious." He suggested that in making Dave a preacher, Lillian was "meeting some need of your own, not some need of the book." That need of Lillian's that Kubie recognized was perhaps responsible for the second, more serious problem he found in the novel, which was similar to the one Fiedler pointed out. According to Kubie's reading, the events in *One Hour* were "predetermined by an array of complex, interacting forces which are under the control of no Man, and equally are under the control of no whimsical and arbitrary Antique God, nor yet under the control of any teleologically purposive force, concocted by frightened men as an ad hoc device with which to quiet their fears." How then, he asked, could she find a place in the novel, and in her own philosophy of life, for "God Forces"?[6]

Lillian decided that the reason most of the reviewers in and around New York disparaged *One Hour* was "because it had hope in it." She noted that the book had been released "at the peak of the Negation period among our reviewers, critics and not-so-young writers." All of them, including "that nasty Fiedler," were trying to be nihilists, imitating Sartre and Genet. "Hope is about the most unfashionable thing among the New York literati at present," she wrote her literary agent, Joan Daves. Sounding rather like William Dean Howells, who theorized that "the more smiling aspects of life" were "the more American," she insisted that in their enthusiasm to adopt the views of the "nihilistic existential school," writers and critics had failed to take into account the context in which it had developed. "I can understand what happened to writers in Europe, after the Second World War, after the concentration camps," she wrote. "But in the United States the boys are mere copy-cats. They have not experienced these traumas; indeed I think their imaginations shun them." Not only were the American nihilists phony, they were also pitiable. They were "the whimpering generation," who were "determined to be miserable, determined to lick their own sores and insist there is no penicillin in the world." They feared hope and, she thought, resented her for offering it, "for if they once accept hope . . . they must accept their responsibility as human beings to do something about the human condition. As long as they can think of the human condition as totally evil, totally absurd, totally unreasonable, totally without sense and totally unchangeable, then why not lie down and suck the nipple of self-pity."[7]

Lillian's concern about the influence of nihilism dated back to the middle 1950s. She had been dismayed to see how pervasive it was among the young women she taught at Vassar in the winter of 1955. She had had them read *The Journey* and remembered that some of them could not abide its optimism. In *One Hour* she drew a portrait of these young women in Katie. Dave describes her as "just out of an Eastern college and girded with pessimism" and contends that she is using existentialism as an escape technique. "Existentialism gave her a place to run to," he muses. "What she longed for, I think, was security from hope. If she felt hopeful she'd have to assume her share of responsibility for the mess the human race had got itself into." Dave does not agree with her but understands her and admires her for protesting complacency.[8]

Lillian thought of herself as "an existentialist of sorts," not of "the Sartre variety" but what she called a "more hopeful brand." Her existentialism was the outgrowth of extensive reading in literature, theology, and philosophy during the 1950s, including Martin Heidegger, Karl Jaspers, Gabriel Marcel, and Miguel de Unamuno, as well as existentialist theologians such as Paul Tillich and analysts such as Rollo May. These thinkers, she declared, had "more depth, more of a sense of wonder, more love and faith" than Sartre.[9]

In *One Hour* she attempted to dramatize the more hopeful brand of existentialism by showing man's capacity for courage, compassion, and transcendence. By the same token, the novel was an effort to combat the threat posed by nihilism. The nihilists were "dynamiters," she told literary critic Maxwell Geismar, and as harmful in their way as "the hoodlum dynamiters of the South. . . . Iconoclasts are for tranquil, peaceful times," she explained; "there are plenty of things they can dynamite then without doing the world any harm. But in this time of stupendous, shaking change, when evil and good thrust up new forms so alike that they are like twins—then is when the human race must hold to nonrational words like hope and faith, love, and compassion. Without them, we die; the race dies; the earth will die."[10]

Lillian's condemnation of the nihilists as dynamiters recalls Van Wyck Brooks's and Archibald MacLeish's earlier condemnations of Modernist writers as "irresponsibles" whose preaching of despair and degradation had undermined the moral and spiritual foundations of the American people, leaving them unprepared to deal with the threat of fascism. While she was partly in the Modernist/existentialist camp in her concern with irrationality and the evil in man and the world, Lillian shared Brooks and MacLeish's opinion that art and society were, or should be, mutually reinforcing and that literature should be a regenerative force which, as Brooks put it, "in some way conduces to race-survival."[11]

Although dismayed and hurt by the way the New York reviewers treated *One Hour*, Lillian was somewhat consoled by the positive response it evoked in other quarters. While he had criticized some aspects of the book, Lawrence Kubie had praised her characterization. Rollo May, an existential psychologist, also liked the book. The response that Lillian valued most came from theologian Paul Tillich, to whom she had sent a copy of the novel. He wrote that he admired her "profound psychological insights," her knowledge of "the ambiguities of life generally—and especially of the human heart," and expressed gratification "that we are so near in our theological outlook." She was also pleased at the book's favorable reception by young clerics and theologians and at seminaries such as Union, Drew, and Boston University.[12]

Even more, she enjoyed the response of her own South. "All the South has given the book good reviews," she exulted in a letter to Dorothy Norman. A review in the Memphis *Commercial Appeal* by Ruth Ballentine of Sardis, Mississippi, especially delighted her. Ballentine wrote that the theme of *One Hour* was "man's endless struggle to know himself, the immemorial search for good in the evil that lies both within and without"—in some ways the most astute and discerning review the book received, Lillian declared. The notice *One Hour* received in Atlanta also pleased Lillian. Margaret Long and Eddie Barker praised the novel in their columns in the Atlanta *Journal;* the newspaper also ran a favorable review by Sam Lucchese. Clayton, too, responded enthusiastically. Lillian reported that the ten-cent store manager had ordered one hundred copies and sold seventy-four, there was a six-month waiting list for it at the public library, and one of the English teachers in the high school had urged all her seniors to read it. Lillian said the townspeople were reading the novel "with grave interest and mature reactions" and seemed to like it.[13]

Lillian admitted being surprised by the southern reaction. She had not set out to write a southern novel—she had decided some time ago that as far as fiction was concerned she was finished with the South— and she had not wanted *One Hour* advertised as such. However, when favorable reviews began coming in from the region, she began to reconsider. The reason southerners liked the book, she decided, was because "for the first time in literary history the 'heroes' are liberal, cultured, almost erudite Southerners." She had not thought of them as southerners, but now realized that southern readers and reviewers did. She believed she had discovered a new and receptive audience made up of educated, cultivated, sophisticated southerners who were sick of being depicted as Tobacco Roaders, Snopses, and lynchers and who identified with Dave and Mark and Grace and Katie.[14]

The brief attention shown *One Hour* in the South and Midwest (it was on the Chicago *Tribune*'s bestseller list in October) was not enough to offset the negative response of the New York reviewers and what Lillian regarded as desultory promotion efforts by Harcourt, Brace, and Company. For a few months, she vented her feelings in long impassioned letters to the president, William Jovanovich, and a few close friends, analyzing and refuting the unfavorable reviews, explaining and justifying the techniques she had used in the novel, quoting the letters from Rollo May and Paul Tillich. "I have to jeer back to keep from bursting into tears," she confessed to Jovanovich. "They can shake you, review after review after review." She admitted she had some weaknesses as a writer, "but I can't let the meanies break my nerve as they are trying to do—the whole damned mess of them—so I have to shout back at them—at least in letters to my publisher and two or three close friends."[15] She wanted desperately to be recognized as a distinguished serious writer, and she never got over the disappointment at the critical reception of *One Hour*.

Refusing to give in to depression, Lillian turned to her time-proven remedy, a new writing project. It was a sequel to *One Hour* in the form of a monologue by Grace offering her view of "the hour." She also resumed work on "Julia." Besides working on the two fictional pieces, she began thinking, reading, and taking notes for a book she had agreed to do for the World Perspectives series edited by Ruth Nanda Anshen. The fact that the series included works by Werner Heisenberg, Paul Tillich, and Jacques Maritain was somewhat intimidating. On the other hand, Lillian believed that being in the series would give her prestige and, she hoped, would encourage critics and readers to view her "as someone who has a gravity of purpose, and perhaps a subtlety of mind, and perhaps a certain quality of imagination." She wrote Anshen that she planned to work on "Julia" in the mornings and "our book" in the afternoons. She wanted to finish "Julia" first, partly because she had been working on it for many years, but also because of the income it would bring. She had had to borrow money while writing *One Hour*, and its sales had been the lowest of any of her books. And she doubted the World Perspectives book would make enough money "to depend on for my living."[16]

While thinking about the World Perspectives book, Lillian resumed her study of philosophy and religion. She described herself as seeking answers to questions that had arisen during the writing of *One Hour*. In one sense, she explained to her friend the Reverend Henry H. Crane, the theme of the novel was "Where is God and where are we? how can we feel a part of cosmic affairs, cosmic destiny? . . . how can a person become strong save as his strength comes from a transcendent God?" Now that the book was finished, she said she was "still asking questions that my growing Dave should be asking," but she had also begun to ask "new questions that Dave did not know to ask, and I, his author, did not know while I wrote the book." When Paul Tillich sent her a copy of his *Theology of Culture* in November, 1959, she felt it had arrived at just the right time, when she was asking questions the book was able to answer.[17]

She had been reading Tillich's works for several years. The two of them had several friends in common, including Ruth Anshen, Rollo May, and Dorothy Norman, and Lillian first met Tillich and his wife at a tea in East Hampton in the summer of 1957 or 1958 when she was visiting Norman in New York. Lillian liked him immediately and remembered how he laughed "with such deep understanding" when she told him about the "Protestant fears" of her childhood and her "horror of those old evangelical 'revivals.'" Reading Tillich in the 1950s seems to have helped her in her search for religious understanding and faith. Since adolescence, she told him, she had "struggled with God . . . asking clumsy, crude questions"; then she had become an agnostic, "achieving a kind of amnesia about God and religion and asking nothing at all"; and now she was "beginning again: to ask questions that maybe are more valid and therefore can draw forth valid answers." Tillich's theology satisfied a deep-seated need for an intellectually as well as emotionally satisfying way of thinking about God. On the one hand she was indebted to Tillich's doctrine for her own notion of God and of the "impenetrable" between him and man. In both *The Journey* and *One Hour* (through Dave) she expressed her belief in God as a transcendent and absolute being and her conviction that man's knowledge of God is necessarily finite, relative, and ever-changing. Dave says, "God means to me the unknown, the eternal mystery beyond the certainty; all that is yet to be learned about our universe and ourselves, and all that is beyond the human capacity to learn; God means to me both the Ultimate Form and the Forming Power beyond the chaos and the order." Citing Tillich's notion that "'God' is a symbol for God," he goes on to reflect that "it is a symbol of a truth that must be created anew—for it cannot be discovered—by each of us and as continuously as our bodies and minds and spirit are re-created."[18]

On the other hand, and perhaps more importantly, Tillich helped Lillian regain the religious feeling she remembered from childhood— and apparently regretted losing—but unencumbered by the anti-intellectualism that had repulsed her as a young woman. The appeal of Tillich's thinking is seen in her response to a sermon he preached in the chapel of Union Theological Seminary in March, 1960. She described the occasion some years later in a letter to a mutual friend, Sara Terrien.

> I had not been in a church in a long time. I turned with fear against churches after my Methodist small-town upbringing; at eighteen I stopped going; since then, I have gone to Catholic churches and sat for hours thinking, looking, listening; I've slipped into Episcopal churches and have done the same thing; I have rarely gone to a Methodist church since I was eighteen—to funerals of the family, yes; now and then to an Easter sermon and always I have sat there weeping heavily but silently, thinking of my mother and father, their life, their death; while everybody else was happy about the Resurrection.

But that day at church at Union Theological! . . . as Paul Tillich preached about God, (what I had always believed an impossible thing to do) . . . I was drawn by his hypnotic voice, his right words to the deepest feeling I had had about God since childhood. . . . there was Paul, so beautiful, so masculine, so warm, so sexy and sensual, so spiritual too, telling us perhaps it would be best never to say the word God for a long long time; and he was quoting from the Old Testament that passage about not looking if one felt the presence of God near. . . . And all the time, the old Protestant music, the church itself, the pews, the old conformations that had been familiar to me from childhood were pulling me back to my parents' home, my parents' religion (so real it was, so deep in spite of the silly non-intellectuality of it) and I was weeping silently inside for that old hurt childhood, that old beautiful sweet tender childhood, that old faith which my imagination felt so completely but which my mind shunned. It was a terrible hour for me in many ways and one of the most awesome and beautiful of my life.[19]

Besides Tillich, another important influence on Lillian's thinking was Pierre Teilhard de Chardin. In 1959 she read the newly issued English translation of his *The Phenomenon of Man*. Although she found the book difficult, it made an immediate and profound impact on her. She later declared it "truly the great work of this century," and she told Margaret Long that it had influenced her more than any other book.[20] In the 1960s she reread it several times, read Teilhard's other works, and commented extensively on his thought in letters to friends and in several book reviews.

Teilhard's philosophy appealed to Lillian for a number of reasons. Preoccupied with overcoming the fragmentation and estrangements of the modern world, she could not help being sympathetic to his discovery of wholeness and unity. She found in his philosophy what she had been groping toward intuitively for many years, she said. Also, Teilhard's style of writing, which Roland Stromberg has described as "a kind of mystic poetry, a pantheistic hymn to the marvels of nature, man, and God," appealed to Lillian. Because Teilhard was "a poet as well as a scientist, the richness of his imaginative vision and his deep feelings get into his writing; and it is this that gives it its special quality," she told Rochelle Girson of the *Saturday Review*. But probably what appealed to Lillian most was his optimism about man and the future. Teilhard provided her with what she regarded as a scientifically grounded rebuttal of the nihilist view and reinforced the feeling of hope she had expressed in *The Journey* and *One Hour*. She thought no writer had written so persuasively and elegantly of man's future as he had. Teilhard insisted that there was purpose in humanity's presence on earth, that life was involved in an evolutionary process that was moving over billions of years toward ever higher states of consciousness and organization. Moreover he described twentieth-century man as on the verge of a tremendous acceleration and proliferation of thought that would ultimately bring him closer to other men and to God. His prophetic vision enabled Lillian to view the present age not with despair but with exhilaration. She regarded it as a crucial time in human history, when mankind was about to make a great leap toward unity and perfection.[21]

Yet another reason Teilhard's philosophy appealed to Lillian was that it seemed to dovetail with new ideas she found attractive in the field of psychology. She admired existential psychologists like Rollo May because of the emphasis they placed on what she called man's "commitment to a future" in shaping human behavior.[22] Their concept of existence as a process of "becoming" echoed her belief, expressed in *The Journey* and *One Hour,* in man's ability to discover and create meaning in life. She also found attractive their notion of man's freedom and responsibility to shape his own existence and, consequently, the desirability of his being open to all the possibilities of existence and not allowing fears, delusions, or compulsions to block their realization. Such a notion was congruent with Lillian's concern to eliminate the internal and external barriers preventing people from achieving their full humanity.

Lillian's literary philosophy in the late 1950s and early 1960s reflected her religious and philosophical thinking. She insisted that writers should deal with "the larger aspects of human experience," with the predicament and potential of modern man. And, like many of those who had opposed the granting of the Bollingen award to Ezra Pound, she was unwilling to dissociate art from moral perception. In an article for the *Saturday Review* entitled "Novelists Need a Commitment," she disagreed with those who she said insisted, "'Of course you can be a great poet and still be a Fascist; you can write a great novel and still cling to nihilism or to segregation.'" She retorted, "I don't believe a word of it." She also dismissed the "nonsense" being published about the need of artists and writers to isolate themselves from society and its problems. Although she did not name names in the *Saturday Review* article, it is clear from her other writing that she especially blamed the Agrarians and their New Criticism for persuading a whole generation of college students to avoid the political and social arena. In the revised edition of *Killers of the Dream,* she drew up a two-page indictment of the Agrarians/New Critics for arguing that "the role of the artist does not embrace concern and action" and for urging their students to "busy themselves with literary dialectics, to support the 'New Criticism' instead of a new life."[23]

She continued to lament the influence of nihilism on modern literature. She held it responsible for what she called the "dehumanization of the novel" during the last half-century. She admitted that nihilism had served a purpose in helping people become aware of what she regarded as the chief problem of the modern age, the fragmentation of the self and the estrangement of man from his fellow men and God. Now the time had come for restoring man's humanity, for portraying the "whole human being." In doing so, writers would not only be delineating a truer picture of man; they would be contributing to his higher evolution. She explained her view in a speech she wrote in March, 1965, entitled "The Role of the Poet in a World of Demagogues." In it she argued that although the present was a time of violence, hatred, and confusion, it was also a time when men everywhere were seeking to "become more human." We live "in the midst of the greatest transformation the human race has ever experienced," she observed, citing Teilhard's prophecies regarding the evolution of humanity. The role of the poet was to reveal "the meaning of what is happening to us," to show the human spirit evolving toward perfection.[24]

Lillian contended that contemporary writers had not fulfilled their responsibility. "What are they saying?" she asked.

> What are novelists and dramatists saying about this tremendous thing that is happening to us? I'm afraid they are saying almost nothing. Most are still talking the old nihilisms of the nineteenth century redressed in new clothes; most are still fixated on narcissistic problems that have sloshed over from Victorian days; most are still moaning about the human condition, the tragic absurdity of man's plight, the hideous lack of cosmic purpose; most mistake an earth-size movement for no motion at

all. I cannot think of one who is creating characters who might have qualities needed for this adventurous age. What has Albee given us? Genet? Sartre? Mailer? Self-absorbed, most cannot tear their eyes from their own small depravities. So they are giving us fragmented sketches of sick people; they hold before us in play and story a never-ending bleak view of miserable, lost, lonely schizophrenics.

They gave the impression that the "splintered, sick, empty people" in their novels and plays were the whole of contemporary life and "all we have to count on for the future." At the same time, by "turning small issues into large" and equating "fleeting problems" with the "human condition," they suggested that humanity had reached a dead end, that "'This age has no exit.'"[25]

"We cannot act as if this is all; as if there is nothing more to count on," Lillian declared. She urged writers to make a "commitment to the future." She did not invoke William James, but what she was asking involved a willing of belief such as he described in his famous essay, and with the expectation of the results he anticipated from such an effort. She stated her view most clearly in *The Journey*. "To believe in something not yet proved and to underwrite it with our lives: it is the only way we can leave the future open," she wrote. She believed with James that faith creates its own verification. To realize Teilhard's prophecy, people must believe in and act upon it, and it was the responsibility of writers to offer a new vision that would enable them to understand and contribute to the transformation of the human spirit.[26]

Just as the will to believe was at the heart of Lillian's religious, philosophical, and literary thinking, it also figured in her personal life. Her first bout with cancer occurred in 1953 while she was writing *The Journey*. After the second attack, in 1955, her doctor at Emory Hospital in Atlanta offered a bleak prognosis. At first Lillian decided to try to accept death, but then she said she realized that "this quiet acceptance would bring death on; that I was the type who had to fight something, not accept passively." She went to Memorial Hospital in New York City where she found a surgeon, Dr. Henry Randall, who encouraged her to fight. "He talked to me for hours," she recalled; "he told me that only I could really keep myself alive; that I had to want to live; had to see some reason to live; and that if I did that, he and the staff at Memorial would devise ways and means of extending my life from six months to six months etc." Randall advised her to go on to Vassar as planned and to load herself up with future commitments and fill her days as full as possible. In later years Lillian maintained it was because she always wanted to write another book that she survived four more malignancies. In July, 1965, after she had been hospitalized for a particularly severe attack, she wrote Harry Golden that she no longer dreaded death and thought she would be able to accept it when it came. But she had not given up even then. "I really want to live and write four or five more books," she declared.[27]

# IX Woman Born of Man

> Women are so secretive; we have not told what we know of life. . . . we
> women must somehow learn to stop lying and tell ourselves and others
> the truth. Our mystery lies in part in our giant-size talent for fooling
> ourselves as well as our men.

"I want now to write about a woman," Lillian declared in a
letter to William Jovanovich in January, 1960. She had not decided
whether to start on Grace's monologue or try to finish "Julia." The former seemed more exciting. "It would be a deeply feminine book; full
of all kinds of disclosures. It will be a woman writing all she knows
about a very real woman," she added.[1]

Following the publication of *One Hour*, Lillian became increasingly
interested in the subject of women. As her letter to Jovanovich suggests,
her interest partly grew out of her desire to elaborate the character and
perceptions of Grace. It may also have been provoked by the critical
response to *One Hour*. Lillian reacted to hostile reviews of the novel
differently from the way she had responded to earlier criticism. In
letters to friends she speculated that some of the reviewers had denigrated the book "simply because I was a woman." She wrote Dorothy
Norman that there were "five or six book editors and critics around
New York who seem to hate me (not personally, they don't even know
me) but ideologically, perhaps; and perhaps there is some sex hostility." She thought possibly the reviewers resented her because she had
dared to create a man as a major character and to "probe into men's
souls," or because she had presumed to "encroach on the masculine
field of philosophy."[2]

178

Lillian also thought that reviewers disliked *One Hour* because it spoiled their image of her as "that nice little woman who does so much about racial segregation." Beginning in the early 1960s, she became increasingly resentful of the stereotype. She decided it had been in the making since *Strange Fruit*, which too many people had read as propaganda rather than serious literature, and had been reinforced by *Killers of the Dream* and *Now Is the Time*. By the time *One Hour* appeared, the stereotype was fixed, according to Lillian, and it played a crucial role in shaping the critical reaction to the novel. "Critics did not try to understand it," she declared. "It was not about race—how dare L. S. write a book not about race! . . . They couldn't bear the knowledge that they had so falsely stereotyped me. Here I was; knowing in the fields of modern music, modern art, existential philosophy—how dare she be so widely informed, so profoundly interested in life as it is experienced at its depths! They simply refused to really read that book."[3]

Even after becoming involved in the civil rights movement of the 1960s, which further reinforced the stereotype, Lillian continued to resent it. She believed people used it to diminish her achievement—by limiting her concern to the Negro and overlooking her interest in the human condition, by focusing on her protest against racial segregation and ignoring her discussion of the dehumanization of man. It enabled them to ignore the Mary side of her nature and what she termed her "deep creative concerns." That "so many people refuse to treat me like a serious and good creative writer" constituted "the hurt of my life," she confided to Rochelle Girson in November, 1964. "I am that or I am nothing," she continued. "What breaks my heart has been this deliberate forcing me in a false category, refusing to see what I have actually done, how I have done it, the quality of my mind and imagination." The following year she vented similar feelings in letters to Lawrence Kubie and Wilma Dykeman Stokely. The National Women's Division of the American Jewish Congress had awarded her the first Queen Esther Scroll for her "creative genius," but in reporting it, the press described it as an award for her "courage and commitment." To her such reporting proved that the press was determined to diminish her. "They have stereotyped me as a propagandist and friend of the Negro Cause and they are determined that I not be looked at as an important writer," she wrote Kubie.

It seems impossible for them to admit either my intelligence or my creative ability. It hurts. Isn't it strange? one is always punished at the place in one's personality where it hurts the most. How can "the enemy" so instinctively find the most vulnerable spot! Somehow, the hostile male group have seemed to know . . . the truth of my being which is that I want above all else to be genuinely creative and discerning and sensitive; I want to be considered as a writer—and as woman; but not as "woman." They know it and they have seen to it that I am not considered so. This has been the unhealing wound in my life.

Writing to Stokely, Lillian compared the deep hurt caused by the stereotyping to the lesser wounds inflicted on her. The fires on Old Screamer, the dynamite threats, the hundreds of nasty letters and phone calls—none of them really hurt, though they sometimes scared her. "What hurt was the fact that 'nice people' took away from me my talent as though I didn't possess it; they stole my creativity from me; that is, they say I am not creative, not talented, not 'a writer' just a nice woman helping Negroes find for themselves a better life. They somehow found exactly the way to crush me."[4]

Perhaps Lillian became interested in the subject of women because she saw a parallel between her own stereotyping and the way women over the centuries had been stereotyped. She addressed the latter theme in several speeches and articles in the early 1960s. Since the beginning of human history, she observed, men had been conjuring up images of women as Madonna and Bitch, as Goddess of Mercy and Terrible Witch, and, more recently, as sacred woman of the South and domineering Mom. Each of these images was based to some extent on reality, but none was true to the whole of it. This kind of stereotyping of women was one of the reasons Lillian faulted contemporary writers such as Tennessee Williams, Arthur Miller, Ernest Hemingway, and especially William Faulkner. None of them understood "women or WOMAN," she declared. Williams did not see women's "awful strength and blindness." Faulkner, she insisted, not only did not understand women but "hated and disesteemed" them, with the result that his women characters were all "dreadful creatures" and "cartoons of women, nothing else."[5]

Women knew how they looked to men, but they had not yet discovered their true identity, according to Lillian. The fault lay partly with them, for they had only begun to break a "million-year silence" about themselves. For centuries women had refused to "tell the truth about themselves"—some because they had no awareness of themselves, others because settling for the men's view seemed "the simplest way to live and often the only way to keep the bread buttered," still others because they feared telling the truth "might radically change male psychology." Whatever the reason, the result was that "we women don't know who we are. Not only are we bereft of a public image we like; we don't have a private image of ourselves either."[6]

Lillian thought of herself as specially qualified to help break the long silence about women. The subject she knew best, she wrote Rochelle Girson, was "women and their curvatures of soul and twisting relationships." The subject also appealed to her because in writing about women she believed she was expressing the Mary side of her nature. "I am part Mary and part Martha," she explained. "As Martha I have written about segregation, the South, etc. etc.; as Mary I know best girls, women, artists."[7]

Circumstances prevented Lillian from realizing her desire to do a substantial work on the subject of women. She became caught up in the civil rights movement of the 1960s and toward the middle of the decade was increasingly incapacitated by her struggle with cancer. So she never wrote the novel about Grace or finished "Julia," the manuscript on which she worked intermittently for some thirty years.[8] Although she contemplated writing her autobiography, the closest she came was to set down her recollections for her biographers Louise Blackwell and Frances Clay.

But if the subject of women only came to the forefront of her thinking in the early 1960s, it was not a new concern, and some idea of her view of women may be gained from looking at her writing before 1960. In the 1930s and 1940s, for example, Lillian and Paula made *South Today* different from other southern journals not only because of their treatment of the race issue, but also because they gave more space and encouragement to women writers, both white and black, and more attention to such subjects as women, the family, children, and education. The two editors presented their own view of women and feminine nature in an article entitled "Man Born of Woman," which appeared in the Winter, 1941, issue of *South Today*. In it they attributed war partly to man's displacement of his "unending secret enmity against woman" onto his fellowmen. Exhorting women to work for world peace and against war, they insisted that women were particularly fitted to extirpate men's destructive impulses because, whether as a result of biology or cultural conditioning, they were psychologically different from men. Women were not given to the kind of abstract thinking that enabled men to rationalize their destructive impulses, and they were more able than men to resist the pull of group loyalty. Moreover, because of their reproductive and nurturing function, women did not share "man's affinity for death." Among the "polarities of the universe," Lillian and Paula cited masculinity and death on one hand and femaleness and life on the other.[9]

While contending that women were specially qualified to save men from their destructive impulses, Lillian and Paula admitted to being less than confident that they would. This was because women had for centuries used their maternal role "as an excuse for [an] empty mind." They had taken pride in their "obscurantism." Despite their talent for plumbing men's hearts, they understood little of their own. Despite their ability to view the world realistically, unencumbered by man's romanticism, they did not value the knowledge gained and made no effort to acquire more.[10]

Lillian and Paula conceded that women were an oppressed group, "that man put our mind in prison," but, they added, "we have grown to love our chains." They urged women to strive to become civilized, humane, informed world citizens, disdaining their former provincialism of thought and feeling. Only then would they be able to take up the difficult task of saving civilization from destruction. Finally, in keeping with their notion of feminine uniqueness, the two editors also urged women to employ their special powers over men. They must "learn again the ancient ways of the female," the "subtle strengths" of their sex, "birthrights . . . sold for the pottage of a specious 'equality' in man's world." By substituting "for a competitor's tricks the old wisdom and versatility," they would be able "to play with brilliant virtuosity the complex, modern role of mother-companion-lover." Women who did this, Lillian and Paula seemed to be saying, would be realizing their true and complete feminity. They cautioned women against abdicating that "magnificent role" by choosing a lesser or partial one, vacillating "between the sinuous acts of Delilah and the parasitic ways of a child," or denying their own femaleness by taking on mannish characteristics, or betraying man "by bestowing the love that is rightly his upon his sons."[11]

Besides *South Today*, Lillian also expressed her view of women in her novels and nonfiction. In several works she introduced the subject of lesbianism. The novel she wrote about China, for example, contained "a good bit of homosexuality" based on the relationships she had observed between the female missionaries and students at the Virginia School in Huchow, and she thought that was the main reason the publishers rejected it. In 1934, she noted, when Henry Miller had not been able to publish in the United States, the subject of lesbianism and her candid treatment of it was "hair-raising." Although some people regarded lesbianism as a taboo subject, she saw nothing wrong with writing about it. She seems to have thought of it as one of those secrets women had refused to divulge. It was entirely different from male homosexuality, she declared in a letter to Rochelle Girson. Commenting on Dorothy Baker's *Cassandra at the Wedding*, she wrote that she was not at all surprised that the men who had reviewed it had not had "the faintest notion of what the book was about." She praised the novel as "the most candid and perceptive account ever printed of girls and women and their feelings for each other and themselves" and "an astute revelation of female homosexuality."[12]

Lillian treated the subject of lesbianism in both of her published novels, focusing not on the relationship itself (as she apparently had in "Walls") but on the effect of society's labeling or tabooing it. Thus in *Strange Fruit*, Alma Deen worries about her daughter Laura's attachment to Jane Hardy, an older woman who teaches school in Maxwell and who has encouraged Laura's artistic ambitions. Why does Laura prefer her to her other friends, Alma asks. What do they talk about? Having found a clay figure Laura had made—a female torso for which Jane had posed—Alma insinuates that there is something wrong with Jane and her friendship with Laura. "There're—women, Laura, who aren't safe for young girls to be with," she warns. "There're women who are—unnatural. . . . I don't believe a woman is the right kind of woman who talks about the naked body as Jane does." Laura reacts to her mother's questions by thinking, "you knew you could talk to Jane, you could tell her about your sculpture and your verses, about your fears and your feelings. . . . And you loved her. Yes, you loved her and wanted to be with her. And now Mother was labeling it with those names that the dean of women at college had warned you about. . . . if Mother made an issue, if she labeled this feeling for Jane with those names, there'd be no more feeling. . . . You wouldn't want it. You wouldn't want your relationship with Jane when Mother finished with it. You wouldn't want—anything."[13]

The story of Alma and Laura Deen and Jane Hardy is best understood in terms of Lillian's broad definition of segregation. In the context of *Strange Fruit,* Alma's insinuation about Jane and Laura's friendship with her is a kind of segregation in that it involves setting up walls (in the form of a sexual taboo) that prevent or destroy human relationships. The novel suggests that sexual taboos have as crippling an effect on the people of Maxwell as the racial taboos separating blacks and whites.

Lillian treated lesbianism more explicitly in *One Hour* than in *Strange Fruit,* including in an early draft of the novel a segment in which Grace Channing describes her seduction at age fifteen at summer camp by a counselor she refers to as "the Woman," a "fabulous creature" who awakened her intellectually and aesthetically as well as sexually. Lillian omitted the segment from the final draft. "Not because the publishers wanted me to," she explained, "but because I myself felt it swept the book beyond the book's place." Consequently, the focus in *One Hour* is similar to that of *Strange Fruit*—not on the relationship between Grace and the Woman, but on the torment Grace suffers when she learns from a doctor's lecture at school that her experience was abnormal and immoral. "She learned during that lecture on 'normal love' that this amazing creature who had seemed to her to have come out of a myth, who did not quite belong in the ordinary world, was nothing but a homosexual." Grace tells Dave, "I struggled to hold on to my image of her, to cling to the validity of what I had experienced, but I couldn't. I fought that word the doctor had used, but it whipped me after two or three weeks, lying awake at night looking, listening to Her, then remembering what the doctor had said." Grace's experience reminds us not only of Laura Deen and the anxiety her mother's questions produced, but of Tracy Deen and his relationship with Nonnie. Just as words or thoughts like "colored girl" and "Negro" jolt him out of thinking that his love for Nonnie is right and good, so Grace tells Dave how she would keep "thinking of Her . . . and all she had told me and it seemed good and true and wonderful, then in a split second, it seemed ugly and dirty and horrible. It would zigzag like that, day and night, day and night." And just as Tracy ultimately allows white society's definition of his and Nonnie's relationship to destroy it, so Grace finds that her feeling for the Woman has been destroyed. "The shell lay there in my mind," she says, "but the living part of it was gone. The pain had left, and the wonder of it; the mystery, the ecstasy were gone and the love I had felt. The new way of looking at Indian pipes and caves and thunderheads and rocks and poetry stayed, but I forgot who had opened my eyes so I could see. I existed, she existed, but the relationship did not exist."[14]

As Grace recounts her experience, she remembers that only after talking about it some years later with Jane Houghton was she able to see it in proper perspective. Jane told her, "It is the quality of a relationship that counts; easy to paste a good label on something spurious and cheap, easy to paste a bad one on something fine and delicate. . . . Not one incident, not one point in your life but the whole structure is what counts: what you are moving toward and away from—what you are forming altogether; not this mistake or that sin or virtue, but your whole way of looking, the depth of your longing, the vision you hold to." Lillian presents Jane's view as a sharp contrast to that of the doctor at Grace's school (and, thinking back to *Strange Fruit*, of Alma Deen). Because Jane is clearly autobiographical (she lives on a mountain where she directs a camp for girls and is an avid reader of Karl Kraus, Lao-Tse, and Kierkegaard), we may assume that she voices Lillian's opinion of lesbianism and the taboos against it.[15]

Lillian's treatment of lesbianism in her novels was part of a more comprehensive challenge she directed against sexual convention. As Morton Sosna has observed, her view of sexuality in the 1930s and 1940s was almost as unorthodox as her view of the race question. In *South Today*, for example, she criticized the sexual stereotyping of young children. Citing a neighbor who called his four-year-old son a sissy for playing with dolls, she noted that in American culture, little boys "are taught in a thousand ways that all that concerns babies, all that has to do with early growth and habits, with tenderness, is 'sissy business'. If they do secretly develop a protective interest in babies, if they furtively learn even such basic skills as cooking and health care (which every man and woman should know), they tend to feel a profound shame for their 'abnormal sex deviations' which only a strong ego can come to terms with." She commented on the difficulty some young men encountered in living up to "the American notion of the male as a kind of half-back-gentleman-cowboy-quick-on-the-draw." The writer Lafcadio Hearn, she noted approvingly, "gave up the miserable business and fled to Japan where small stature, interest in books, flowers and painting, did not prohibit him from finding a woman who could deeply love him without feeling shame in her choice and where he could live with prestige the way of life that he believed in."[16]

Lillian also challenged sexual convention at Laurel Falls Camp, offering a kind of informal sex education as part of the campers' program of intellectual, emotional, and physical development. She and the counselors apparently made a conscious effort to help the young girls overcome fears and guilt regarding sex or the body. Similarly, in *Strange Fruit, Killers of the Dream,* and *The Journey,* she decried various types of sexual repression, especially taboos against talking about, touching, and looking at certain parts of the body. In her view, the notion that parts of the body were "segregated areas" derived from the same mode of thinking that produced racial separation and was just as harmful to human growth.[17]

Besides criticizing sexual conventions, Lillian also challenged traditional notions of women. In *Killers of the Dream* she described various types of southern womanhood. One represented a small minority of white southern women, those who rejected "their womanly qualities," envied and yet hated men, and often filled the ranks of feminists in the cities who championed women's equality. Another type represented the majority of white women in the South, what might be called the hollow women. They accepted the image of sacred womanhood prescribed by their menfolk. "They listened to the round words of men's tribute to Sacred Womanhood and believed, thinking no doubt that if they were not sacred then what under God's heaven *was* the matter with them!

Once hoisted up by the old colonels' oratory, they stayed on lonely pedestals and rigidly played 'statue' while their men went about more important affairs elsewhere." They lived in a fantasy world of flower gardens and gracious homes and shut their minds and hearts against anything ugly, unpleasant, or evil, such as sex, segregation, and poverty. They "convinced themselves that God had ordained that they be deprived of pleasure, and meekly stuffed their hollowness with piety, trying to believe the tightness they felt was hunger satisfied." The one thing they could not ignore was the "secret wound" festering in their hearts—the humiliation of having to give up their children and menfolk to the black women whose nurturing and sensual qualities they lacked.[18]

The castraters represented a third type of white southern womanhood. Psychically and sexually crippled like the hollow women, they became hateful and destructive. "Their own dreams destroyed, they destroyed in cruelty their children's dreams and their men's aspirations." In the name of "what is right," they set up a kind of police state in the home, enforcing rigid obedience to all sorts of racial, religious, and sexual taboos. "Many a man went into politics, or joined the KKK, had a nervous breakdown or forged checks, got drunk or built up a great industry, because he could no longer bear the police-state set up in his own house. But this would have been a hard thing for these good mothers and wives to believe, and for the men also." The effect on the children was equally deleterious.

> [The castrating women] did a thorough job of closing the path to mature genitality for many of their sons and daughters, and an equally good job of leaving little cleared detours that led downhill to homosexual and infantile green pastures, and on to alcoholism, neuroses, divorce, to race-hate and brutality, and to a tight inflexible mind that could not question itself.
>
> They did a thorough job of dishonoring curiosity, of making honesty seem a treasonable thing, of leaving in their children an unquenchable need to feel superior to others, to bow easily to authority, and to value power and money more dearly than human relations and love.
>
> They did a thorough job of splitting the soul in two. They separated ideals from acts, beliefs from knowledge, and turned their children sometimes into exploiters but more often into moral weaklings who

daydream about democracy and human dignity and freedom and integrity, yet cannot find the real desire to bring these dreams into reality; always they keep dreaming and hoping, and fearing, that the next generation will do it.[19]

Yet another type of white southern womanhood was the reformers, who refused meekly to accept the place defined for them by men and southern tradition. They felt compelled to question, and "their questions and answers told them that all a woman can expect from lingering on exalted heights is a hard chill afterward; that indeed, white women had not profited in the least from the psychosexual profit system which segregation in the South supported so lavishly; and that furthermore, no bargain had been made with them in any of these transactions." So they climbed down from the pedestal and went forth to commit treason against southern tradition. At first they worked stealthily, and always decorously. Then the "lady insurrectionists" gathered in one of the southern cities in 1930 to form the Association of Southern Women for the Prevention of Lynching. "They primly called themselves church women but churches were forgotten by everybody when they spoke their revolutionary words. They said calmly that they were not afraid of being raped; as for their sacredness, they could take care of it themselves; they did not need the chivalry of lynching to protect them and did not want it. Not only that, they continued, but they would personally do everything in their power to keep any Negro from being lynched and furthermore, they squeaked bravely, they had plenty of power." Once they had accomplished their revolt against "the sleazy thing called 'chivalry,'" they set to cleaning up other dirty spots on the fabric of southern culture, always "prim and neat and sweet and ladylike and churchly," sometimes using those "ancient ways of the female" and "subtle strengths" Lillian and Paula had urged women to use against war.[20]

The last type of southern womanhood Lillian described in *Killers of the Dream* was the Negro women who mothered the children of the South, white as well as black. They were the nurturers; and in their warmth, serenity, and sensuality, they were the opposite of most white women in the South. While not minimizing the effect of segregation on

them, Lillian argued that they did a better job of child rearing than the
white women.

> Unconfused by a church's rigid system of splitting spirit from body and
> injecting sin into bodily needs, unconfused by a patriarchal-puritanic
> system which psychically castrated its women, who in turn psychically
> castrated their children, male and female, by the burden of anxiety they
> laid on their minds—these women knew intuitively, or from old lore,
> the psychosomatic truths that we whites are groping awkwardly toward
> today. The results in their children were a stability, a health, a capacity
> for accepting strain, an exuberance, and a lack of sadism and guilt that
> no Anglo-Saxon group, to my knowledge, has ever shown.[21]

In *Killers of the Dream* Lillian exploded the myth of southern womanhood, replacing the idealized Southern Lady with four types of
white women—feminists, hollow women, castraters, and reformers.
But while she broke down one stereotype, she helped to reinforce another—the black mammy. Richard King has suggested that her image
of the black mother "edged toward a sort of inverted sentimentality."[22]
Certainly her description of southern Negro women in *Killers of the
Dream* failed to do justice to the range of types they actually represented. However, the black female characters in *Strange Fruit* are more
varied and complex than the black mothers in *Killers of the Dream*.

Most of the types of southern womanhood described in *Killers* appear in Lillian's two novels, *Strange Fruit* and *One Hour*. Significantly,
the fictional counterparts are not specific to one race or the other as
they are in *Killers of the Dream*. In that book Lillian was describing
types of white and black womanhood, whereas in her novels she created characters who epitomized general types of womanhood and
merely happened to be southern or black or white. The women in the
novels also exhibit more complexity than the types described in *Killers*, partly because Lillian often combined the traits of two or more
types in a single character. To be sure, in *Strange Fruit* there is a character who perfectly embodies the black mother described in *Killers of
the Dream*. Sam, the black doctor, remembers Mrs. Anderson, Nonnie's
mother, "reaching out and pulling everybody, everything, the whole
world, to her, and sort of nursing it in her big lap—all of it, good
and mean, its nastiness and its brightness, drawing it in against her

breast."[23] However, Nonnie, the main black character, is much less stereotyped, much more complex than her mother. She combines the warmth and sensuality, the nurturing capacity Lillian attributed to black women in *Killers*, with the willful blindness to reality seen in the hollow women. Bess Anderson, Nonnie's sister, has warmth and sensuality, but she is much more realistic than Nonnie. Her anger at the Jim Crow system makes her a black counterpart, at least potentially, of the white women reformers described in *Killers*. They worked with the Association of Southern Women for the Prevention of Lynching; Bess seems a likely candidate for CORE or the NAACP.

Alma Deen in *Strange Fruit* challenges the stereotype of the Southern Lady. Lillian described her as "the other side of the coin of 'sacred womanhood.'" Every member of her family—her husband, her daughter Laura, and especially her son Tracy—has been scarred by her manipulation and destructive cruelty. Renie Newell and Miss Hortense in *One Hour* illustrate the same type, the frustrated, castrating woman. Like Alma they represent what Lillian called "the poison in the juices of the flower of Southern Tradition."[24]

A character who exemplifies Lillian's positive view of womanhood is Grace Channing in *One Hour*. She is certainly not sacred womanhood or the Southern Lady. Rather, she is the "mother-companion-lover" Lillian and Paula described in "Man Born of Woman"—intelligent, mature, with a strong sense of identity and open to a variety of human relationships. She is the only one of Lillian's white female characters who exhibits the sensual and nurturing qualities associated with black mothers in *Killers of the Dream*.

Although Lillian challenged conventional notions of sexuality, women, and womanhood, she did not think of herself as a feminist, and rightly so. As a young woman around the time of World War I she was embarrassed by the strident zeal of the women's rights advocates and took for granted the gains they made in the 1920s. Although the doctrine of feminine uniqueness she and Paula enunciated in *South Today* was a stock item of early twentieth-century feminist ideology, they probably got it from reading Freudian psychology rather than feminist literature. Even in the late 1940s, describing various types of white southern womanhood in *Killers of the Dream*, Lillian painted an unflattering picture of the woman's movement, referring to the feminists as "a grim little number" who rejected their "womanly qualities" and adopted a mannish appearance. "Not daring in the secret places of their minds to confess what they really wanted, they demanded to be treated 'exactly like men,'" she wrote. "They were . . . a part of the psychosexual, economic, political protest of women arising throughout Western culture, a kind of fibroid growth of sick cells multiplying aggressiveness in an attempt at cure."[25]

Rejecting public, organized feminism, Lillian adhered to a kind of private feminism, seeking personal autonomy and self-fulfillment. Her mother had raised her to be a southern lady, but Lillian refused to play the role, even though she retained some of its attributes. While she did not preach feminism at Laurel Falls Camp, the programs promoting emotional and intellectual growth were aimed at liberating the campers from the constraints of the southern lady. "So much of our effort here is spent in trying to wake up these little sleeping beauties that our Anglo-American culture has anesthetized, or rather put in a deep freeze," she wrote to the parents of one of the campers. Lillian also prosecuted her private war against what she liked to call sacred womanhood in the columns of *South Today*. Eschewing the sentimental fiction and poetry associated with most southern women writers, she specialized in reportage and editorial comment. When she took up fiction, she refused to be typed as a typical lady novelist, focusing on social problems and ideas instead of the usual interpersonal relationships.[26] However, she was clearly not a feminist writer, for lesbianism was only a minor theme in her novels and none of her works was written to promote women's rights or liberation.

Although defying sacred womanhood was not her main purpose, Lillian inevitably threatened two of its major supports by challenging white supremacy and racial segregation. Indeed, she was one of the first to note the connection between the protest against segregation and the challenge to sacred womanhood. According to Lillian, southern white women fought against Jim Crow—in many cases before or in a more open manner than white men—because unlike white men, they felt personally injured by the system of white supremacy. It meant supremacy of the white male, not the white female, and women had known this in their hearts long before they uttered it in words, she contended. That knowledge, once kept secret, was now "bursting open like an old boil." As they protested segregation, southern white women were stepping down from the pedestal and refusing to "play statue." The result, she observed, was a cultural revolution in the mid-twentieth-century South that was transforming not only race relations but relations between the sexes.[27]

Lillian believed the condition of southern women mirrored that of American women as a whole and that all women were victims of the kind of dehumanization that crippled blacks and whites living under the Jim Crow system. "It is a curious fact about the human being," she wrote; "you cannot wisely segregate him from society nor can you segregate parts of his organism from other parts. A man is whole or he is a poor thing; and what goes for men goes for women, too." Until women were free to realize all their capacities—emotional, sexual, intellectual—they could not become whole; they could not become fully human. The first step was for women to recognize their own responsibility for their condition. "It is our fault—nobody else's," she declared in one of her university speeches. "We gave up; we took the rights we had gained for granted; we fell for the feminine mystique." She urged women to rebel against the crippling restrictions of the feminine mystique and seek their full humanity.[28]

When Lillian expressed such views, the women's liberation movement was just getting underway. Had she lived into the late 1960s and early 1970s, she might have become deeply involved in it. Indeed, she once remarked to Rochelle Girson that the racial situation in the United States paled in comparison with the woman situation.[29] However, in the early 1960s she continued to devote the larger share of her attention to the cause of black civil rights, as she had in earlier decades.

# X Relationships

I am intense and have lived intensely with relationships to both men and women, children and grown-ups; all kinds of relationships. So in a sense I know people very well from having suffered with them, from them, having inflicted pain, and having enjoyed delicious and delicate pleasures.

In characterizing women as secretive, Lillian was surely thinking of herself as well as other women. For while she believed herself capable of divulging the secrets of women and devoted a share of her writing to that endeavor, she was quite reticent about her own personal life. In *One Hour* Dave thinks about Jane Houghton. "Tell me about you, Jane: what men, what women have you loved? how many have you hurt? and what has hurt you so much that you are compelled to find a place to abide where you cannot be hurt again? are you sure you are safe there? She knew so much . . . but would it ever be told? Do women ever tell? They were bred to secrecy for ten thousand years—will they ever tell? They know so much—but will they tell?" Like Jane Houghton, Lillian chose to present only one layer of herself to the world and seemed rather proud of her inscrutability. In a letter to George Brockway of W. W. Norton in which she observed that her life had "been kept so secretive," she quoted the minister of All Souls Unitarian Church in Washington, D.C., as saying in a sermon, "I have talked with her several times for an hour or two, had dinner with her once, read her books; but I have the strange feeling I know absolutely nothing about the personal, the 'real' LS." She added, "He sent me a reprint of that sermon but I still didn't tell him anything about the 'real' LS."[1]

193

When she first began writing, Lillian was not especially reluctant to reveal aspects of her personal and family life. The two novels and three novellas she wrote in the 1930s were all firmly grounded in personal experience. However, after two publishers rejected the China novel because of its discussion of homosexuality, and when she realized that it would be easy to recognize the real-life counterparts of many of its characters, she decided not to try to publish it. Similarly, since the novellas were based on her family life and were "obviously autobiographical," she decided that although she would not be hurt if they were published, some members of her family would be; so she put the manuscripts away and did not submit them for publication. Her decision not to write about her personal and family life seems to have stemmed from a concern for the privacy and feelings of others who might be hurt by her disclosures.[2]

The storm of controversy raised by the publication of *Strange Fruit* reinforced Lillian's reluctance to subject her personal life to public scrutiny. She discovered that whether people praised or damned her, they failed to see her, or did not really want to see her, as a person. So she decided to give out as little information about herself as possible and to withhold any that might be distorted. In adopting this policy in the late 1940s, she sought to protect not only her sense of identity but the cause to which she was linked. Even before *Strange Fruit*, she had anticipated that people opposed to her antisegregation stand in *South Today* might try to tarnish her reputation or suggest impropriety, and she had determined to outwit them by being "cagey and shrewd." After *Strange Fruit*, when her enemies charged her with obscenity and advocating miscegenation, she decided she must be even more cautious and discreet. Perhaps that is why she avoided calling attention to the biracial gatherings on Old Screamer. They were, after all, as much a part of her crusade against segregation as an element of her social life. She could have publicized them as the kind of individual effort against segregation she had been championing since *South Today*. But by choosing not to draw attention to them, she deprived her enemies of incidents they might have used and perhaps even distorted to damage her cause. Interestingly, Lillian also cautioned members of her family to be discreet about her, the camp, the magazine, and *Strange Fruit*. In August, 1944, she wrote them, pointing out that her public support of the reelection of President Roosevelt, in combination with *Strange Fruit*, had made her especially controversial—and vulnerable. Warning them against speaking to unprincipled or malicious reporters, she suggested they reply to questions about her by saying, "I am sorry I have nothing to say about this matter—my sister speaks for herself." If they wished to say that they were proud of her and the novel that would be fine. On the other hand, she observed, it would be "a bit indiscreet" for any of the family to admit not having read the book, for the press would surely play that to the limit.[3]

Besides hoping to protect her cause, Lillian had another reason for avoiding unfavorable publicity. She wished to remain in the South and continue to operate Laurel Falls Camp, which she regarded as her livelihood. She did so until 1949 when she published *Killers of the Dream. Strange Fruit* had not harmed the camp, but Lillian believed the reaction to *Killers* would. "I knew even my most loyal parents would simply find it too hard to fight their neighbors' opinions of me and them," she explained. Reasons of health also persuaded her to close the camp, but they were probably secondary. She would not abandon her policy of discretion, but she thought that discretion would not be enough to counter the reaction she anticipated against *Killers of the Dream* and to save the camp from ruin.[4]

Just as Lillian was secretive about her personal life, she was selective in revealing information about her family life. In *Killers of the Dream, The Journey*, and *Memory of a Large Christmas*, she wrote about her mother and father (not always favorably) as well as Little Grandma and other members of the Smith family. But when it came to family members still living and her relations with them during adulthood, she was reticent. Her correspondence and the autobiographical reminiscences she prepared for Blackwell and Clay contain only fragmentary comments on that subject. She seems to have been closest to her sister Esther. Although as a child Lillian may have envied, even resented her, the two girls developed a strong bond of affection after the family moved to Clayton. It became even stronger when Esther took a year's leave of absence from Western Maryland College, where she taught drama, to collaborate with Lillian on the play *Strange Fruit*. While working together in New York City they shared an apartment. Lillian found Esther easy to get along with because "Es" did not invade her "psychic privacy." She also valued Esther's dramatic expertise and no doubt looked to her for emotional support in those dreary weeks when it became clear the play was a failure. Next to Esther, Lillian probably felt closest to Frank. She seems to have regarded him as the male head of the Smith family after her father died, and she admired the projects he instituted as Rabun County Ordinary in the 1930s and 1940s—a county library, a hot lunch program in the schools, a maternity home open to both blacks and whites—and his later work with the Georgia Mental Health Association.[5]

Lillian described the Smith family as a clan "somewhat like the Kennedy family but without the Kennedy money." She admitted the "pleasure in this clan business" of knowing intimately so many people— seven sisters and brothers (one brother, DeWitt, had died in college) and fourteen nieces and nephews—all of whom put her in touch with "a wider arc of life" than a small family might have. But a large, close-knit family imposed burdens as well. The Smiths had "the oldfashioned way of feeling responsible for each other," she observed. Lillian seems to have played the Martha role with her sisters and brothers and nieces and nephews, just as she had with her mother and father, and with the same ambivalent feelings. Although she loved her family and felt responsible to and for them, she sometimes resented the demands they placed upon her. After their mother and father died, the Smith brothers and sisters looked to the mountain as their symbolic or psychic home and sometimes they made Lillian's home theirs, without her encouragement. On one occasion after a visit from the Smith clan, Lillian confessed to Lawrence Kubie that she was "touched and pleased to be cherished by all these nephews and nieces and their children but I could wish sometimes for just a little less affection. It is so damned wearing." She adored the children, but they insisted that she tell them all the old stories about the camp and their parents and aunts and uncles, and then the elders wanted to talk about "momentous things," and she did that too, "and suddenly I want[ed] to yell out and say, Darlings, please all of you go back to Washington, and New York and Jacksonville and Memphis and leave me alone with my thoughts and my dreams and my writings." Moreover, among the Smiths, troubles were legion, she confided to another friend. Lillian remembered a few occasions when she and Frank and Esther had been burdened almost beyond their resources by other family members' financial difficulties or ill health. She thought that too often the mountain became a womb to such troubled people, and it became necessary for her to push them out when she thought they were ready to leave.[6]

Lillian's closest friends outside her family were women: Dorothy Norman, Ruth Nanda Anshen, Margaret Long, Helen Bullard, and Paula Snelling. Her friendship with Norman dated from the *South Today* period. A New York *Post* columnist in the 1940s, Norman was active in civic and cultural organizations in New York City. Lillian visited her many times in the 1950s and 1960s, once for a month at her summer home in East Hampton. They delighted in long, intimate conversations about literature, art, and ideas. Having just returned from a visit with her, Lillian wrote that she had "thought so much about all we discussed together, the ideas: the existentialism; Rilke; Paul Tillich's ideas; our musing about the Guernica; those marvelous photographs of yours of the bull, the lion, the rest of it; the Sumerian ones; something about them I liked especially; your absolutely right quotes. I still think of it all and am sure I have been deeply touched by it, pressed in here, pulled out there, shaken—and changed." At the time Lillian was working on *One Hour* ("I did a wonderful two pages which I think you, especially, will like," she wrote), and when she published it she dedicated it to Norman. Lillian and Norman also had mutual friends in Eleanor Roosevelt, Frank Taylor, Paul and Hannah Tillich, and Rollo and Florence May. Through Norman and another close mutual friend, Ruth Anshen, editor of the World Perspectives series for Harper's, Lillian was introduced to scores of literary, scientific, and academic people. On one trip to New York City in February and March, 1960, she met the brother of the poet García Lorca, Hans Kohn and his wife, Sir Hugh Taylor, Dr. Florence Powderisker, and Dr. Kurt Goldstein through the two women. Both Norman and Anshen wrote Lillian long, effusive letters expressing their love and admiration for her. Perhaps because of their familiarity with the New York publishing world and because she felt confident of a sympathetic hearing, Lillian often wrote them long letters venting her irritation at the way New York newspaper editors and book critics treated her.[7]

"Maggie" Long was a columnist for the Atlanta *Journal* and also worked for the Southern Regional Council. She admired Lillian unabashedly, both as a civil rights activist and a literary artist, which was why she could joke about Lillian as "the nice lady who has done so much for race relations" and sympathize with her when she complained about Ralph McGill. Lillian in turn praised Long's outspoken columns on segregation, civil liberties, and government corruption. She seems to have seen her as a kindred spirit. Long had authored two novels, one of which had cost her her job on the Macon *Telegraph*, and as a *Journal* columnist she came under fire from the Ku Klux Klan, the White Citizens Council, the governor, and even some of her newspaper colleagues. When Lillian nominated her for the 1961 Florina Lasker Civil Liberties Award offered by the New York Civil Liberties Union, she wrote that to appreciate Long's courage and determination as a columnist, "one has to remember that I was smothered in the South and am still smothered and Margaret Long knows this. No other writer in the South has dared to speak so plainly since I burst out twenty-five years ago; so I have a special feeling of admiration for her determination, her wit and intelligence and her plugging at it during the years."[8]

Helen Bullard, another Atlantan, Lillian described as someone "who has not only stood by me through all the southern pressures but is a friend, too." Like Margaret Long, Bullard often visited Lillian and Paula on the mountain and frequently invited them to parties at her place to meet interesting people and enjoy "much to drink and little to eat." A public relations consultant who worked for Charles Rawson and Associates and later established her own one-woman firm, Bullard was a formidable person in many ways. Although she was only five feet one inch tall, immensely fat, with a soft voice and gentle manner, she could be toughminded and shrewd, as many of her political opponents and friends were aware. For many years she was an adviser and campaign manager of Mayor William Hartsfield, and like many Atlantans, Lillian credited her with being the impetus behind his increasingly liberal stand on the race question. Lillian also applauded Bullard's political acumen in helping the even more liberal Ivan Allen win the mayoral race against Lester Maddox in 1961. Bullard in turn admired Lillian's work and was proud of their friendship. When one of her friends, unaware that she knew Lillian, expressed admiration for *Strange Fruit*, Bullard said, "Well, I'll call the author and you tell her so."[9] Like Lillian's other women friends, she seems to have recognized how much Lillian desired approval and praise.

Lillian's closest woman friend was Paula Snelling. The two met at Laurel Falls Camp in 1921, when Mr. Smith hired Paula, a Wesleyan College graduate and high school math teacher, as a tennis, swimming, and riding counselor. They did not get to know each other very well until the summer of 1925, when Lillian returned from China and began directing the camp. At the close of that season, when she fired most of the other counselors, she put Paula in charge of athletics, and three years later made her assistant director, in which post she continued until the camp closed.[10]

During the early years of managing the camp, when Lillian was fighting to save her Mary side from suffocation, Paula proved to be a godsend. Lillian discovered that she was intensely interested in books and ideas, and the two began reading and discussing literature together. Partly as a result of those discussions Lillian decided to channel her creative impulses into writing. Then during the five winters she and Paula spent in Macon in the early 1930s, Lillian wrote the novels about China and the Tom Harris family and the three novellas. Paula praised her writing and provided the encouragement and emotional support Lillian needed as she struggled to become a writer.

Lillian recognized Paula as an important source of support throughout her writing career. "She has always been the best critic I ever had," she wrote in 1965. But, she added, "she criticizes rarely and usually praises." Paula offered what Lillian wanted and needed most, unqualified approval. Lillian admitted as much. "I need the praise sometimes more than I need the criticism as I often don't get much praise," she confessed. "Paula's staunch belief in me and what I have tried to do has been a precious thing to me; I don't know that I could have stood the vicious gossip, the terrible snubbing of old friends, the nasty insinuations, and the burying process of the past twelve years (especially) had she not firmly and with intelligence and love stood by me."[11]

In the middle 1930s the two women's friendship almost foundered as a result of Lillian's driving ambition to be a writer. After they started *Pseudopodia*, Lillian was dismayed to find that readers liked Paula's articles more than hers. "It hurt like hell, hurt *me*, when the letters came in praising P.'s writing and not saying a word about mine," she remembered. "I was furious; I always am when I am deeply hurt. . . . Here I was working day and night, I muttered, not only to myself but alas to P., paying for the mag out of my camp profits which were usually less than $3000.00 (and we had to live on this, too); and here she was getting all the praise. I sort of hated her, for a few minutes, now and then; but I tried to face up to this: that she really did write non-fiction better than I did." Lillian remarked it was a wonder their relationship survived those first two or three difficult years of the magazine, and observed that Paula "was wonderful about it, of course; and we both could laugh even when tears were dribbling down my face." Ultimately she found satisfaction in thinking that she had surpassed Paula as a writer. "I finally found a certain kind of 'success,'" she remembered, whereas Paula "stayed about where she was," a fine book critic but unable to write fiction.[12]

Paula seems to have been less adventurous and imaginative than Lillian. Both she and Lillian described her mind as critical, not creative. Lillian was the more volatile and aggressive of the two, more the dreamer and plotter. She remembered that sometimes Paula had difficulty coping with her energy and aggressiveness, her constant need to be doing something. "She . . . said she often just had to go to bed because I was so strenuous and working so hard; it tired her to watch me."[13]

Although Paula and Lillian were coeditors of *South Today*, when the magazine ceased publication Paula did not pursue a literary career. In the late 1940s and 1950s, after the camp had closed, she received a small salary as Lillian's assistant, doing research for her writing projects, editing and supervising the typing of her manuscripts, and handling her income tax returns. Lillian referred to her in the 1950s as her "long-time helper and companion."[14]

What began as an intellectual and professional partnership between the two women in the middle 1920s developed into a deep emotional attachment. Paula described their friendship to Louise Blackwell and Frances Clay as "a rare spiritual and intellectual comradeship" and observed that it was "so subtle, deep and beautiful that neither of us likes to talk much about it. Nor to hear it talked about on the basis of rumor or third-hand gossip." There was gossip, a "tremendous amount" in the 1930s and 1940s according to one of Lillian's associates in the

Southern Conference for Human Welfare; and a former Laurel Falls counselor contended it was generally assumed Lillian and Paula had a lesbian relationship. It would not be surprising if Lillian's lifelong struggle to break down walls of all kinds included the conventional sexual barriers. Her writing suggests that she did not disapprove of lesbianism and accepted it as part of the whole of human sexual experience. Moreover, her antipathy toward her puritanical upbringing and her openness to experience may have encouraged her in that direction. However, other people who knew the two women did not think they had a physical relationship. Glenn Rainey, an English professor at Georgia Tech who was a contributor to *South Today* and a good friend of Lillian and Paula's, described Lillian's love for Paula as "a protective love." Initially she valued Paula as an assistant because of her outdoor, athletic orientation, Rainey thought. They saw that they "complemented each other," and from their association at the camp they "moved on into a sort of partnership which came to involve their sharing living quarters and working together on all aspects of their lives—most notably the camp and the magazines."[15]

Although the two fires on the mountain destroyed most of their correspondence before 1955, some insight into Lillian and Paula's relationship may be gleaned from the letters they wrote in the late 1950s and early 1960s. It is clear that they loved and depended on each other and were open in declaring their affection, addressing one another as "Paulie" and "Tut" (which was also Dr. Deen's nickname in *Strange Fruit*), each writing that she loved and missed the other. A few letters Lillian wrote in 1961 and 1962 are especially revealing of the nature of their relationship. At the time, Lillian was undergoing another siege of cancer and having financial difficulty as a result of high medical bills; she had had to borrow several thousand dollars. Paula had just accepted a position as a librarian at Tallulah Falls School a few miles from Clayton, and Lillian had experienced a tremendous sense of release from the tension and ill feeling that had developed in their relationship. She had apparently felt guilty that after *South Today* Paula had not pursued a literary career. She feared that it was her fault, that her career had overshadowed, even swamped Paula's. Paula protested against such thinking, and Lillian herself believed that Paula looked upon writing as a hobby rather than a vocation and did not feel driven to improve or enlarge her talent. But her guilt feelings persisted, reinforced by comments others made about her negative influence on Paula. Paula's getting a job relieved some of those guilt feelings.[16]

When Paula obtained the librarianship, Lillian also recognized and felt relieved of her resentment of Paula's psychological and financial dependence upon her. She remembered that after her riding accident, Paula had quit teaching and stayed with Lillian on the mountain, working at the camp and helping edit the magazine. "It was partly because I needed her and we enjoyed working on South Today and our other projects, but it was partly because after this accident she seemed unable to take a job; just went to pieces at the idea," Lillian explained in a letter to a friend. After the camp closed Paula continued to feel unable to work except as Lillian's assistant. "I knew P. should get out on her own—because it would be better for her and because I was not making a big income," Lillian continued. "But by that time, she couldn't get out; or felt she couldn't." By 1961 Lillian's finances were so shaky she felt she could no longer afford the small salary she was paying Paula. Then, at a dinner party, they heard of the position at Tallulah Falls School. "We stared at each other hard," Lillian remembered; "on the way home, [Paula] said quietly, 'Maybe this is it.' I breathed, 'Yes.' And she applied and got it." Nevertheless, Paula remained apprehensive, and while she was at Emory taking some courses in preparation for the job, Lillian wrote her a long letter to reassure her. "Honey—I know it is hard as hell. But any new step is," she wrote.

> You are bound to have hours and days when you . . . panic a little; or feel it isn't "worth it" or something. But in the end, I believe you will be deeply thankful that you took this step. It is a step toward saving our deep, good relationship; it is a step toward taking care of your financial future; it is also a step toward freeing your perdonality [sic] from the pressure my personality puts on you. You realize this, but you hate to acknowledge that my personality does weigh yours down. I have known it for years; and sometimes I have mnaged [sic] to deliberately lift that pressure from you; but I have had too many things to manage; I just can't work when half sick, make a living, and change my personality all at the same time. At least, I have not been able to. I know living with me has extended and expanded your life in a thousand different and fascinating and rewarding ways. I understand all this. But my "fame" and

loss of fame, my position, my special work, and my kind of personality have pushed you in the background when you should not have been pushed back. And at the same time, it has made people look down on me for putting you in such a difficult position. And this has seemed unfair to me; and I have resented it. This kind of moral-psychological-physical-spiritual-financial tangle can destroy both of us and our relationship with each other. When such a situation gets like this, there is one thing to do; change it. . . . And this is what you and I are now trying to do.

By working at the school, Paula would be able to share their financial burden. "This I shall deeply appreciate and you will feel my appreciation and this will, in turn, make you feel better," Lillian wrote. The job would also provide Paula with a livelihood in case anything should happen to Lillian. (That, Lillian confided to a friend, gave her "enormous peace of mind.") Lillian also thought Paula's job would enable her to make her own friends and decisions and to "plan things without always consulting me, etc. You do not yet realize how much you will welcome this freedom from a kind of subservience to me and my life," she continued. "You will like it fine; you will have growing pains for a while; but you will like it. For I have at times felt your resentment toward our way of life. It is one reason you have been smoking so much. You are under tension here on the mountain. This tension will disappear when you have your own work, your own money, your own liberty to do as you dam [*sic*] please."[17]

Lillian admitted the new situation would be almost as difficult for her as for Paula. "We shall miss each other dreadfully," she observed. But she insisted again that it would help their relationship. "Most of all, it is going to bring our relationship in the clear: we shall have a chance of making it the deep, rich, mutually rewarding relationship it has been. Money will get out of it; and 'working for me' and all that which in your *heart* you have never really wanted to do. But all that has been frustrating to both of us will be *cleared up completely*."[18]

The last paragraph of Lillian's letter to Paula reveals how great a strain Paula's financial dependence had placed on Lillian and how much she cared for Paula and their relationship:

I love you better than anybody in the world. I want you to know that. I respect and honor you as a person. I have realized even in my

angriest moments, my weakest times when I felt I could not work another hour or take another step, that you wanted to help me in every
way you could. During my cancer years you were a tremendous help to
me; I leaned on you heavily at that time; very heavily. I always lean on
you as to your criticism of my work: your criticism is the only one I
truly want or value. I think you leaned on me during your years after the
accident and after the hysterectomy. We have been mutually helpful to
each other and mutually understanding. My only worry has been debts.
I have felt disturbed by your not working when we so desperately
needed money to pay these debts. The debts worry me terribly as I
think you know. And when I have got mad, and blazed out, it has been
because of these debts. But I also realized that you went through a hard
time psychically when a job was an impossible word to you; this is easy
to understand; and I was grateful that I could help you at this time. I
did not always understand—only in retrospect, have I really seen the
dilemma for what it was—but I am grateful that I could help however I
did help. Now, however, the time has come for a new, mutually helpful
but largely independent life for us. We shall be far better friends because of this change; we shall both suffer in making the change; but we
shall be glad, I am sure. And I want you to know that I could not do
without you as a beloved person; nor do without your criticism of my
work and your encouragement and psychic support. I need all that desperately. And I hope to give you what you need from me in a personal
way. Everybody in my family loves you greatly, and deeply respects you;
and are grateful to you for living with me when I was sick. They appreciate all your fine qualities. But they are glad *for your sake*—and for the
unknown future—that you have a job for they know my income is
dwindling. Or seems to be. And they have worried about your future. I
love you very much and care deeply. [signed] Lil[19]

After Paula began working, their relationship did become less
strained. In the middle 1960s, in the last years of her struggle with
cancer when she became increasingly isolated on the mountain, Lillian
was especially grateful for Paula's companionship and fidelity. Her job
kept her away from Old Screamer most of the day, but, Lillian explained to a friend, "she has a little house on this ridge; we have dinner
together every night at my house; we are connected by phones and
push-buttons; and when I am very ill she comes down to see about
me."[20] Except perhaps for her sister Esther, Lillian had no more devoted and faithful friend than Paula.

Eleanor Roosevelt was another woman friend who offered Lillian

considerable approval and emotional support. Their friendship began
in the early 1940s when Lillian wrote Mrs. Roosevelt about her work
for the Rosenwald Fund and sent her some issues of *South Today*.
Lillian recognized a kindred spirit in Mrs. Roosevelt (throughout their
correspondence she used the formal salutation in addressing her), and
the president's wife seemed to have had a similar feeling for Lillian.
Mrs. Roosevelt's devotion to the Negro cause was well known. In 1938
at the Birmingham meeting of the Southern Conference for Human
Welfare, she had offered dramatic proof of her opposition to segregation. Police Commissioner Eugene Connor had ordered black and
white delegates to sit apart in the Municipal Auditorium, and the conference had acquiesced but had resolved not to hold segregated conventions in the future. Mrs. Roosevelt indicated her disagreement with
the concession by refusing to sit with the white delegates; instead she
placed her chair in the aisle separating the two races. Because of these
and other demonstrations of Mrs. Roosevelt's commitment to civil
rights, Lillian felt assured of a sympathetic hearing when she began
writing to her about race relations. Mrs. Roosevelt was among the
many people to whom Lillian sent a copy of her letter to Guy Johnson
declining to join the Southern Regional Council because it had not
taken a stand against segregation. Her trust proved well-founded when
Mrs. Roosevelt wrote a note warmly praising the letter.[21]

Like many racial liberals of the 1940s Lillian looked to Eleanor
Roosevelt as a conduit to the president and the higher levels of his administration. Mrs. Roosevelt used her good offices to help Lillian on at
least two occasions. In December, 1943, when the Clayton and Atlanta
postmasters held up the mailing of *South Today* and it appeared likely
that Lillian and Paula would be investigated by the Georgia legislature
and the Federal Bureau of Investigation, Lillian visited Mrs. Roosevelt
in Washington to discuss the problems. After Mrs. Roosevelt telephoned Attorney General Francis J. Biddle, the two editors' difficulties
quickly dissipated.[22] Lillian also benefited from Mrs. Roosevelt's influence in 1944 when she persuaded the president to get the Post Office
Department to revoke an order banning *Strange Fruit* from the mails.

Initially Lillian valued Mrs. Roosevelt's friendship because of the
support she provided in the fight for civil rights. But as Lillian enlarged her own concern to take in all human rights, she came to see

Mrs. Roosevelt as the embodiment of that larger cause. In her Chicago *Defender* column she praised Mrs. Roosevelt as "a symbol of the future" and declared that she pointed "the way to a new world in which men will live as integrated personalities, free to grow, to believe as they wish, to say aloud what they believe, free not to bow to any great power or authority whether of state or church or economic power."[23]

There were other, more personal reasons why Lillian came to admire and love Mrs. Roosevelt and to cherish her friendship. She was flattered by and grateful for Mrs. Roosevelt's genuine concern for her, especially after she began her bout with cancer. In 1954 when Mrs. Roosevelt wrote praising *The Journey* and wishing her a quick recovery from cancer surgery, Lillian replied that she was deeply touched by the letter. She wrote that she had always felt close to Mrs. Roosevelt, even though they had met and talked together only a few times. She remembered that Mrs. Roosevelt had feared for her safety after the publication of *Strange Fruit*, but, she observed, instead of violence southerners had chosen more subtle ways of hurting her—by silence and ostracism. "I have felt the loneliness down here that comes to a person who says what people are not quite ready to hear," she wrote. Mrs. Roosevelt, of course, knew well the pain of such loneliness, and in replying she agreed with Lillian about its coming to people who said things others were not ready to hear.[24]

In expressing her gratitude, admiration, and affection, Lillian came close to idealizing Eleanor Roosevelt. She seemed to embody the feminine ideal Lillian and Paula had described in the *South Today* article, "Man Born of Woman." "What a wonderful thing it is for the world that you exist," Lillian exclaimed in a Christmas card. "In a sense you have created a new kind of woman: you have shown the feminine possibilities that did not exist before—they inherently existed but had not found their way into the personality of a woman before." In her Chicago *Defender* column she described Mrs. Roosevelt as "a simple, quiet, strong, kind woman, accepting all human beings on this earth, wanting for all a good life of dignity and freedom. A woman without personal ambitions, without greed, without vanity, without hunger for power, mothering a world of hurt people." Emphasizing Mrs. Roosevelt's nurturing qualities, she declared in the last paragraph, "She is

Woman, protecting the world's children, trying to keep harm from coming to them, trying to hold a broken world together."[25]

Lillian was not alone in emphasizing Mrs. Roosevelt's nurturing qualities or viewing her as a mother figure. But her description of Eleanor Roosevelt takes on added significance in light of her uncongenial relationship with her own mother. Lillian's feeling of being rejected by her mother apparently lasted long after Mrs. Smith's death, and she seems to have looked to Mrs. Roosevelt as someone who gave her everything she had wanted from her mother, someone who not only cared about her well-being but shared her political and social views and admired her literary ability. Mrs. Roosevelt's regard for Lillian may have offset, if it did not eliminate, that feeling of rejection that had developed in the mother-daughter relationship and was reinforced by the criticism Lillian received from political opponents and literary critics.

Lillian seems to have been more trusting and open with women than with men. Sara Terrien, who had seen Lillian only twice before, remembered a long conversation they had one afternoon in March, 1960. The two women were sitting near a piano in the Terrien home and Lillian asked which of the children played it. Reminiscing about her studies at Peabody Conservatory, Lillian said she had had difficulty memorizing piano scores. Her hopes of becoming a concert pianist were dashed when, at a recital in Washington, D.C., her mind went completely blank as she sat before the keyboard. That was why she made the sudden decision to go to China to teach music, she confessed. As Lillian was telling about the incident that had occurred almost forty years earlier, Mrs. Terrien was struck by her intense feelings about it and realized "how acutely the pain of disappointment with herself was still there after all the years." Mrs. Terrien recognized, and Lillian allowed her to see, a side of her character she revealed to only a few people—her vulnerability and besetting feeling of disappointment.[26] Most people knew only Lillian's public self, the strong-willed crusader and polemicist.

People who knew Lillian generally agree that she found men attractive, enjoyed being with them, sometimes even flirted with them. A former counselor at Laurel Falls remembered that she kept a framed photograph of Frank Taylor on the bureau in her bedroom. Even after their dispute over *Now Is the Time* destroyed their friendship, Lillian could write to Dorothy Norman, "I can name every sin he has but I still miss him and I suppose I still care about him in a shamefaced way." Lillian told several people that one of the Menningers had proposed marriage to her, and she told others that she thought José Ferrer had fallen in love with her when they were working on the play *Strange Fruit.* She and Paula once had a party on Old Screamer to which they invited twenty-two men. We "forgot to ask their wives or I think we just didn't want them," she remembered. Only the wife of the director of the University of North Carolina Press attended. "Nobody seemed to mind—the men not at all, and their wives we hope took it all right," she added. They had become acquainted with the men through *South Today;* they were businessmen, politicians, professors, and writers, "men who were changing the South" and who Lillian and Paula thought should get to know each other. Describing the party, Lillian remembered that the camp had just closed for the season and about forty drums, which the girls had made to use in one of their dramatic productions, were still around. "So, Friday afternoon (or maybe Saturday afternoon, after some had been here overnight and had got the spirit of the place) we were high up on the ridge . . . beating the drums. Everybody was drumming. The men, some of them stodgy old professors at home, were sitting on the ground or kneeling drumming away with a glass of bourbon or scotch nearby. . . . It was fantastic—and fantastic fun."[27]

Lillian had a good relationship with her father and five brothers and counted a number of men as close friends.[28] However, some of her relationships with men seem to have been difficult, frequently involving some tension or animosity. Perhaps her notion of an inherent enmity between the sexes, noted in "Man Born of Woman," contributed to such situations; on the other hand it may have been the result rather than the cause.

As a young woman she had what she called her "first and most intense love affair" with a musician twice her age whom she met while working at a hotel in Daytona Beach in 1917. She became deeply involved before he told her he was married. Many years later she compared their relationship to that of Tracy and Nonnie in *Strange Fruit* in that "there were dreadful barriers between us, and I could not break them." A few years later, during the summer of 1920, she had another love affair, again with an older man, which continued for about a year and a half. Then, as she told George Brockway and Margaret Long, she "ran away to China" partly to escape that relationship.[29]

Lillian admitted that she was reluctant to commit herself to a long-term relationship—a "psychological quirk," she called it, that kept her from marrying. "I cannot bear to be tied up with anybody . . . too far into the future," she commented. "All my life, I have felt burdened by having to make promises that extend too far into the future. To be brutally frank about myself, that is why I never married. My family did not believe in divorce (of course now, nobody cares—but then they did) and I could not commit myself wholly and irrevocably."[30] Possibly Lillian's aversion to such a commitment derived from her ambivalent feelings toward her family; to enter into marriage would be to assume the sense of obligation she felt, and sometimes resented, toward her mother and father and sisters and brothers.

On another occasion she explained that she had not married because it was difficult to find a man who appreciated intelligence in a woman. Speaking at Stetson University in May, 1963, she said of herself and her generation of women:

> We wanted two things: we wanted an interesting career and we wanted an interesting man to live with. It was easier to find the interesting career than the interesting man. . . . we discovered men did not want their women to have brains; or if they had them they mustn't use them, and it hurt, it hurt like hell if I may say so, to find that the interesting men liked us in the office and laboratory and on the stage but most of them didn't want women like us in their home. So we finally had to swallow hard and admit that while we had won the battle we had lost the war.[31]

The disappointment Lillian felt may have influenced her relationships with men. She wanted them to appreciate both her womanly qualities and her intelligence, and when they ignored or belittled the latter, she felt hurt and resentful. On occasion she seemed to feel the need to prove her intelligence by deliberately challenging or arguing with men. When George Brockway came to Clayton to work with her on *Killers of the Dream*, they did not talk together about the manuscript until late in the evening of the night he was to leave. Before that he had seen her only at mealtimes. Lillian had closeted herself away, still writing and revising portions of the manuscript, and Paula brought parts of it to him and relayed his comments back to her. He remembered that when he and Lillian finally did get together to talk, "inside of an hour, we two unlikely people got into an argument about Lincoln." Lillian developed a headache, the meeting ended, and Paula drove him to the railroad station. The next day Lillian telephoned to say that he was right about Lincoln, but not Beethoven's Seventh![32]

As Lillian grew older she became increasingly sensitive to criticism and even the slightest hint of condescension. Criticism from Ralph McGill or the New York book critics infuriated her, but even when it came from a close friend whose respect and affection was not to be doubted, she found it difficult to accept. Lawrence Kubie, a New York psychoanalyst, was a long-time friend who greatly admired her writing but sometimes combined criticism with praise. Lillian admitted being especially sensitive to his reaction to her work. While writing *The Journey*, she feared he would not like parts of it, and while working on *One Hour* she confessed she was wondering, anxiously, whether he would like it. "You know how much I value your reactions," she wrote in August, 1956; "I remember telling you once that a criticism from you can dash me down hard; I don't quite know why; I mean, I am usually independent of criticism but yours I have during the years taken very seriously. So, naturally, I want you to like it; but if you don't, I want to know that too." However, when Kubie did respond, Lillian welcomed the praise but became defensive about the criticism. She apparently wanted him to be like Paula and her other women friends who usually praised but rarely found fault. Kubie had pointed out certain weaknesses in the novel, including Lillian's appeal to religious faith as a source of meaning in life. Lillian complained to Dorothy Norman that Kubie's "imagination simply cannot grapple with the word, God. . . . He wrote a very long letter trying to *convince* me that I had made some radical mistakes in the way I wrote the book. He has somehow set himself up as my mentor which I find myself resenting rather strongly at times." She went on to dismiss the validity of his criticism, declaring, "Larry seems to me to know so little about the creative process, so little about art, music, writing, dancing that I find myself feeling I am talking to a Philistine at times." She admitted he had praised her handling of character in the novel, but she gave more weight to his negative comments, even while dismissing them.[33]

Lillian's tendency to read a negative element into an otherwise friendly and caring relationship with a man is also revealed in an incident with Rollo May, the psychologist. After she sent him a copy of *One Hour*, May expressed admiration for the book and in December, 1959, wrote to ask her to read the manuscript of a novel he had been working on for some years. Lillian did so and gave it high praise, first in a telegram calling it superb and fascinating and then in a long letter in which she reiterated her admiration and suggested a few minor revisions. When she met May and his wife, Florence, at a dinner party given by Dorothy Norman in February, 1960, the three quickly became close friends and began exchanging affectionate letters in which they talked about their writing, health, and family life. Then in the fall of 1961 Lillian wrote May asking him to read the newly revised edition of *Killers of the Dream* and to write an advertising blurb for it. She also wanted him to review it for the *New York Times Book Review*. May replied that he would be happy to read the book and write a blurb and would also consider reviewing it. However, because of what he described as a falling-out with the *Times Book Review*, he doubted it would accept something from him. Perhaps he could do a review for the *Saturday Review*, he suggested. He did none of the things he had agreed to do; as he explained in a letter dated December 22 he had not gotten around to reading the book because of his involvement in the peace crusade and then, later, as a result of being hospitalized for a lung hemorrhage. Perhaps his explanation assuaged Lillian's annoyance at his inaction. Before that, not hearing from him, she had interpreted it as a kind of betrayal, part of the general effort of critics to smother her or ignore her literary achievement. In a letter to Harry Firestone early in December she had recounted the incident as follows.

> Last year . . . a famous psychoanalyst told me in New York that Killers of the Dream was the most terrific book he had ever read about the South, and too, about the whole American scene. He was having difficulty getting a somewhat offbeat (but very good) manuscript looked at with interest. He told me of his troubles; asked me if I would read the manuscript. I said yes. I read it; wired him that it was top stuff, that I

was very enthusiastic. Then I sat down and wrote three publishers who are my friends and asked them to look at that ms seriously. They did, and one took it. Next time, he saw me he said it was the "most generous thing" that he was deeply touched, that my telegram pulled him out of a deep depression, etc. etc. etc. Yet, this fall, when I asked him to help blurb *Killers of the Dream,* and asked him as a big favor if he would ask to review it (he stands well enough to do this) he edged out. I suppose because his book will soon be out and he did not want to be caught on a limb praising the controversial L. S.[34]

One can understand Lillian's irritation with May for not doing what he had promised to do, especially considering his and Florence's effusive protestations of affection. What is puzzling and revealing is that Lillian could have attributed his inaction to mere forgetfulness or distraction, even without knowing the exact reasons, but instead chose to view it as a personal affront, the result of May's not wanting to be publicly associated with her because she was controversial. She seemed to expect ill treatment from people, especially men, and purposely looked for indications of it to confirm her suspicions. At least some of the frustration and disappointment marking her life and career was of her own making and the result of an inability to take satisfaction in anything less than unconditional praise or loyalty.

# XI A Strange Kind of Love

The South is full of excitement. These Negro students are forcing the South to turn a corner. It is an irreversible journey and things are going to be different. The question is: are we going to turn blind and stubborn as has South Africa or are we going to see that this ordeal must be met creatively, with the doors wide open to the future.

The student sit-ins that began in February, 1960, at a Woolworth lunch counter in Greensboro, North Carolina, were "the first movement in the South that I have ever had a sense of excitement about," Lillian wrote to Paul Tillich. In April she delivered a speech in All Souls Unitarian Church in Washington, D.C., praising the movement and urging support for it. When it spread to colleges and universities in the Atlanta area, she offered assistance and advice and hosted several groups of students on visits to the mountain. On October 16, she addressed a regional meeting of the sit-in groups called by the newly formed Student Nonviolent Coordinating Committee (SNCC) in Atlanta. Her speech, entitled "Are We Still Buying a New World With Old Confederate Bills?" was addressed to the young blacks who made up most of the gathering. "I am glad to see old friends again; and proud to speak to this group of students," she began. She said she was proud of their courage and their willingness to run risks for something important. She regretted so few southern white students had joined the movement, but predicted they would, once they realized segregation was their enemy too. Lillian made it clear that she agreed with the students' opposition to Jim Crow. At the same time she pointed out some of the dangers and temptations that were likely to confront the new

movement. She warned the students to be on guard against the desire
for individual publicity and the temptation to take money with strings
attached or "to sell out big causes for little ones." She offered the warning as a member of an older generation that seemed incapable of
making the new and better world of the future. "For the river Jordan is
a chilly place," she explained in the conclusion to the speech.

> Full of whirlpools and quicksand. Only the young and the brave can
> cross it and still have strength for their new jobs. But you must do it if
> you are to bring not only your race but all our people to the Promised
> Land, the new world the youth of the entire earth must make together.
>     We of the older generation cannot go on that great journey with
> you. . . . But there is something we can do: We can make of our lives,
> our knowledge, our experiences, our wisdom and our hopes and faith
> and insight a *bridge*, a strong sure bridge, over which you can cross into
> the new unmade world. Perhaps in this way we who are older can help
> keep you out of the quicksands and the worst whirlpools. Perhaps by
> our firm support, our unwavering belief in you we can give you that
> extra lift you are going to need. I hope so.

The students' response to her warning gratified Lillian. "I wanted
them to know I was with them; and they do know this," she wrote
Tillich; "but I wanted, also, to help them see what the temptations are
in all movements. . . . And bless them, they took it from me; and told
me afterward (and I could have wept, so touching it was) that they
didn't want power, they didn't have ambition (or if they did, they'd fight
it), that they wanted only to help all southern people, white and
colored."[1]

Three days after the sit-in groups meeting, the students staged
demonstrations against Atlanta variety and department stores, including Rich's and Davison's. Thirty-five were arrested and jailed, along
with Martin Luther King, Jr. Although Lillian had not shared in planning the demonstrations, she supported them wholeheartedly. She also
agreed with the students' (and King's) decision to refuse bail and to
continue putting pressure on the stores by picketing and sitting in.
"They are using a good technic," she reported to Marvin Rich of the
Congress of Racial Equality (CORE). "They are being arrested only

when they do not leave a store after being asked to by the top management. So today, when asked to leave, they left; then in twenty minutes a new batch was there; they left when requested to, then a new batch came. To me, this is a terrific war of nerves and might work beautifully anywhere. It can go on and on until Rich's nerves break."[2]

Lillian considered joining the demonstrators herself but decided against it. She explained why in a letter to Jane Stembridge, the young white secretary of the Atlanta office of SNCC, who apparently had expressed a desire to join the other activists in jail. "I know how you feel about going to jail," Lillian wrote; "I feel I should go, too; it is very hard for me to stay up here and write letters to important people, and phone others, and write speeches, etc. and keep in touch with news media. It would feel better to me to sit-in and go to jail." But she believed that she and Jane were doing equally important things in behalf of the movement. "One acts in the mind, in the imagination, in the heart as well as out in the world with one's body. You are making an impact with your ideas, your guidance, your suggestions, your restraints, your values," she insisted. Besides, she feared that for her or Jane to go to jail would "split the sympathies of white people." The sit-ins were "symbolic acts which white people can respond to with their hearts and minds if the young Negroes do it," she explained. "When a white woman does it, or a white girl, the symbol splits; it is still a good symbol to those who understand that segregation hurts the whites as much as the Negroes, but since most whites do not yet understand this, we confuse them in their symbol-making." If the time came when their sitting in would have symbolic significance, "then we can and must do it," she concluded, but she did not feel that that time had come.[3]

To aid the students' war of nerves against Rich's, Lillian wrote a long letter to the owner, Richard Rich. It was a model of the kind of letter she had long been urging decent, intelligent white southerners to write—polite but firm, balancing a clearly articulated threat with several pages of gentle persuasion. Unless the store stopped discriminating against Negroes, she would withdraw her account, she declared. Twenty years ago, she continued, Rich's had shown a most enlightened attitude by being the first department store in the South to give Negroes courteous treatment, and thoughtful, responsible Georgians had applauded its action. Now, when other stores in other southern cities were opening their lunch counters and restaurants to blacks and even hiring them as salespeople, Rich's policies had become archaic. What would happen if the Magnolia Room served Negroes, quietly and without publicity, she asked. "At most, you would have a few well dressed, well educated Negro women come in for lunch; there would be a few stares from white customers, but hardly more than if a Balinese in costume had walked in. Now and then, a few well dressed, well educated Negro men would come in; but only now and then. The prices are fairly high and the Negro community as a whole—90 percent of them—cannot afford to eat there." But if few Negroes would be directly affected by the change, why did they want it? "Because of its symbolic significance. It hurts to feel shunned; hurts to feel second-class; hurts to be pushed around." The Negro community "wants this *symbol of degradation* removed." She assured Rich that once segregation had been eliminated, "you will find the Negro community cooperative, sensitive, courteous, unwilling to force its members on people." Moreover, she insisted, Rich's best patrons and most responsible citizens would stand by the store.[4]

The letter to Rich was one of several Lillian wrote in late October while the student demonstrations were going on. She sent copies of it to Frank Neely, chairman of the board of Rich's, and to William Hartsfield, mayor of Atlanta. "You may or may not approve," she wrote Hartsfield; "I simply want you to see this point of view." She used the occasion to praise Hartsfield's "tremendous courage and integrity" and to tell him that she was thankful he was Atlanta's mayor, saying, "It has given all thoughtful citizens of the state a sense of security that you are in charge of things." She then went on to suggest that it was "both rather futile and dangerous to fight back at the young Negroes." They had an inalienable right to protest segregation, she declared. "What better way than by a dignified, nonviolent, cooperative attitude and method!" She urged the mayor to meet them halfway and to do so before white "toughs and roughnecks" began to make trouble.[5]

Two days after writing Rich, Neely, and Hartsfield, Lillian sent two long letters to Eugene Patterson, editor of the Atlanta *Constitution,* and Dale Clark of WAGA-TV. Like the other letters, these two were friendly, almost personal, but firm. Lillian represented herself as a southerner and as someone who was concerned about the reputation of Atlanta; she urged Patterson and Clark, as individuals who wielded "great influence over good decent people," to reconsider their editorial policy. Instead of opposing the student demonstrations, they should seek to calm people's anxieties by pointing to the peaceful desegregation of restaurants and department stores in other cities.[6]

The response of Atlanta's leaders to the student sit-ins was not encouraging. Lillian decried their lack of imagination in dealing with the demonstrators. Many of the leaders were "fine people," she told Henry Hart Crane, but their childhood training had made it impossible for them to think creatively and so they were responding "with their reflexes, as if they were well trained animals." The department store heads and city officials had reacted to the demonstrations exactly the way the "unenlightened British" had in India. They could think of nothing more creative than to jail the demonstrators for trespassing.[7]

Four days later the demonstrators were released from jail, and Mayor Hartsfield announced a cooling-off period during which the students would not picket or sit-in and there would be negotiations with the department store heads regarding the desegregation of lunch counters and restaurants. However, Martin Luther King remained in jail, having been turned over to DeKalb County authorities for violating probation for a traffic conviction handed down the previous spring. Lillian had been in the car with King when he was arrested for the traffic violation. She was in Atlanta for a check-up at the Emory Hospital; they had had a meeting and he was driving her back to the hospital. A policeman, seeing a white woman riding with a black man, stopped them and discovered that King's Alabama driver's license had expired and that he had no Georgia license. King was fined twenty-five dollars and placed on a year's probation. On October 25, 1960, Judge Oscar Mitchell found him guilty of violating probation and sentenced him to four months at hard labor. The action of "the bigoted little judge in DeKalb County" and the way King's jailers treated him, handcuffing him "as if he were a murderer," incensed Lillian. However, she was delighted when, a few days later, Senator John F. Kennedy and his brother Robert Kennedy intervened—"in a most brave way," she said—and persuaded Judge Mitchell to reverse his decision and release King on bond.[8]

When the month-long cooling-off period ended, negotiations had broken down and the situation in Atlanta had not changed at all. The students resumed their demonstrations, at which point all the downtown stores closed their restaurants and lunch counters. "And the managers, owners, etc. are being congratulated by the KKK and the GUTS (a rough, crude, sex-ridden group of men) for their brave stand against Negroes!" Lillian fumed. "Well," she wrote Tillich, giving way to an uncharacteristic expression of despair, "this is my South; the South I was born in and still love. Full of cruelty and blindness; stiff and rigid in some of its ways, so resilient and warm in others; dragging itself and the whole country toward chaos. Sometimes I am not confident that we shall make it. Sometimes, I feel that the white race has had its day; its chance; that it cannot measure up to the ordeal now confronting it." Not just the failure to desegregate the department store restaurants and lunch counters discouraged her. She also feared that it doomed the forthcoming and more important effort to desegregate the city's public schools. Eating at lunch counters and restaurants is a "sometime thing," she pointed out to Eugene Patterson.

> Going to school is *every day*. If Atlantans cannot move this one small step by opening their lunch counters and restaurants then God help them next fall. The GUTS and White Citizens Councils will have won; they will grow strong on their victory; the good decent people of Atlanta will already have lost. If we can't win this small battle, the big battle next fall will be inevitably lost to the mob. If we win on this small thing . . . then we shall be prepared morally, psychologically, strategically to carry through our hope of open schools into a reality.[9]

Shortly before the Atlanta sit-ins, Lillian had become involved in the Kennedy presidential campaign. In September she wrote to Chloe Fox Zerwick, a worker for the Kennedy Steering Committee, offering advice regarding Georgia and the South. She had been horrified to learn, upon talking with people in Atlanta, that many liberals and moderates favored Nixon because they doubted Kennedy was a true liberal. "I said I felt he was, and I knew he was an honest man while Nixon was a man still in search of his soul," she wrote. Adlai Stevenson was "the one man who could swing the decent element in Georgia over to the Democratic ticket," she declared, and advised sending him to Atlanta to speak. She was even more concerned about Kennedy's losing the black vote in the South. Many Negroes were planning to vote for Nixon, she reported, because they thought he would keep the United States out of war and that they could depend on a Republican to alleviate the racial situation. They had lost faith in the Democratic party. For that reason she thought Lyndon Johnson would not be of much help in campaigning among blacks "because no matter what he says he is a symbol to the Negroes *of what has not been done for them.*" On the other hand, if Hubert Humphrey could be persuaded to come to Atlanta and speak plainly on the subject of race and violence, that would help immensely, especially among the younger Negroes. She seemed to think that Kennedy could offset the loss of wealthy southern men (who, though they cited civil rights, opposed him mainly on economic grounds "because they secretly like the Republican idea of money, of capitalism, etc.") by gaining the votes of blacks, student activists of both races, and women in the South.[10]

Lillian did some campaigning for Kennedy on her own among the black students involved in the sit-ins. When some of them were arrested, along with Martin Luther King, she wrote Eugene Patterson that the action was bound to hurt the Democratic cause. She had been pleading with the young blacks to support Kennedy, but they could see "only Johnson, only southern demagoguery" and feared Kennedy would be dominated by the southern wing of his party. Kennedy's Warm Springs speech had helped, as had the telegram he sent to the October meeting of the sit-in groups, but still they were not completely persuaded. "I said, 'Don't you see? Kennedy is really interested in you.' Their answer was: 'Oh, we'll get a telegram from Nixon, too.' But they didn't, thank God. Nixon forgot to send it or was afraid to send it." At that point, she observed, "things were set for us to really work on them politically and get them over to the Kennedy side." Then came the arrests in response to the department store demonstrations. "What can we say to them now?" she asked Patterson.[11] But then Kennedy intervened to secure King's release from jail, which she thought was exactly the kind of symbolic action needed to win the black vote.

About six months after the sit-in movement began, Lillian decided that the time was right for *Killers of the Dream* to make a comeback, and she wrote George Brockway of W. W. Norton about reissuing it. She sensed a real awakening in the South. People of both races were asking questions about the origins of the race problem. Whites, in particular, were less defensive and trying to see the problem more constructively. They had not been especially concerned about race relations when *Killers* came out in 1949. But now they were, and the only book on the market was W. J. Cash's *Mind of the South*. While she respected Cash's book, she thought it "too distant from today's psychological problems to be of much help in giving insight." *Killers* "should be *the* book on the southern mind and soul," she told Brockway. She considered it one of her best books, a classic. "Rarely in the history of Western writing has anyone chosen to write of moral and political and social affairs in direct terms of his own personal experience of them. This book is a kind of existential confession; this is life in a segregated culture as I saw it, heard it, felt it, experienced it, and was shaped by it. Therefore it has a lasting quality, as do honest memoirs, a lastingness that no other writer from the South or about the South has been able (up to now) to give a book." All it needed was a few revisions to eliminate repetition and fuzziness and some new material on the current situation to bring it up to date.[12]

Brockway agreed to publish a revised edition, and Lillian began working on it. She wrote a new foreword in the form of "A letter to my publisher" in which she emphasized the urgency of dealing with the race problem. Americans needed to eliminate racism and segregation at home in order to win the trust of the emerging nations of Asia and Africa and prevent their turning to communism, she wrote. All the efforts of the president, the State Department, the United States Information Agency, and the Peace Corps in offering help and friendship to such countries would not change their feelings about the United States as long as Americans continued to act out the notion of white supremacy in their schools and parks and buses and restaurants. Already, ninety miles away, Cuba had established a communist government. How could it have happened? "Why are we so blind to each disaster as it begins slowly, slowly, and then rushes toward us?" Was it because of a tendency to blindness in those who overvalued their whiteness? "If we were not blocked off by our racial feelings would we not realize that segregationists, South and North, are our country's dangerous enemies, even when unwittingly so? . . . For the sake of a mythic belief in the superiority of their 'whiteness'—a strange mad obsession—they are willing to drag us to the edge of destruction." Time had run out, she declared. The United States faced "probable extinction as a free nation" if it failed to adjust. Yet so few people seemed aware of the danger. They remained silent, refusing to leave the dead world of the past to take their place in the new world of the present. "Are we—the nation that first embarked on the high adventure of making a world fit for human beings to live in—about to destroy ourselves because we have killed our dream? Can we live with a dead dream inside us? How many dead dreams will it take to destroy us all?" It was the apathy of so many Americans, more than the fanaticism of the rabid segregationists, that disturbed her. "There are so many people who are determined not to do wrong but equally determined not to do right," she wrote.[13]

The big question posed in the foreword, Lillian told Brockway, was why Americans, and especially southerners, remained apathetic about discrimination and segregation. Her answer was contained in the body of the book. All but the last two chapters were the same as those in the first edition. Lillian decided to revise the last two chapters because she had written them hastily and without the usual polishing. She thought them eloquent and moving, but also somewhat muddled and so worked to make them clearer and more cogent. In the next to last chapter she presented an impressionistic survey of changing race relations in the South, updated to include events of the 1950s and the sit-ins of early 1960. In the last chapter she speculated on the future. Therein lay the main difference between the first and revised editions of *Killers*. Whereas in the first edition she had expressed a tentative and somewhat abstract hopefulness about the future, in the revised edition her hopefulness was not only more assured but more firmly grounded, in the philosophy of Teilhard de Chardin on one hand and the emergence of the civil rights movement on the other. Lillian believed that many people throughout the world had begun to realize "that from here on out we have our destiny in our own hands," that mankind was "evolving a new being," and that compared to "this gigantic purpose," the current battles over armaments and skin color and capitalism or communism were "mere epicycles that have had their day." From the larger view she drew her optimism regarding the world situation. As for the South, she wrote, "our big hope lies in the fact that ten years ago, only a few saw things clearly; now, thousands see." They included not only lonely individuals but groups like the Southern Regional Council, the Human Relations Councils, civic clubs and the League of Women Voters, and an increasing number of newspaper reporters and editors. Perhaps the most hopeful sign was that "just plain people, men and women, rich and poor, are searching for the right questions." She also drew hope from the abrupt and dramatic change that had taken place in the Negro. "There is, today, a revolution going on in the Negro's mind," she wrote. "He is discovering his powers: moral, economic, psychological, political. . . . Realizing his strength, he has begun to resist the old segregated way of life." More than anything else, the new awareness on the part of blacks and whites seemed to assure the eventual triumph of the dream of freedom and human dignity over those who sought to kill it.[14]

Lillian's experience in the civil rights movement during the early 1960s generally confirmed the optimism she had expressed in the last chapter of *Killers*. She continued to work with students, securing contributions for the Student Nonviolent Coordinating Committee and inviting groups of young people to visit her on Old Screamer. "We walk around, listen to music, they browse around in my library; I give them a good dinner; then we talk about everything—not just sit-ins," she wrote of a visit in May, 1961. She also spoke on a number of college campuses and before several adult groups: in Jacksonville, Florida, to a meeting of about five hundred blacks and whites; at the Central United Presbyterian Church in Chicago; and to the Coordinating Council on Human Relations and members of the Central Methodist Church in Detroit.[15]

Lillian continued to work with the Congress of Racial Equality, having been a member since the late 1940s. The older civil rights organization had pioneered the strategy of nonviolent direct action. In the early sixties when it devoted much of its effort in the South to training students in nonviolence and organizing the Freedom Rides, she aided it in a number of ways. Perhaps the most important of these was securing money for the organization. The proceeds from her All Souls Unitarian Church speech and part of a collection taken at the Central United Presbyterian Church were donated to CORE; so was a portion of her profit and all of the publisher's from *Our Faces, Our Words,* published in 1964. Lillian also channeled several thousand dollars to CORE and other civil rights organizations from two elderly Chicago ladies, Anna Grace Sawyer and Edna Dunlap, for whom she served as a consultant.[16]

The nonviolent demonstrations of the early sixties gave Lillian new hope that segregation might soon be abolished. She had become a strong advocate of the nonviolent strategy—even stronger than at the time of the Montgomery bus boycott—partly because she believed Negroes were becoming increasingly resentful and impatient, though they were still showing immense self-control. "We are indeed lucky to have Dr. Martin Luther King, jr., leading this movement instead of a southern Adam Clayton Powell," she wrote Eugene Patterson. Instead of hatred and violence, the nonviolent movement emphasized the power of "love and compassion, of forgiveness, of redemption of others by their own suffering," she noted. She also favored the nonviolent protests as being more expeditious than the wearying and costly legal battles waged by the NAACP.[17]

One reason Lillian was so hopeful in the early sixties was that the sit-ins renewed her faith in young people. Unlike the fifties generation of students, the young activists of the sixties did not seem to be obsessed with security or apathetic about important issues. In her All Souls Unitarian Church speech, she asserted that the very suddenness of the student movement, along with its unpretentiousness, insured that it would fire the imagination and stir the good feelings of the southern people. The older generation had hesitated and wavered so long that it was incapable of handling the ordeal of desegregation. If white students would join the blacks, together they might be able to forge a new leadership for the South that would be able to master the ordeal.[18]

In some respects Lillian's enthusiasm for the sit-in movement recalls her initial response to the Southern Conference for Human Welfare. By

1960, however, because of her recognition of what she called in *One Hour* "the unconquerable evil in man," she balanced her optimism with a concern for potential dangers. Thus in her October speech to the sit-in groups she warned of temptations to greed, hatred, and ambition, and the lust for power. In November, in a letter to Jane Stembridge, she broached another more concrete concern, SNCC's association with leftist groups and individuals. She specifically named James Dombrowski of the Southern Conference Educational Fund and may also have had in mind others in that organization, as well as the Highlander Folk School. She said such people disturbed her, "not because they may (or may not) have been Communists or fellow-travelers," but because "I have found their way of working dangerously unreliable, at times . . . unwise, and strategically dangerous to what we are trying to do." She insisted that if any of them were in trouble, she would risk her own "good name" to defend them in court. However, she said she feared working with them as a group because "they don't let you know where they stand; they say one thing and often mean another; they are devious and tortuous and this I do not like in anyone, Methodist, Baptist, Catholic, Communist." Lillian apologized for writing at length on the subject, but defended herself as "an old veteran in these matters" who feared the students would jeopardize their cause by associating with Communists. They would inevitably be accused of being Communists themselves and then, she warned, would have to expend time and energy fighting the red-baiters instead of the larger and more important evil of segregation.[19]

While she thought the leadership of the civil rights movement was passing into the hands of the younger generation, Lillian believed its success still depended on the support of intelligent, decent, responsible white southerners—the same people she had been urging for many years to speak and act against segregation. As in the past, she insisted that they were much more numerous than the demagogues, hoodlums, and crackpots who supported Jim Crow, outnumbering them twenty to one. They had only to speak out against segregation to take the initiative away from the "haters and hoodlums and moral riffraff" whom the demagogues were inciting to violence. Once they broke their silence, change would come quickly in the South, she thought, because so many people were ready for it—including hundreds of ministers who had begun to preach against segregation, women who were willing to give up segregation in all public places including the schools, young men who had become accustomed to integration in the armed forces.[20]

Events of the early 1960s severely tested Lillian's notions regarding the role of intelligent white southerners in eliminating segregation. In January, 1961, she visited New Orleans to do interviews for an article for *Redbook* on the desegregation crisis. It was almost two months after four black children had desegregated two of the city's public schools. Lillian was pleasantly surprised at the warm reception she received from almost everyone she interviewed. Apparently she did not talk with any of the women who had made up the screaming mob that daily taunted the black children on their way to the formerly all-white schools. She said later that she decided that their story was "only head-line stuff and not of real importance." Those "benighted women" be-longed to the past, whereas she wanted to catch "a glimpse of the fu-ture." So the focus of her story was "the women behind the mob"; they were "the intelligent, warmhearted, sensitive women" who were meet-ing the ordeal of change creatively. Lillian was profoundly moved by their candor and lack of defensiveness. She reported that for those women the sight of the screaming mob had been devastating, opening their minds to new questions and shattering old attitudes and beliefs. The women "had been trained since babyhood to believe that segrega-tion is right: trained by family, playmates, school, church, newspapers and the color signs overhead." Yet they were now willing to question segregation; they were now "thinking and feeling deeply and hon-estly—for the first time, some of them—about human relations." Al-though few in number, the women provided a ray of hope in an other-wise depressing situation. Most people in the city had been "too lethargic or afraid" to protest the White Citizens Council or arch-segregationists like Leander Perez, Lillian wrote. The few whites who had spoken out admitted they had acted too late to do any good. Lillian conceded that the new awareness and courage of the women she inter-viewed was not enough to offset the powerful racists who continued to resist desegregation. But she regarded it as a step in the right direc-tion, and thought if others would only follow, possibly "the inevitable change" would come about in a constructive rather than a destructive way.[21]

Atlanta seemed to have learned a lesson from New Orleans. In August, 1961, the city desegregated four public high schools without violence. Lillian gave much of the credit to two organizations formed to mobilize support for desegregation. The Organization Assisting Schools in September (OASIS) included some fifty civic and religious organizations such as the junior and senior chambers of commerce, Civitan, Rotary, and the parent-teacher association. Help Our Public Education (HOPE) was composed mainly of women, many with school-age children, who insisted that the schools should not be closed, even if it meant the end of segregation. Both organizations were made up of the kind of people Lillian thought of as decent, intelligent, and responsible. She thought the work of the two predominantly white organizations especially important because, as she told Edna Dunlap in June, "it is basically the white Atlantan's job to educate, persuade all white Atlanta to do the right thing when September comes." After desegregation, however, Lillian became somewhat skeptical of what groups like OASIS and HOPE had accomplished. She was still proud of what the city had done, she wrote Frank McCallister in late October, "but I have to laugh, too, for it is the old complacent city it always was; everybody's moved over to open schools and no riots but their hearts have not really changed very much."[22] An institutional change, and a token one at that, unaccompanied by a psychological change represented only a partial victory over segregation as far as she was concerned.

Although disturbed by Atlanta's complacency, Lillian was heartened by the change in the political climate of the city. School desegregation had proceeded smoothly at least partly because of the leadership of Mayor Hartsfield, who had not only championed open schools but had urged the state legislature not to interfere with the city's compliance with court-ordered desegregation. Lillian praised him as a man not without racial prejudices in his earlier days who had grown as the world around him changed "to become a bulwark of sanity and honor when racial matters came up." The election of Ivan Allen, Jr., as mayor in the fall of 1961 portended even greater progress in race relations. The former chamber of commerce president had defeated archsegregationist Lester Maddox. Perhaps remembering Ellis Arnall in the 1940s, Lillian observed that "so often winning in the South is done at the expense of real liberalism, and at the expense of the Negro group. Not so, this time. Right up to the end Ivan Allen grew stronger and stronger and stronger in his position on integration."[23]

As Atlanta's ordeal abated, Albany's intensified. Lillian knew Albany well. She had visited there many times and knew several families who had sent their children to her camp. She had long considered it a progressive city. In the fall of 1961, SNCC launched what became known as the Albany Movement, an effort to desegregate public facilities in the city using nonviolent direct action techniques. By December hundreds of Negroes were in jail. The Southern Christian Leadership Conference (SCLC) joined the movement and in July, 1962, following the "jail-no-bail" strategy of the other demonstrators, Martin Luther King chose forty-five days in prison over a $178 fine. Lillian wrote to one of her former campers, whom she described as "a prominent young social leader whose husband is a leading young businessman," and pleaded with her to try to secure King's release.

> Mimi dear—what I am concerned about now is Dr. Martin Luther King's being put in jail in Albany. . . . he is one of my friends and a most wonderful guy; if you only knew him you'd be sure the man is good, honest, sincere, sensitive and full of compassion and also well stocked up with brains. He should not be in jail; he felt he must not pay the fine, however, for Americans do have the right to protest, to work for their freedom and he should not have been arrested in the first place. . . . What may happen is that Albany will get into the New Orleans or Little Rock kind of mess. Now, while I would expect this sort of thing of Americus (my 25 years dealing with Americus people made me know they are historically behind the times etc.) but NOT ALBANY! I said at the time this happened: "Albany will do the right thing; I am sure of it." . . .
> . . . Couldn't you and Bob and your friends do something to make officials in Albany see that this can be worked into a world scandal and poor old Albany will pay for it for years. The right thing to do is to accept integration in the bus stations etc. and quietly let Dr. King and Rev. Ralph Abernathy go back to Atlanta. Dr. King studied at either Yale or Harvard, he is a cultivated man, quiet, gentle, with beautiful

manners and most delightful to talk to. I feel that your little group might be able to put some commonsense into the people who seem to have lost theirs; the whole thing could be quieted down, eased off, the men released, the whole affair of last winter forgotten, and Albany would profit greatly by it. These people are Georgia's best Negroes; God help you if you ever get tangled up with those Black Muslims; these people are trying to keep down racial violence. There is so much anger among the Jacksonville Negroes—you see it on streets, on buses; you don't see any of this in Atlanta for the Negroes there feel they are being given a real break; and God knows they are patient people if they think anybody is helping them.

Thank you for anything you or Bob or your friends can do to ease this situation. Atlanta has eased its hot spots by a few upperclass people like you, quietly talking to the right officials.

Mimi did not reply, which dismayed Lillian. She remembered that Mimi had liked *Killers of the Dream* and had said she would welcome integration in the schools when it came. "She says things like this at cocktail parties, and in her crowd," Lillian wrote to a friend, political analyst Helen Fuller. She decided that Mimi and her crowd misunderstood the nonviolent strategy and did not see that the real troublemaker in Albany was not King but James Gray, a transplanted northerner and outspoken segregationist. "They just don't seem to know what it is all about," she complained. "I told her 40 of them could turn the tide. I do not understand this paralysis for I do not believe it is apathy; it is what happens to some GI's under fire; they go dead, they can't respond rationally."[24]

Although discouraged by the outcome of the Albany Movement, by late 1962 Lillian was gratified to see that enlightened southerners were exerting more and more influence on public opinion. Among other things she cited the recent Georgia gubernatorial victory of the more moderate Carl Sanders over the demagogue Marvin Griffin. Even Albany went for Sanders. At the same time she was disturbed by the fact that many whites, including some who had supported desegregation (like Mimi in Albany), were now attacking the nonviolent philosophy and methods of Martin Luther King and groups like SCLC and SNCC. In an article for the *Saturday Review* she quoted a letter she said she had received from a woman who had frequently spoken out against segregation. "It is not segregation we are defending," the woman wrote; "we were going to accept desegregation of schools quietly . . . until these Negroes started demanding things. Now look at the anger in our town! Is it right to break laws as a protest? Should young Negroes be encouraged to go to jail? Shouldn't they be taught instead to be respectable?" Lillian explained such opposition to nonviolence by pointing out that it shattered the stereotypes whites had made of themselves and of Negroes. White southerners saw themselves as good-hearted people who, if not pushed too hard, would give the Negroes a portion of their rights, "doling them out as we (or our grandfathers) used to dole out fat bacon and sweets and cornmeal at Christmas." Negroes were expected to bow and scrape and thank the whites effusively for whatever small gift they received. But when Negroes sat in, or picketed, or demanded a conference with city officials, they were no longer bowing and scraping but asking "for what is theirs and asking for it now," Lillian observed. And their action caused whites suddenly to see the Negroes and themselves differently.

> Suddenly, the stereotypes we have made of them and of us collide and clash and break into splinters; we feel nakedly exposed as we stare at our real selves, and stunned as we stare at them: these are not "nice Negroes who are satisfied with things as they are" but human beings, wanting for themselves and their children the right to grow, to learn, to question, to become, to feel secure in their home towns. And as we glimpse ourselves we see something queasily dishonest which we cannot bear to acknowledge: how can we be so proud of our kindnesses to the few Negroes we know when we have stubbornly kept from all Negroes their civil rights—rights that are as much theirs as our civil rights are ours.

Lillian also cited the "psychic difficulty" of dealing with the "strange kind of love" represented by nonviolence. "Compassion from someone you consider beneath you, or whom you have harmed, enrages you—if you are easily enraged," she explained. Finally, she noted that most human beings do not like being put in a position in which they feel compelled to act and, if they do not, despise themselves for not acting. The nonviolent protests challenged people's apathy and complacency, their "paralysis in the face of a changing, whirling world that won't wait, no matter how loudly we Americans, South or North, beg it to wait," she observed.[25]

Although mounting white opposition to nonviolence disturbed her, the fact that it shattered stereotypes, disturbed people's complacency and apathy, compelled them to act, whether for right or wrong, persuaded Lillian of its efficacy. As before, in the 1960s she continued to emphasize the psychological dimension of the race problem. "Change comes not only by a few external acts but by a great many internal acts," she wrote in the *Saturday Review* article. The sit-ins, Freedom Rides, and other nonviolent demonstrations were impelling the change of heart and mind she had always believed necessary to eliminate segregation, and accomplishing in a few years what she had been trying to do for decades by explanation and exhortation. She realized that the demonstrators paid a fearful price in the form of beatings, shootings, and other kinds of brutality meted out by public officials as well as private individuals. Nevertheless, she remained guardedly optimistic about their ultimate success. In January, 1963, she sought to console her young friends in SNCC. Reading their newsletter, she had to admit that the racial situation was bad. "But things are breaking and thawing: we must hold on to that," she added. "A frozen river is a quiet thing; in thaw it is a roaring monster. We are in thaw in the South: there is bound to be much noise, much individual cruelty, much collective madness. But underneath, change is taking place—not only in streets and places but in human hearts. . . . If you think this thaw is bad, I wish you could have experienced the hard frozen sterile quality of [the 1940s and 1950s]. I say this not to minimize the horror of today but to give perspective, to help us see that sometimes noise and blood and screams and blows are not a sign of things worsening but of things getting better."[26]

Once again she appealed to the young people as a veteran of the civil rights movement. She closed her letter by urging them to maintain their sense of humor and compassion, to "be wary, shrewd, alert as well as bold and outthrusting," and to "hold on to this 'strange kind of love' which is so mighty in its effect that it is often criticised more than violence itself." Some people wanted them to come down to their level and be violent, "but you won't—of this I am sure," she wrote. "But nonviolence is not enough: the compassion that melts the cruelty not in others but in your own minds and hearts is the big thing, the real thing."[27] As the letter to SNCC indicates, Lillian's optimism regarding the continued progress of the civil rights movement depended as much on the demonstrators maintaining the philosophy and methods of non-violence as on white southerners changing their thinking about race and segregation.

# XII Old Dream, New Killers

> I . . . have been let out from the smothering blankets. Oh, they are scared, and the papers keep the blankets ready to cover my mouth again, but I am at least out.

With the thaw in the South came a lifting of the conspiracy of silence under which Lillian had chafed for almost a decade. The first sign of it appeared in Atlanta. At a Democratic election party in the fall of 1960, the first big party she had been invited to in the city since 1949, she found everybody discussing *Killers of the Dream*. "One business man said he still gets it out every two or three months and reads the final chapters in it which are his favorite," she wrote George Brockway. "Another one said, 'I cry over the damned book; it is so full of my childhood and everybody's down here.'" She also reported that on another occasion some students from Emory and Georgia Tech had told her that everybody was reading *One Hour* and asked how they might obtain copies of *Killers*.[1]

In another indication that the "smothering blankets" were being lifted, the Atlanta *Journal* published a letter to the editor in which Lillian urged support for the student sit-ins. Her relations with the other Atlanta daily, the *Constitution*, also improved. Ralph McGill had become publisher, and Lillian began corresponding with the new editor, Eugene Patterson. Like his predecessor, Patterson disagreed with many of her opinions regarding civil rights, but unlike McGill he did not dismiss them. In thanking her for one of her letters, Patterson wrote, "I do believe this: You are speaking the truth and you are speak-

232

ing it with courage and intelligence, and while it is not the way I can speak, you are just as valuable to mankind right now as I am, if not more so. There is a place for all of us. I only wish there were more like you." A month later, thanking her for another letter, he said it had given him "a good workout of the conscience and a feeling of close kinship with you." Lillian welcomed this kind of recognition and appreciation almost as much as if Patterson had converted to her views. Besides, she believed she exerted some influence on editorial policy. Phrases from her letters often appeared in Patterson's columns, she told Brockway, and instead of ignoring her, the *Constitution* now reported her activities, even quoted her speeches.[2]

On the national scene, the lifting of the conspiracy of silence began when *Redbook* invited her to do the story on the New Orleans school desegregation crisis. She said later that it took five "big name people in liberal circles" to persuade *Redbook* to have her do the story, and she resented the way it was cut and edited "almost beyond recognition," but she considered it a breakthrough nonetheless. In December, 1961, *Life* magazine published her "Memory of a Large Christmas." It was not on civil rights but, remembering how *Life* had scorned her in the 1950s, she was pleased (and surprised) that they accepted it. Then, in the summer of 1962, after she had received the Sidney Hillman Prize Award for the article on New Orleans, *Redbook* published her acceptance speech and ran ads in various magazines publicizing it. She thought that was what encouraged *Life* to ask her to do an article about her reaction to the crisis surrounding James Meredith's enrollment at the University of Mississippi. She wrote it in twenty-four hours and wired it to the editors. "They phoned late that night after receiving it," she reported to Page Wilson of the Americans for Democratic Action, and said that "they were 'thrilled and deeply moved, terribly excited and awed'." A little more than a week after the *Life* piece appeared, *Saturday Review* ran "A Strange Kind of Love." All of this, Lillian insisted, was "a giant step toward breaking the conspiracy of silence which the magazines have clamped down on me." The final breakthrough came in November, 1964, when *McCall's* published "The Day It Happens to Each of Us."[3]

Publication in large-circulation magazines like *Redbook*, *Life*, and *McCall's* not only brought Lillian the recognition she had long craved; it came at a time when she needed the substantial fees they paid. She had been down to "rock bottom" when asked to do the *Redbook* piece, she told *Petal Paper* editor P. D. East; the money she received for it supported her for three months. "Memory of a Large Christmas" would pay some of her bills and "keep me eating for a while," she told Marvin Rich. The check from *McCall's* came just when several hospital stays had almost bankrupted her again. During the 1960s her income averaged about $5,000 a year. With Paula working as a librarian, the two managed as far as living expenses were concerned, but Lillian's increasing medical and hospital expenses were a drain on her resources.[4]

The article *McCall's* published in 1964 was the epilogue of Lillian's last book, *Our Faces, Our Words*, published by W. W. Norton. In October, 1963, Marvin Rich, community relations director for CORE, had asked Lillian to do a little book about the civil rights movement. He had in mind a book with photographs depicting the movement as a whole, not just CORE. Both he and Lillian agreed that it would appeal mainly to college students and young people. Lillian wrote the text for it in between two lengthy hospital stays. The cancer had moved into her lungs and she was having trouble breathing and was also suffering from extremely low blood pressure. She alternated between staying in bed and getting up for brief periods of time to work on the book. When she finished it, she sent the epilogue to Norman Cousins of the *Saturday Review*. Sometime earlier, hearing that she was ill and hard hit by medical expenses, he had sent her a check for a piece to be written when she felt strong enough to write it, and she thought she owed him an article. He liked the epilogue so much that he wanted it to have a broader circulation than *Saturday Review*, and according to Lillian, "he pulled the rabbit's foot . . . and persuaded McCalls to run it." To her friend Frank Daniel of the Atlanta *Journal*, she wrote: "It is amazing to me how the ravens feed me these days; I write a piece, somehow, just in time and then a good angel steps in and persuades somebody to publish it. Well . . . I have things to be bitter about, God knows, things that won't quite go away though I try to bury the hurts but I have so many marvelous acts of grace to remember, . . . how can I be other than humbled and silent about the evil things!"[5]

*Our Faces, Our Words* was composed of photographs from various sources, along with nine monologues by participants in the civil rights

movement and an epilogue in which Lillian offered her own views in
her own voice. The monologues were fictionalized statements by a variety of people, including a black college student who had participated
in the sit-ins, a southern white girl who had gone to jail in Mississippi,
a northern Negro who had worked for SNCC, and a southern minister
agonizing over the murder of three civil rights workers in Philadelphia,
Mississippi. Lillian was annoyed that some reviewers thought they
were transcriptions of interviews with actual people. They were "dramatic monologues of fictional characters," she told Rochelle Girson;
she thought the misunderstanding was one more indication of an un-
willingness by some people to view her as "a serious and good creative
writer" rather than a sociologist or race relations expert. She had created the monologues "out of wisps of dozens and dozens of long talks"
with student activists, she told Wilma Dykeman Stokely; and she had
used her skill as a novelist to express in vivid, intense language "the
struggle of mind and heart" that engaged them. Indeed, the monologues were not really about civil rights per se, she later declared. They
dramatized the role of young southerners in the human evolution described by Teilhard de Chardin. The young people were part of a process of humanization, she wrote, a process that she had come to believe
was "the essence of religion: this 'getting with' the purpose of the divine Creator, this refusal ever to turn backward to things past, conditions less human, less compassionate." The young people were "wonderful; wonderful in their mistakes, even; terrifying, sometimes, to us
older ones, but . . . here to stay and . . . a presage of things to come."[6]
     Lillian viewed *Our Faces* as a piece of creative writing which, like
*Killers of the Dream* and *The Journey*, intermingled imagination and
mythic mind with reason and fact. Nonfiction could be "as creative and
full of art and poetry as fiction," she insisted. She also viewed the book
as an outgrowth of both the Mary and Martha sides of her nature. "I
must admit the 'Martha' in me . . . is always pushing the 'Mary' aside
to clean up the messes, to feed the starving," she wrote Bruce Galphin
of the Atlanta *Constitution;* "but sooner or later, Mary slips inside
Martha and shows her how to take the human 'problems' and trans-
mute them into poetry and art of a sort, at least; and maybe, now and
then, into something really valid and enduring."[7]
     The first reaction to the *McCall's* article was an anonymous tele-

phone call from a man who threatened to dynamite Lillian's home. "It made chills run through me," she told George Brockway. "My heart got very slow and heavy and my hands and arms went icy. . . ." Although she did not publicize the threat for fear of alienating the people of Clayton, she did inform a few male friends in the town. She realized they could not prevent a dynamiting, but their expressions of outrage and concern and the fact that they insisted on informing the Georgia Bureau of Investigation and the FBI somehow reassured her.[8]

Several letters from people who were pleased with the *McCall's* article offset the hostile reaction and led her to hope that more of "the good people" in the South would wake from their apathy and indicate how much they liked it, as she was sure they had. There were also some favorable reviews of *Our Faces*, including one in the Atlanta *Constitution* by Bruce Galphin, whom she described as "very liberal, young, and brave enough to defy McGill and praise me." But she was annoyed that the book was ignored in New York, just as the revised edition of *Killers* had been. The New York book reviewers' long-standing hostility toward her was the main reason, she thought, for the snubbing of both *Our Faces* and *Killers*. The *New York Times Book Review* did finally mention *Our Faces*, four months after its release, but only briefly in a review of five books on American Negroes and race relations.[9]

Although *Our Faces* for the most part celebrated the courage and commitment of participants in the civil rights movement, it also criticized some aspects of the movement. Lillian thought that many participants were unaware of what was happening to the movement and that it was her duty, as one who was not blinded by the smoke of battle, to speak out. Her main concern was the commitment to nonviolence. Without naming individuals or groups, she attacked the "Intruders" in the movement whom she described as hate-filled, violent men pretending to be nonviolent, and as people who were making "a dangerous caricature of the Nonviolent Movement" and assuming "the outer ways [of nonviolence] without making the inner sacrifices and spiritual decisions." The "Intruders" were people in CORE and SNCC who Lillian thought were abandoning the nonviolent philosophy. After CORE's 1961 convention, she had written to Marvin Rich that she wished the New York delegation had more appreciation for the meaning of nonviolence; she also confessed that she had been appalled at the lack of understanding of nonviolence on the part of a group jailed in Mississippi. "Some of the northern young whites seemed to me only rebels clinging to a new, dramatic cause," she wrote. Like the founders of CORE and Martin Luther King, Jr., and many of the early SNCC activists, Lillian viewed the nonviolent philosophy as a compound of Christian-pacifist and Gandhian principles. It taught that the purpose of sit-ins or boycotts was redemption and reconciliation. The un-merited suffering of protestors who were beaten or jailed was supposed to awaken a sense of moral shame, then understanding and friendship in opponents, and ultimately lead to the creation of what King called "the beloved community." However, as Lillian had begun to realize, many people in CORE and SNCC no longer viewed nonviolence as a philosophy based on "a strange kind of love" that appealed to the con-science of white Americans and redeemed both activists and oppo-nents. Instead, they looked upon nonviolence as a useful tactic to co-erce the federal government into legislating and enforcing equal rights. Some, like the Deacons for Defense, went even further, supporting the right of blacks to act in self-defense and to engage in retaliatory violence.[10]

Lillian not only criticized the "Intruders" for abandoning the phi-losophy of nonviolence, she also censured them for alienating support-ers of the civil rights movement. The "Intruders" had joined the move-ment at a "sensitive moment," just after the first successes of the nonviolent protests, she wrote. After hundreds of restaurants, hotels, and parks had been opened, after buses had been desegregated and department stores had begun to hire Negroes, thoughtful whites who were sympathetic to the Negro cause requested a pause, a rest period to give other whites time to adjust to desegregation. Just at that point the "Intruders" entered the movement and launched a wave of demonstra-tions in both the North and South. Lillian apparently referred to the mass protests of 1963 against housing, educational, and employment inequities in northern cities and black demands for "Freedom Now!" in the South. She insisted that such demonstrations had aroused the anger of even the Negro's most loyal friends and had irritated "every fair-minded Negro and white."[11]

Many CORE and SNCC workers abandoned the philosophy of nonviolence because they decided that their opponents—people like the notorious Sheriff "Bull" Connor of Birmingham, Alabama—were incapable of being redeemed and conciliated and that only the intervention of the federal government would bring about equal rights. Lillian denounced white intransigence and violence, but she continued to believe in the power of nonviolence to change hearts and minds. In her opinion, the changing of hearts and minds, and with it the destruction of barriers and the building of relationships between people, remained the primary objective of the civil rights movement. Legal or institutional changes were important and necessary, but their success depended on that psychological change which she believed only the nonviolent philosophy could bring about.[12]

Lillian also deplored the emergence of black nationalism for the same reason she lamented the abandonment of nonviolence—because it strengthened rather than eliminated barriers between the races. She had encountered it at the 1961 CORE convention, when some members of the New York delegation had questioned why she had been chosen to speak instead of a southern Negro. Writing Marvin Rich afterwards, she said she had been shocked to find some of the CORE members thinking in terms of stereotypes.

> Wanting "a southern Negro" for chairman, for instance; wanting one to speak (instead of me, I hear!). Who and what is "a southern Negro"? We are such stupid people when we use phrases like that. What we want is a good person to make a speech, one who can and has the kind of experience and background that can be useful to Core. This same kind of thing I have seen in New Yorkers who hate "all white southerners." Any white southerner, apparently. Many hate me in New York, simply because I am a white southerner, regardless of what kind of person I may be; regardless of what I have done in the segregation fight. It is stupid and dangerous, this kind of silly generalization, this placarding people.

Lillian thought the New York delegation challenged the interracial philosophy that, along with nonviolence, had long served as a cornerstone of the CORE ideology. Malcolm X and "his hate-filled followers," as she termed the Black Muslims, also alarmed her, and for the same reason. They were talking of a new kind of segregation and thinking "on the same splintered level as Klansmen and white racial fanatics," she wrote in *Our Faces*. Black nationalism did not offer freedom, she asserted, but "a flight from freedom, a new form of slavery—this time, slavery to hatred of whites and to black arrogance." What alarmed her most about the Black Muslims was the way they stirred up feelings of hate and resentment against whites, feelings that might be translated into violence even though the Muslims did not recommend it as a policy.[13]

Although she did not mention him in *Our Faces,* it is clear from her private correspondence that by 1963 Lillian regarded the novelist and essayist James Baldwin as more dangerous than Malcolm X and the Black Muslims, primarily because of the influence he seemed to be exerting on young people in the civil rights movement. She admitted that he had done some good in arousing many Negroes and white intellectuals from their apathy. However, she also feared his angry recriminations would "breed a big fire" and render the work of Martin Luther King and others useless. The fact that he had been late in joining the movement against segregation and had not been "on the firing line" participating in the southern protests angered her. Baldwin should picket in Georgia or Mississippi, she told writer John Howard Griffin; it would purge him of his rage and hatred and make him understand that "hate never brings about change but only brings about chaos."[14]

Besides revealing Lillian's apprehension regarding the direction the civil rights movement was taking in the mid-sixties, *Our Faces* evinced her new interest in the so-called poor whites of the South. Previously she had been inclined, despite their numbers, to discount their significance in the struggle to eliminate segregation. They supplied the haters and hoodlums who bombed churches and murdered Negroes, but she did not think they were strong enough to prevent the attainment of equal rights. However, the continuing apathy of the "good, respectable whites" and increasing violence against Negroes and civil rights workers led her to change her perspective and focus attention on the poor white element. She pointed out in *Our Faces* that though many of them suffered glaring inequalities just as the blacks did, they were not all economically poor. Their deprivation was psychological and cultural, not economic. They were "not poor any more in terms of money, but poor and deprived in terms of human culture, of spiritual richness, of civilized morality." Since the late nineteenth century the powerful planters and industrialists had been taking everything from them and feeding them the "drug of white superiority" so that "they wouldn't crave the bread their bodies needed and the values their souls had to have."[15]

She reiterated that theme, which she had first adumbrated in "Two Men and a Bargain," in a letter to Chicago *Sun-Times* book critic Hoke Norris. She said she was thinking of doing a collection of monologues in the voices of the poor whites, expressing their bewilderment, anger, and resentment. Whom did they really hate? Not the Negro, she thought.

> No, I think they hate us: they hate the upperclass whites of the South who fed them the drug of "whiteness" until they have destroyed themselves spiritually. They hate us because they, too, are segregated: segregated as rigidly socially from the Big Wheels and their families as are Negroes. This never talked about segregation which must be like a white fog around the poor whites is the thing that makes them hate Negroes with a psychotic violence; it isn't their competition for jobs—that is a rational fear; this other thing is deep, sick, psychotic.[16]

The 1964 presidential campaign sharpened her awareness of the importance of the poor whites. They were the ones who supported Goldwater and who were joining the John Birch Society—"by the tens of thousands," she noted—and the KKK and the Minute Men, a group she regarded as particularly dangerous in the South. Moreover, she had become convinced that the so-called power structure was "imprisoned and trapped by the poor whites of the South." She still did not believe they could prevent the Negroes from obtaining equal rights. But it would be an empty victory unless white attitudes changed, and that change would require something more than the traditional liberal solution of better jobs, housing, and education. That was but a rational answer to what she regarded as "a profoundly deep problem of the mythic mind." Jobs, housing, and education would help blacks, but they would not help "the white man's trouble," she declared; "the same dirty foul spirit will live in the clean well dressed bodies of these white 'poor trash.'" The main problem for the future was the one she had identified twenty years ago—not the Negro problem, but the notion of white supremacy—and it continued to harm whites as much as it harmed blacks. That was why, in December, 1965, she urged the Southern Regional Council to consider the plight of the poor whites as

well as blacks. "I think we should now—all of us, I in my more creative way perhaps, SRC in its exploratory way, confront the deprived
white, deprived once of money, still deprived culturally and morally
and psychologically. There are as many of these as there are Negroes
and they must be analyzed and their plight—our plight—drama-
tised," she wrote.[17]

After the smothering blankets were removed, Lillian enjoyed a kind
of equanimity, but her psyche remained fragile. Early in November,
1964, the dynamite threat and several nasty letters, coupled with the
lukewarm reception accorded *Our Faces*, plunged her into a depression
that prompted a self-pitying letter to Rochelle Girson, book review editor of the *Saturday Review*. It was in this letter, noting that some of the
reviewers had interpreted *Our Faces* as a sociological study, that she
complained: "Why under God's heaven can't the critics and reviewers
treat me as the artist I really am! This is the hurt of my life." Ten days
later, upon rereading the letter, she sent another asking Girson to forgive her using her as "a wailing wall." After consulting with her spe-
cialist in Atlanta, she decided that some hormones she had been taking
for the cancer had contributed to her depression, and she stopped
taking them. "Better cancer than paranoia—it is as simple as that," she
wrote Girson; "here's hoping—and praying—for a decent disposition
again and a sense of humor and all the rest that all writers need every
day of their lives!"[18]

During the next year she guarded against yielding to what she called
her "sense of persecution." She knew it would destroy her if she let it.
The problem was complicated by the fact that prednisone, which had
been prescribed for the cancer, was known to induce paranoia in some
patients. She recognized, too, that the loneliness which came from
living in semi-isolation on the mountain affected her temperament.[19]

Then in September an incident occurred that revived all the old
hurts and resentments and precipitated the worst spell of self-pity
she had ever experienced. Felicia Geffen, assistant secretary of the National Institute of Arts and Letters (NIAL), sent her a check for five
hundred dollars from the literary committee of the Artists and Writers
Revolving Fund "as a gesture of appreciation for your accomplishments." Lillian responded with a letter saying she could not accept the
check because she regarded it as charity rather than an award recognizing her accomplishments as a writer. The NIAL had never accorded

her recognition for her literary achievements, she pointed out, either by granting an award for any of her books or by inviting her to become a member. To accept aid from "a group who has in no way acknowledged my worth as a writer" would be humiliating, she declared. While she appreciated the committee's concern for her, she felt she must return the gift.[20]

Initially the NIAL gesture made her angry. Then she went into a severe depression. "I was paralyzed and could not write," she told George Brockway; "somehow I felt almost for the first time in my life that I really couldn't write, that it had been a dream-nightmare, an illusion and a damned silly one. It all seemed so Kafkan . . . for they chose the only way they could truly hurt me and hurt bad, by diminishing me to exactly nothing as a writer."[21]

During this period of depression she wrote long letters about the matter to several close friends. She had managed to be courteous and restrained in the letter to Geffen, but in these she unburdened herself completely. The day before she wrote Geffen, she sent a letter to her attorney, Donald Seawell, asking for advice on how to respond. She did not want to be rude and return the check, she said; she simply wanted the NIAL people to accept her and read her books. Because of the influence the Agrarians wielded after they went North ("over the crowd at Yale, Columbia, Harvard, Princeton"), the literary people had not read or appreciated her books, she explained. "Nobody got anything that this crowd didn't want them to have. So—when I dared write Strange Fruit and publish South Today they were in for me for they were very white indeed in those days. . . . They fought me hard then and they have fought me ever since." She contended that the NIAL committee had listened to "their hurting conscience (they won't face why it is hurting which is because if they had promoted me my books would be selling and would be used in English classes in the universities) and listening to their consciences they decided (as do upper-class people) to fling a little charity to a 'lower-class writer.'" She wanted Seawell to talk the matter over with George Brockway of Norton and William Jovanovich of Harcourt, Brace. "Bill does not recognize my worth either; he has a golden egg there that he is treating as a bad egg, yet he doesn't see it," she wrote. "But this might help him see his way to do something to change the picture." She remembered how, after *Strange Fruit* was published, Random House had reissued several books by

William Faulkner and got Malcolm Cowley to write an introduction, which initiated the Faulkner revival. "Publishers have to help with these things; they can't leave it all to luck and fate, etc. All they have to do, really, is set me up against all living southern writers (and some of the dead, too) and see what I've done, the kind of writing I've done, the terrific vocabulary, for instance, that everybody uses now but I inserted into all talk of human rights, segregation, etc." She also wondered whether Brockway and Jovanovich "might with tact arouse something over at the Institute that would help? or whether two or three members of the literary committee could be talked to."[22]

The next day, and the next letter to Seawell, found her in a different frame of mind. It really did not matter, she assured him, apologizing for her long, hurt, angry letter. She had never written for money or prestige but "because the artist in me wanted to write, felt almost driven to write of all that life had shown me; and I write because my spirit does long for a better world for all of us to live in, and I keep thinking that maybe 'the truth' as I see it (which is only in fragments here and there) can help others see, can help others want to create a better world inside them and outside them." She continued to insist that the NIAL committee had acted to assuage its bad conscience, realizing that she had had "a rough time of it for the past few years" mainly because the institute had not given her the recognition she deserved. "Had they made me a member or given me an award then professors in the colleges would have used my books and I should have made a better living and not been so completely ignored by the literary critics." But, returning to her initial statement, "it just doesn't matter." She had decided: "It is not up to me to try to push people into recognizing my worth as a writer; if I die before they do, all right. Just turn away, I told myself, and devote all your remaining strength and time to writing what you really want to say." Seawell was not to bother with the matter. She was going to return the check with a note letting the institute know she was hurt but without being defensive or angry.[23]

On December 1 Lillian reported to George Brockway that she was wrestling hard with her demons. "Where is my soul? where has it gone to?" she asked.

> Do I really want prestige more than anything else? If so, then I am damned. If I don't, then why am I ryining [sic] my last years, maybe my last months, ryining [sic] and wasting them on grabbing, desperately,

ferociously for something that never in my life have I (before) put first!
This I must answer. . . . Always I did what I did because I wanted to,
or because it seemed right to do so in my very depths; I often wrote for
an obscure magazine that would pay me nothing while the big-time
magazines begged me to write for them (after Strange Fruit.) Even before S. F. when I had no money I never once chose the way of prestige as
against what my whole organism wanted to do. And it was not "conscience." It was something deeper, it was something close to the whole
of me. Then why now does it mean so much? Realistically, I do need
money (but not badly as I did too [*sic*] years ago; Esther has helped and
Paula has now that she thank God has a good job); it isn't that; it is
prestige I hunger for. I want to be called a novelist, a critic, a writer. I
don't care if they criticise me just so they accept me. Now this is dam-
foolishness. I know it. I think it comes from the fact that all my life the
creative Mary had to give up for the grubby, doing Martha. Now, in my
old age I want Mary to have her day.

That month two incidents exacerbated her anger and hurt feelings.
One was a telegram from a prominent Negro (who had earlier refused
to write a blurb for *Our Faces*) saying how grateful she was to Lillian for
all she had done to help her in her writing career. The other was a gift
of candy from a reporter for the Atlanta *Journal* who had published an
article naming several southerners, including Carson McCullers, as
important writers, but not mentioning Lillian. The fires on Old
Screamer, the nasty letters, and the dynamite threats "make you feel
you've accomplished something; to be hated by the right people can
seem honorable," she observed to Brockway. The little humiliations,
"people being sweet to you and then denigrating your life's work," were
what hurt. Like the NIAL check, the telegram and the candy constituted "backdoor treatment," she explained. "Backdoor giving of
presents instead of prestige—just as we whites used to do our servants,
our mammies." And the contempt it implied hurt her just as it hurt
Negroes, she said. But, she added:

> I am fighting this out; it will destroy me as a person and maybe as
> writer, too, if I don't; I must be full of messy stuff inside that I didn't
> know was there; I need this humbling, I suspect; and must accept it in
> the most profound way possible. I'm just not as "nice" as I thought I
> was; just not as devoted, as committed as I thought; I want too much to
> be a good good writer; I should care only about leaving the world of
> relationships better, more subtle, more loving, than I found it. I should

> toil over my words, my thoughts, my feelings, my visions: this counts;
> nothing else does.

Not until early January was she able to report that she was busy writing
again and watching the prednisone to see that it did not play tricks on
her temperament. She credited Brockway, more than any other person,
with helping her through her "spiritual debacle" by offering understanding as well as the "firm shake of the shoulder" she needed to
bring her back to her senses.[24]

During the last two years of her life, civil rights remained Lillian's
primary concern though other Americans were focusing their attention
on Vietnam. Lillian did not say or write anything justifying United
States involvement in Vietnam, but neither did she join the protests
against it. While she defended pacifists and conscientious objectors
and while she believed in the philosophy of nonviolence, she was not a
pacifist herself. "I am wholly against nuclear war," she wrote; "and
99½ percent against any form of war whatever." The other half percent
led her to view some wars as justifiable, a notion she explained in neo-
orthodox terms. "Sometimes we human beings sin so deeply that we
are compelled to sin even more; this is a dreadful thing, a heart-
chilling thing but I believe it is true," she wrote. She claimed she was a
perfectionist by nature and had had to struggle to see the world as it
really is: "there is no clear evil and no clear good, no clear black and
clear white: it is wrapped together in a terrible tangle; and it is our
duty—I think it is God's purpose!—for us to have to unwrap it, learning more about the good because of the evil meshed with it."[25]

In explaining her position on Vietnam, she pointed to her early experience and long-standing interest in Asia, which she thought made
her more aware than her fellow liberals of the complexities of the Vietnam issue. In her opinion, involvement in Vietnam arose out of the
many failures and missed opportunities of the United States in China.
Now that the United States was involved, it must continue ("with as
much daily mercy and compassion as possible for all concerned") until
a solution was found. "There come times in individuals' lives—and
nations' lives—when they have postponed doing the right thing for so
long that there is no choice except the lesser of two evils," she wrote the
social philosopher Lewis Mumford in November, 1965. In her view,
involvement in the war was a lesser evil than a Communist take-over of

South Vietnam. She admitted she did not have a solution to "this hideous situation," but neither did she approve the solutions proposed by the antiwar people. "How can we just walk out and dump everything?" she asked. "How can we negotiate when nobody wants to negotiate?" She believed the real solution existed and would ultimately be found. "I pray we shall soon find it," she wrote. "Nobody has the right answer, as yet; neither government or its opponents; it is wrong to be there, God knows; but the suggestions for getting out are equally wrong in terms of who will be hurt."[26]

Because of her long-term interest in China, she was inclined to think that the real problem, and the solution, lay with that country rather than Vietnam. "It is China that we need to deal with," she declared to Norman Cousins in March, 1966. "Viet Nam will slowly straighten itself out if we can just change the situation of our relationship with China." To that end she advocated opening trade with the People's Republic, extending diplomatic recognition, and supporting its admission to the United Nations, policies she had favored since the 1950s.[27]

Lillian may have been reluctant to join the antiwar movement because it reminded her of the position she had taken regarding United States intervention in World War II. Then, she recalled, her abhorrence of war had caused her to err in thinking that the United States should not get involved in a war with Hitler. "I was wrong there," she confessed to Ruth Nanda Anshen. "I did not really know what Hitler was doing to the Jews and to all of Europe." Another and probably more important reason was that, unlike many of the antiwar protestors, Lillian believed in the integrity, goodwill, and decency of the United States in Vietnam. This was largely because she liked and trusted President Johnson; her regard for his achievements in the area of civil rights colored her view of his policies in Vietnam. He had done more than any other president in a hundred years to see that Negroes got their rights and privileges, she declared. She wished her "liberal friends" as she called them would be fairer and less prejudiced toward him. She was convinced that, although they did not realize it, they hated him because he was southern. Moreover, she argued, Eisenhower and Kennedy had gotten the United States into Vietnam, and "Johnson was left with the bag to hold" and with "no easy and no right way out."[28] Her argument did not address the fact that Johnson was expanding the war far beyond what his predecessors had authorized. Nor did Lillian criticize Johnson for diverting attention and resources from the struggle for civil rights to the war in Vietnam.

Although she supported street demonstrations to protest domestic issues such as segregation, she did not think they were justified where foreign policy was concerned. She took an essentially elitist view of foreign policy. Explaining her refusal to support an antiwar march on the White House, she argued that international matters "must be handled with care, with finesse, keeping all the subtle complexities in mind." A march could not do this; moreover, if it were publicized throughout the world, it could do the government great harm. By contrast, thoughtful spoken or written criticism (presumably by people like herself) not only did the government less harm, it also educated "the minds of our people." Marches were not educational, she insisted; "they push toward action, but in international affairs 'the people' cannot act—except through their President." Moreover, she declared, "the people marching hardly know where Viet Nam is; they couldn't give us 25 important facts about Asia's history for the past 60 years; they are screaming and yelling about something they know nothing much about." She was also disturbed by the language and anger of the antiwar demonstrators, shocked to hear "so-called nonviolent people, pacifists etc." using "four-letter words" and "stridently violent adjectives," and dismayed by their hatred of the government and President Johnson.[29]

Some of the tendencies she disparaged in the antiwar movement were similar to those she had criticized in the civil rights movement. By 1965 she was even more concerned than before about the direction the latter was taking. Although she still supported the Student Nonviolent Coordinating Committee, its tendency toward racial separatism troubled her. She had begun working with the Southern Student Organizing Committee (SSOC), founded in Nashville in 1964 to bring southern white students into the civil rights movement. No significant change would occur in the South without the efforts of young white students, she explained to Sue Thrasher, executive secretary of the new organization. "It is impossible for the Negroes to do it alone; it is hard to accept the fact (hard for some of them) that the young whites must help, that it can't be done either by a group of Negro college students or the Negro 'masses.'" Her reference to "the Negro 'masses'" indicates her disagreement with SNCC workers who believed in the necessity of militant mass action to effect social change. "Masses can't do anything; they have force and power but they are always led—and who leads them in the South is terribly important," she commented. Still committed to the philosophy of nonviolence, Lillian also continued to be alarmed that more and more civil rights workers, especially young blacks, seemed to be abandoning it. She understood why. She too was horrified by the brutal attack by deputies and state troopers on civil rights marchers at the Edmund Pettus Bridge and the murders of Jimmy Lee Jackson and the Reverend James Reeb during the Selma, Alabama, demonstrations. Incidents such as those, as well as the reluctance of white Americans to grant equal rights to Negroes, were causing the young blacks to abandon the nonviolent philosophy, she contended. "We whites have had our chance now for five years to do something wonderful and what have we done?" she wrote a friend in October, 1965. "We've made the young civil rights workers force us into every step we've taken! And they are hurt, they are resentful, they are angry kids now: they are saying What the hell is nonviolence, anyway? just a state of comfort for the whites? And inconsistently, of course—but we are all inconsistent—they become violent here at home and insist that we not be violent at all in Viet Nam!" Many of the young Negroes with whom she had worked in the early sixties were becoming "nihilistic revolutionaries" or were leaning toward anarchism, she observed. However she was not sure how to write about the matter, since to criticize any aspect of the civil rights movement was to give aid and comfort to the segregationists. Having expressed her criticisms somewhat obliquely in *Our Faces*, now, a year later in October, 1965, she was thinking that she ought to express them more openly.[30]

On January 14, 1966, the Atlanta *Constitution* published a letter by her under the headline, "Old Dream, New Killers." She had written it in response to two incidents. On January 6, John Lewis, chairman of SNCC, held a press conference and released a statement on behalf of the organization's 135 paid staff members opposing United States involvement in the Vietnam War. The conference was reported on the front page of the *Constitution* the following day. The organization had been considering taking an official stand on Vietnam for several months, and at their November, 1965, meeting the staff members had authorized the executive committee to draft an antiwar statement. According to Clayborne Carson, what triggered the January press conference was the shooting of Sammy Younge, a black SNCC worker, while he was attempting to use the whites-only restroom at a service station in Tuskegee. To the SNCC workers, Carson explains, Younge's death symbolized "the racism and hypocrisy that infected the nation." In its statement, SNCC charged that the United States government was being deceptive in claiming a concern for the freedom of the Vietnamese people, just as it "has been deceptive in claiming concern for the freedom of the colored people in such other countries as the Dominican Republic, the Congo, South Africa, Rhodesia, and the United States itself." As evidence of such deceptiveness, SNCC cited the experience of its own workers. "Our work, particularly in the South, taught us that the United States government has never guaranteed the freedom of oppressed citizens, and is not yet truly determined to end the rule of terror and oppression within its own borders." Workers for SNCC "have often been victims of violence and confinement executed by U.S. government officials," the statement noted. The United States government bore "a great part of the responsibility" for Younge's death, it declared. His murder was no different from the murder of people in Vietnam, "for both Younge and the Vietnamese sought and are seeking to secure the rights guaranteed them by law. . . . Samuel Younge was murdered because U.S. law is not being enforced. Vietnamese are being murdered because the United States is pursuing an aggressive policy in violation of international law. The United States is no respecter of persons or law when such persons or laws run counter to its needs and desires. We recall the indifference, suspicion and outright hostility with which our reports of violence have been met in the past by government officials." As further evidence of the government's lack of concern for freedom, the statement declared that "elections in this country, in the North as well as the South, are not free," and noted that the 1965 Voting Rights Act and the 1964 Civil Rights Act "have not yet been implemented with full federal power and concern."[31]

The Atlanta *Constitution* story included some of the portions of the statement quoted above, but focused on those regarding the military draft. The lead sentence of the story declared, "The leader of the militant Student Non-Violent Coordinating Committee Thursday urged 'all Americans' to use any method they see fit to avoid being drafted," and the story quoted that portion of the statement which said:

> We are in sympathy with, and support, the men in this country who are unwilling to respond to a military draft which would compel them to contribute their lives to United States aggression in Viet Nam in the name of the 'freedom' we find so false in this country. We recoil with horror at the inconsistency of a supposedly free society where responsibility to freedom is equated with the responsibility to lend oneself to military aggression. We take note of the fact that 16 percent of the draftees from this country are Negroes called on to stifle the liberation of Viet Nam, to preserve a "democracy" which does not exist for them at home. . . .
>
> We, therefore, encourage those Americans who prefer to use their energy in building democratic forms within this country. We believe that work in the civil rights movement and with other human relations organizations is a valid alternative to the draft. We urge all Americans to seek this alternative, knowing full well that it may cost them their lives—as painfully as in Viet Nam.[32]

The other incident that provoked Lillian's letter involved Julian Bond, whom she had known since the student sit-ins of 1960. The son of the well-known educator Horace Mann Bond, he had been elected to the Georgia House of Representatives in June, 1965. According to Carson, he had been on leave from SNCC since the political campaign and had not helped write the statement on Vietnam. However, the *Constitution* reported that Bond, who was identified as SNCC's information director, had said he concurred fully with the SNCC statement; he was quoted as saying that although he would not burn his own, he "would admire the courage of anyone who burns his draft card." He was denounced for this in most of the Georgia newspapers and by the governor and other state officials, and then, on January 10, the members of the House of Representatives denied him his seat in the legislature.[33]

Lillian had written her letter as a personal communication to Eugene Patterson. He telephoned for permission to publish it in the *Constitution*, and it appeared on the editorial page. In it Lillian denounced the action of the Georgia legislators as hypocritical and unconstitutional. What right had they to "judge Bond's belief in democracy when for much of their lifetime they've done all they could to keep us from ever living a real democracy in the South?" she asked. She described Bond as naive in opposing the Vietnam War, but insisted on his right to oppose it. She then outlined her own opinion of the war, noting that she disagreed not only with "those who want to burn draft cards" but also with "the leftists, even some of my friends, who I had thought about as moderately liberal." Involvement in Vietnam was the result of mistakes dating back to the 1920s, she argued, all of them made "long before Johnson came in." The Vietnam War was "an enormously complicated matter." She wished it could stop today, that negotiations could begin tomorrow, but, she wrote, "I simply know too much about it to take the simplistic position (and the highly angered and discourteous position) that so many of my friends in the North have taken." She believed President Johnson was earnestly trying to find the right solution. "I want us to speak against war, to urge negotiations, but to respect his efforts to bring these matters about," she declared.[34]

In much of the remainder of the letter Lillian attacked SNCC. What had started out as a "starry-eyed and pure-hearted movement" had deteriorated for lack of discipline and good leadership and because the young Negroes in the organization had accepted "the advice of men like Staughton Lynd and others who came South and infiltrated the Movement. . . . They've been listening for three years now to a mixed up mess of 19th century anarchism and 1930's communism (several of their most popular young northern helpers are children of the old Commies well-known in the '30's)." She said she had hoped they would take note of her warning in *Our Faces,* but they had not. "I've warned them; but they don't listen," she wrote. She explained SNCC's statement against the war in Vietnam as an application of the anarchistic theory "that it is a good idea to cook up a revolutionary incident, then let things fly and hope out of the mess something good will come." And, she warned, the Georgia legislators, the newspapers, and "many decent whites" would be "walking right into the trap" if they tried to punish Bond for supporting the statement. The best thing to do would be to ignore the whole matter; she urged the legislators "to admit he has the right to be wrong, just as they in the past have been wrong, and are now wrong about freedom to dissent."[35]

Lillian's criticism of the Georgia legislators and her vindication of Bond's right of dissent were predictable, and the opinions she expressed on Vietnam were those she had already stated in private correspondence. The main significance of her letter lies in what she wrote about SNCC. To understand what she said and why she said it, it is helpful to look at her correspondence following the publication of the letter. During January and February she wrote numerous lengthy letters to various friends elaborating her views on SNCC and the Bond affair.

It is clear from both the published letter and her private correspondence that she felt disregarded by the leaders of SNCC. "I mothered SNCC during their first three years"; "I went out on a limb for it before any magazine or other writer did"; "I helped get them quite a few thousand dollars," she wrote in letters to Arthur Raper, Karl Menninger, Norman Cousins, and others. That was when SNCC's leaders "honestly wanted to be nonviolent; they yearned to feel real compassion for whites; they were willing to suffer in order 'to redeem themselves and their enemies,'" she remembered. But then the "Intruders," as she had called them in *Our Faces*, came down and took over SNCC. They were James Forman, a black schoolteacher from Chicago, and "three or four white men from the North (one of them this mentally sick Staughton Lynd)," she told Menninger. She disliked and distrusted Forman the most. "That tricky Foreman" (she consistently misspelled his name) "is not basically interested in bringing civil rights to the South," she advised Bruce Galphin; "he has bigger game in his mind: a world-size racist revolution and he wants to be one of its leaders." She admitted this was intuition, but, she insisted, it was "intuition based on 35 years of study and absorption in what is happening in black and white minds all over the world. I believe this." In describing the ideological orientation of the clique that now controlled SNCC, she used such terms and phrases as "New Leftists," "sort of Castro revolutionaries," "sort of Pan-Africanists," "neo-nihilists," "partly 19th century anarchists," and "following the Maoist racist line." The word she used most often to describe them was "revolutionaries."[36]

As she had noted in the published letter, so in her private correspondence she pointed out that she had described and warned against the take-over two years earlier while writing *Our Faces*. "Maybe I should have written it straight, not in the quiet, half-creative way I used," she reflected. At any rate, SNCC had not listened. By that time, she said, "SNCC feared me." They would not promote the book, even though she offered them a percentage of the royalties—"not to 'promote it,'" but "without strings," she told Norman Cousins. "The only thing I asked for was a conference with Foreman and Bond to 'find out what their philosophy was, what they were really after.' They refused to come up and talk to me; although always saying they'd come 'one of these days.'" Now, she pointed out to other correspondents, "they refuse advice from anyone older" and had no sponsors who were older citizens.[37]

Lillian refused to consider the antiwar statement official, arguing that it had been drawn up and announced by the "revolutionary clique" without being authorized or voted upon by the SNCC membership. She insisted that the Forman clique had deliberately staged the press conference four days before the opening of the Georgia legislature in order to provoke the legislators into censuring Bond and creating "a new cause." Forman and the others, she explained to Harry Golden, thought up the one thing the legislators would find hardest to take.

> This was "disloyalty" to the USA in wartime. Brought up under a totalitarian regime[,] to these Georgians "loyalty" meant no dissent; this is the way they had felt about the southern "way of life." Now, in wartime, they (all southerners tend to) felt "loyal" to the USA government; and this meant, of course, no dissent. It is easy to see how the smart boys could figure this out; only one other thing could have upset the clods and that was a declaration for intermarriage which these SNCC revolutionaries did not dare try to put over. So: they took the second best: suggesting that they were not "loyal" and did not want other young people to be "loyal."

All this seemed obvious to Lillian, though she observed that "our northern friends saw it simply as another act on the part of the legislature against 'Negroes.'" The revolutionaries got what they wanted, she noted: "front page news and a tie-up with Asian and African revolutionaries. . . . And the poor white fools in the legislature were 'had' and they know they were; but accustomed to conditioned reflexes they reacted just as the revolutionaries counted on their doing."[38]

In telling the story of the coup staged by the Forman clique, Lillian exempted Julian Bond from any part in the machinations. She had described him in the *Constitution* letter as "pulled this way and that" by conflicting ideological currents, implying that he, too, had walked into the trap; and though the newspaper had attributed the statement about burning draft cards to Bond, she had attributed it to John Lewis. In her private correspondence she portrayed Bond as "the innocent in this picture; the young poet who has been deliberately sacrificed by the machinations of a very clever and very small group of men." He was "a sweet, clean-minded 'nice' C.O. (truly one from childhood)," she told Harry Golden, and he had reacted to the SNCC statement "just like a Billy Budd might have done." Now his political career was ruined—and along with it the opportunity to be a "creative force" in the Atlanta community. The Student Nonviolent Coordinating Committee had been harmed, too, as had the whole civil rights movement, she thought.[39]

Reading Lillian's letters on the SNCC antiwar statement, it is impossible to avoid the conclusion that like the Georgia legislators she had walked into a trap, and a trap of her own making, not one set by SNCC. Just as the legislators overreacted by denying Bond his seat in the legislature, Lillian overreacted by viewing the SNCC statement as part of a conspiracy planned and executed by dangerous revolutionaries. Her reaction was conditioned by two feelings: the feeling of being disregarded by SNCC, already mentioned, and a feeling of pride, even arrogance, which made her think that she knew better than most other people what was going on—and what should be going on—in the civil rights movement. It was not just that she considered herself a veteran of the movement. She had come to believe that living on the mountain offered her a vantage point from which to appraise the civil rights movement. Instead of feeling isolated and out of touch with what was happening, she felt she had attained a more accurate and comprehensive view than other observers of the political and literary scene.[40]

In fact, she badly misunderstood and misinterpreted SNCC and its antiwar statement. But she was not alone. Eugene Patterson and some of the Georgia legislators also viewed the antiwar statement as a trap. What distinguished Lillian's view from theirs was her notion that the trap had been set not only to catch the legislators, but to carry out a coup within SNCC. She saw it as a conspiracy hatched not only to antagonize the white legislators, but to commit SNCC to a new cause in alliance with Third World revolutionaries. Probably the impetus behind this notion was her concern about the reorganization of SNCC. By 1965, SNCC had been transformed from a loosely organized, unstructured student movement to a political organization of full-time, professional activists under increasingly centralized authority. Forman was the principal agent of the transformation, but the restructuring of SNCC hardly involved the kind of take-over that Lillian depicted.[41]

Lillian also misinterpreted SNCC's ideological orientation. Compared with other civil rights organizations, SNCC was radical—but not revolutionary. Although illegal, neither burning draft cards nor counseling avoidance of the draft was revolutionary. Indeed, both activities could be viewed as forms of nonviolent civil disobedience similar to those SNCC used in the struggle for civil rights. Nevertheless, by 1966 Lillian seemed to agree with the editorial writer in the Atlanta *Constitution* who asserted that SNCC wanted "to tear down the whole structure and start anew." She allowed her emotional reaction to what Carson has called SNCC's "verbal militancy" to influence her thinking. She admitted being antagonized by the insulting words and the nasty, "Castro-style adjectives" employed in the antiwar statement to describe "our government's dishonesty, its cynical manipulating of the situation in . . . Viet Nam." She wrote in the *Constitution* letter that the talk of burning draft cards had shocked and outraged her.[42]

Perhaps another reason she regarded SNCC as revolutionary was that its radical perspective was so inimical to her own political outlook. As a liberal she was unable to countenance SNCC's contention that the federal government could not be counted on to protect civil rights workers or enforce equal rights. As an adherent of the Cold War orthodoxy that supported involvement in Vietnam, she disagreed with SNCC's condemnation of American imperialism.

Lillian also erred in overemphasizing the influence of communism, Castroism, Maoism, and Pan-Africanism within SNCC. As a one-time supporter of the organizaton, she, more than other observers, was in a position to see that, as Andrew Kopkind noted, "SNCC's radicalism is its own, not of another society's or another generation's making." Instead, her conviction that SNCC was a revolutionary group, combined with her long-standing suspicion of communism, led her to engage in the very red-baiting she had deprecated in earlier years. In doing so, she joined the growing chorus of critics of SNCC, which by 1966 included not only southerners but northern liberals and most civil rights leaders.[43]

Lillian had few, if any, misgivings about her criticism of SNCC. Patterson and others had given her the impression that Georgia was on the verge of hysteria and that publication of her letter would calm people down. "It seemed to do just that," she said later. She was delighted to have the letter appear in the *Constitution*, along with an editorial praising it as an eloquent, accurate and profound analysis of the Julian Bond incident. "The first nice word [about me] that has ever appeared on the editorial page of the Constitution," she remarked to Arthur Raper. She was also pleased with the many letters and phone calls she received from both Negroes and whites, including Mayor Ivan Allen, praising her statement. As more and more favorable letters came in, she confessed to Karl Menninger, "I grew restive and began to think I had been too conservatively 'reasonable'—but maybe not; maybe I put the wiggly little ducks in rows that somehow made sense to people."[44]

Shortly after her letter on SNCC appeared in the Atlanta *Constitution*, Lillian submitted a longer article on the Julian Bond affair to the *Saturday Review*. Although the magazine rejected it and it was never published, it is a revealing piece of work, the last full-length article she wrote before she died. Entitled "Orpheus and Roast Pig," it offered what she called an "intuitive" interpretation of the Bond affair.[45]

People in Georgia had been craving "symbolic roast pig" for some time, she noted. On one hand, white rural Georgians and some state legislators, resentful of the changes wrought by the civil rights revolution, were hungry for "the old demagogic barbecue hate-feasts" they had enjoyed for decades. On the other hand, members of SNCC were resentful, too, not only because of jailings and beatings, but also because of the indifference of whites who should have helped them but had always turned away at the moment of need. They "urgently wanted an emotional barbecue," she wrote, and, being activists, they arranged for one to happen. In the process, the "shadowy revolutionaries" of SNCC, the "four or five so-called 'New Leftists' (most from the North)," sacrificed Julian Bond, their Orpheus, and he became the "roast pig" of their emotional barbecue as well as white Georgia's demagogic feast.[46]

Lillian sharply contrasted Bond and the other SNCC officers, describing him as "an intelligent, sensitive, courteous, quietly poised young poet" who had left college to work for civil rights in the early days of the student sit-ins. His handsome "Ivy League look" set him apart from most of the other SNCC people. Moreover, she insisted, Bond was a true conscientious objector, whereas the shadowy revolutionaries were not, for they did not believe in nonviolence as a "way of life," but "use it as a tactic and strategy when they think it will 'work.'" Given the great difference she perceived between Bond and the other SNCC officers, Lillian could not understand his response to reporters' questions about the SNCC antiwar statement. Something seemed to be compulsively pushing him to say that he admired those who burned their draft cards, she wrote. When he tried to explain his views, he only made matters worse. "Like Prince Myshkin in Dostoievski's novel, this sincere idealist kept finding the wrong words: words that betrayed his own inner beliefs." She held James Forman responsible, noting that Bond seemed "curiously susceptible" to his influence. She claimed to have been told "on excellent authority" that one of the Georgia legislators had sought to resolve the controversy between Bond and the men who had denied him his House seat. But, she wrote, every time the legislator and Bond got close to agreement, Forman "would barge in, take Bond off for a talk—and suddenly, the chasm would widen again." With just a few words, the "racist revolutionary" Forman was able to "swing Bond back into what seems at this distance to be a stubbornly perverse, self-destructive stand."[47]

Whereas in her Atlanta *Constitution* letter, Lillian had emphasized Bond's right of dissent and criticized the Georgia legislature, in "Orpheus and Roast Pig" she clearly sympathized with the unnamed legislator who had sought an accommodation. While she admitted Bond's right to dissent, "even . . . in an ugly way," she also defended the reasonableness of the legislator's appeal. "This . . . highly thought of legislator did not ask Mr. Bond to crawl," she explained; "he asked him only to explain, with Bond's natural courtesy, his real beliefs about

nonviolence and to state his feeling of loyalty to his country—not loyalty, 'right or wrong,' as the hypocritical segregationists now demanded
of him, but honest, essential loyalty." She apparently did not consider
it a violation of Bond's rights to demand that he publicly affirm his
loyalty as a condition for taking his seat in the legislature.[48]

Lillian also downplayed the issue of dissent in explaining the general significance of the Bond affair.

> Once more the poet was sacrificed to the demagogic mob; it has hap-
> pened throughout human history. In this one fact lies the real tragedy of
> the Bond affair—not in his "right to dissent" (important as it is, in the
> long view it is a secondary problem) but in the fact that flaming hate of
> white and black, streaked with repressed attraction, combined to de-
> stroy the innocent, the dreamer. Of all the issues in the world today—
> most of them spurious or already dead—the big one is this deep con-
> flict in the human race between the demagogue and the poet; on this the
> moral (and political) polarities swing; on the outcome of this Big Con-
> flict the human future depends.

"Orpheus and Roast Pig" may be seen as another of Lillian's efforts
(like *Our Faces, Our Words*) to resolve the Mary/Martha split in her
character by writing creatively about civil rights. In "Orpheus" she interpreted the Bond affair from an essentially literary point of view,
seeing Bond not only as Orpheus destroyed by the Maenads (the
SNCC people) but also as Prince Myshkin and Billy Budd, characterizing Forman as the sort of "daemonic personality" described by
Goethe, and viewing the whole affair as an archetypal tragedy. She
transmuted a concrete civil liberties issue into a rarefied, mythic drama
and in the process changed Bond from victim to victor. Whereas in the
Atlanta *Constitution* letter she criticized the denial of Bond's rights, in
"Orpheus" she ignored that issue, indulging the sentimental notion that
Bond, though destroyed, like Orpheus and Billy Budd would ultimately exert an influence. "The thing to remember," she wrote, "is that
although the Maenads cut off the head of Orpheus, it floated down the
river still singing its songs, still telling the poetic vision. Julian Bond is
not going to be forgotten. I do not know that he will ever become a
great poet or even a good one; but his poetic vision will not die." Thus
the lesson offered in "Orpheus" is similar to that in *One Hour,* but
quite different from that offered in *Strange Fruit.* In *Strange Fruit,*

Lillian presented the lynching of Henry, an innocent black man, as stark injustice. In "Orpheus" she interpreted Bond's victimization just as Dave Landrum interpreted the deaths of Andy and the church organist—as a moral triumph. Whether she intended it or not, "Orpheus" diminished the significance of the injustice visited upon Bond by diverting attention to the notion of an ultimately intangible victory over his enemies.[49]

In early 1966, when she wrote her Atlanta *Constitution* letter criticizing SNCC, Lillian insisted that CORE was different. Six months later, however, she changed her mind and sent a telegram to Floyd McKissick, CORE's national director, announcing her resignation from the national advisory committee. She protested what she called "the dangerous and unwise position CORE has taken on the use of violence in effecting racial change." Delegates to the annual convention had just voted to eliminate adherence to nonviolent direct action as a requirement for chapter affiliation and had approved a resolution stating that "the concept of nonviolence and self-defense are not contradictory" and upholding "the natural, constitutional and inalienable right of self-defense." The fact that the convention also embraced Black Power, condemned United States involvement in Vietnam, and pledged support of draft resisters undoubtedly influenced Lillian's decision; but she did not concern herself with those policies in the telegram. Explaining her decision to resign, she noted that for many years CORE had held to a belief in nonviolence and had "refused tactics dictated by anger and hate." But "now we have new killers of the dream," she wrote. "CORE has been infiltrated by adventurers, by nihilists, Black Nationalists, and plain old fashioned haters who have finally taken over." She emphasized the responsibility whites bore for the change. Their stubbornness, complacency, and violence had made it easy for the "haters" to take over from "more wise and patient leadership." But this was no excuse. "I do not believe in the use of violence, however great the temptation," she declared. "We are working for something bigger than civil rights; we are working for better human beings, we are working for excellence in our cultural life. How can we achieve these goals unless all of us meet this challenge with honesty and intelligence and good will and speed?"[50]

In criticizing SNCC and resigning from CORE, Lillian aligned herself with the more moderate wing of the civil rights movement, including such organizations as the NAACP, the Urban League, the Southern Regional Council (of which she had recently been made a life member), and the Southern Christian Leadership Conference, and such civil rights leaders as Roy Wilkins and Martin Luther King, Jr. During the 1960s she maintained essentially the same position on the race problem she had taken twenty years earlier, but the changed context meant that she was no longer regarded as a radical but as a racial moderate or liberal. Nothing so well illustrates the changed context of the sixties and Lillian's place in it as the policies of the Atlanta *Constitution* during the last years of her life. When the paper published her letter on SNCC, she interpreted it as a capitulation. "Ralph McGill actually broke a taboo of 22 years and let me be heard in the Atlanta Constitution," she crowed to a friend. McGill had caught up with her position. By the mid-sixties he had become known as the "conscience of the South." Lillian conceded that he had done "tremendous good" in writing in favor of civil rights. However, she resented the fact that he had won the recognition and awards, including the Pulitzer Prize and the Presidential Medal of Freedom, that she thought she deserved because she had spoken out against segregation long before he had and when there was more risk involved.[51]

What meant even more than publication of her letter in the *Constitution* was the editorial praising it and describing her as "one of the distinguished women of American letters" and one who "has devoted much of her life to social protest against injustice to Negroes." It was the recognition of her literary achievement, even more than the praise for her work as a social reformer, that delighted her. It was "a beautiful editorial," she told a friend, writer Dorothy Bromley, "called me one of the nation's most distinguished writers, a woman who loves the South and has worked for both Negroes and whites all her life, a woman who has been scorned, isolated, treated badly but never wavered, etc. etc." She said that after it appeared, the "telephone rang all day—long distance; Lillian has been made respectable in Georgia, and before her death; friends called to say they were weeping, they were so glad, it had happened while I was alive. It was touching."[52]

# Epilogue

On July 4, 1966, less than three months before she died, Lillian received the Charles S. Johnson Award, named in honor of the noted black social scientist and former president of Fisk University. Her acceptance speech, which she was too ill to deliver in person, was a kind of valedictory. She had always contended that her concern was not just race relations but the whole range of human relations, and in the speech she focused on the larger theme. Citing the evolutionary philosophy of Teilhard de Chardin, she argued that mankind was entering a "new age of human relations" in which the main task would be improving "the quality of our relationships with each other, with all men, with knowledge and art and God." That had been her own life's work, she declared. "What I have tried to do during these many years has been to give vision, to open up a wider path toward man's future: I have tried to arouse hope that the future holds a wondrous challenge for our children. It is not something to dread. It is something to prepare for by increasing our knowledge, polishing our intelligence, cultivating our love and compassion and humor and patience and fortitude and courage." The search for ways of improving human relations she termed "the big job of our age." "As one writer," she said, "I have tried, only to work toward this end."[1]

It was like Lillian to describe her life's work in expansive philosophical and literary terms, for she wanted above all to be recognized as a significant thinker and writer. Regrettably, her philosophical thinking was generally derivative and superficial and her literary effort unexceptional. Her primary significance lies in the role she played in the southern civil rights movement of the 1940s, 1950s, and 1960s. Long before other white southern liberals, she spoke out publicly against segregation and called for its immediate abolition. Even more important, unlike other critics of Jim Crow, she emphasized the harm it did to whites, not just to blacks. This was something she had learned from her own personal experience with all kinds of segregation—racial, sexual, and intellectual. As she once declared, she wrote from "the personal point of view of one who has experienced a hundred kinds of segregation, not merely race segregation." Unlike many other liberals she did not feel guilty about segregation and, significantly, did not try to persuade whites to abolish it by arousing guilt feelings in them. Emphasizing the harm segregation did to whites, she urged them to eliminate it in their own and their children's interest. "When the imaginations of white people are stirred, when they become aroused to the great injury being done to their own children, they will have a more profound motivation for changing our segregated way of life than simply that of sporadically doing a 'good deed' for the Negro," she wrote in the *New Republic* in 1945.[2] By "white people" she meant the intelligent, decent white southerners to whom she consistently directed her appeals. They were the ones she believed would act against segregation once they realized the harm it did to them as well as blacks. Like many American reformers, Lillian believed people only needed to be shown the way to act rightly. Her thinking on the race problem in the United States rested on a paradox: while emphasizing the role of irrational fears and anxieties in maintaining segregation, she nevertheless insisted that whites would abolish it out of a rational concern for their own interest and general welfare. Even the rise of massive resistance in the middle 1950s did not diminish her faith in the decency, reasonableness, and intelligence of middle- and upper-class whites in the South. Only in the 1960s did she abandon her essentially elitist, individualistic approach to the race problem when she endorsed nonviolent direct mass action by blacks to overturn segregation. Even then she overestimated the power of nonviolence to change whites' minds peaceably.

In her life as a whole, although she did not succeed in eliminating all the walls in her life, Lillian did open herself to a broader range of thought and experience than most white women of her generation. Molding her life out of the clay of southern culture and her own character, she validated her belief in the power of an individual to surmount the self-created or culturally sanctioned barriers that cut people off from other human beings, new ideas, and new experiences.

# Notes

## Prologue

1. Margaret Sullivan, "Lillian Smith: The Public Image and the Personal Vision," *Mad River Review*, II (Summer–Fall, 1967), 6.
2. Charles K. Piehl, "Telling About the South on Paper and Canvas," *Reviews in American History*, XII (December, 1984), 544. Three recent interpretations of Lillian's crusade against racism and segregation are Morton Sosna, *In Search of the Silent South: Southern Liberals and the Race Issue* (New York, 1977), Chap. 9; Richard H. King, *A Southern Renaissance: The Cultural Awakening of the American South, 1930–1955* (New York, 1980), Chap. 8; Fred Hobson, *Tell About the South: The Southern Rage to Explain* (Baton Rouge, 1983), 307–323. Sosna and, to a lesser extent, Hobson exaggerate Lillian's sense of guilt and the influence of southern evangelical religion on her thinking. King, on the other hand, emphasizes Freudianism to the exclusion of other important influences. Daniel Joseph Singal, *The War Within: From Victorian to Modernist Thought in the South, 1919–1945* (Chapel Hill, 1982), 374–75, treats Lillian's role in the development of Modernism in the South.
3. LS to Maxwell Geismar, January 1, 1961, in the Lillian Smith Collection, Special Collections, The University of Georgia Libraries, Athens.

## Chapter I

1. Unless otherwise noted, all quotations in this chapter are from unpublished autobiographical materials in Box 1 of the Lillian Smith Collection, Special Collections, The University of Georgia Libraries, Athens, Georgia, hereinafter cited as autob. mats., LS Coll. The materials consist of numerous publicity and information sheets prepared by LS for various book reviewers, interviewers, and writers.

The largest and most valuable item in the box is a manuscript of over one hundred pages containing autobiographical information and recollections prepared by LS in 1965 for her biographers, Louise Blackwell and Frances Clay.

2. Kathleen Atkinson Miller, "Out of the Chrysalis: Lillian Smith and the Transformation of the South" (Ph.D. dissertation, Emory University, 1984), 39. Miller offers a detailed and insightful discussion of Lillian's childhood and early family relationships, based in part on interviews with her sister, Esther Smith, and her girlhood friend in Jasper, Marjorie White.

3. LS to Sarah Patton Boyle, August 14, 1962, in LS Coll.; LS, *The Journey* (New York, 1954), 63.

4. Esther Smith to the author, October 31, 1985; LS to Sarah Patton Boyle, August 14, 1962, in LS Coll.; LS, *Journey*, 118.

5. LS to Robert Coles, September 27, 1961, in LS Coll.; LS, *Killers of the Dream* (Rev. ed.; New York, 1961), 85, 87, 89, 90, 91.

6. LS, *Killers*, 110–11.

7. LS, "Growing Into Freedom," *Common Ground*, IV (Autumn, 1943), 47, 49; LS to Sarah Patton Boyle, August 14, 1962, and to Rollo May, December 26, 1959, in LS Coll.

8. LS, *Killers*, 130–31; LS, "Growing Into Freedom," 48.

9. Miller, "Out of the Chrysalis," 60–61, and for an illuminating discussion of Lillian's early relationship with her mother, see also 55, 57–59; LS, *Killers*, 110.

10. LS to Elmo Ellis, February 24, 1965, in LS Coll.

11. LS to Wilma Dykeman Stokely, October 30, 1965, in LS Coll.

12. "Psychology Teaching Stressed at Lillian Smith's Girls' Camp," New York *Herald Tribune*, August 27, 1944, Sec. 2, p. 4. On Laurel Falls Camp, see also LS, "Summer Camps for Boys and Girls When the Children Come to Rabun County" in Andrew J. Ritchie (ed.), *Sketches of Rabun County History* (Clayton, Ga., 1948), 433; Rose Gladney, "The Liberating Institution: Lillian Smith and the Laurel Falls Camp," *Proceedings of the Southeastern American Studies Association* (1979), 33–39; Miller, "Out of the Chrysalis," Chap. 5.

13. LS to Robert Coles, September 28, 1961, and see also LS to Willa L. Currier, February 17, 1965, in LS Coll.

14. LS to Wilma Dykeman Stokely, February 24, 1965, in LS Coll. Arthur Raper, who worked with Lillian in the civil rights movement during the 1930s and 1940s, thought that her concern for blacks was a result of her empathizing with them. See Interview #3 with Arthur Raper, April 23, 1971, in Southern Oral History Program 4007, Southern Historical Collection, University of North Carolina Library, Chapel Hill.

## Chapter II

1. Autobiographical materials in Box 1 of the Lillian Smith Collection, Special Collections, The University of Georgia Libraries, Athens, Georgia, hereinafter cited as autob. mats., LS Coll.; LS and Paula Snelling, "Yes . . . we are southern," *South Today*, VII (Spring, 1943), 42–43.

2. *Pseudopodia*, I (Spring, 1936). (The early volumes of *Pseudopodia* and *North Georgia Review* had no printed page numbers.) Helen White and Redding Sugg,

Jr., have edited *From the Mountain* (Memphis, 1972), an anthology of selections from Lillian Smith's magazine. Since *South Today* is available in so few libraries, if an article has been reprinted in *From the Mountain,* I have cited the anthology (with magazine title and date in parentheses) rather than the original.

3. George Brown Tindall, *The Emergence of the New South, 1913–1945* (Baton Rouge, 1967), 580, 666.

4. *Pseudopodia,* I (Spring, 1936); LS, "Dope with Lime" (*North Georgia Review,* Spring, 1939), in *From the Mountain,* 12. *North Georgia Review* is hereinafter cited as *NGR.*

5. LS, "Dope with Lime" (*NGR,* Spring, 1939, and Spring, 1938), in *From the Mountain,* 12, 11; LS, "An Open Letter to Mr. Caldwell on Child Care," *Pseudopodia,* I (Summer, 1936); LS, "Book Buyers' Millennium," *NGR,* II (Winter, 1937–38).

6. LS, "Dope with Lime" (*NGR,* Spring, 1939), in *From the Mountain,* 13.

7. LS, "Dope with Lime," *NGR,* II (Summer, 1937); LS, "Dope with Lime" (*NGR,* Spring, 1937), in *From the Mountain,* 7.

8. LS, "Dope with Lime," *South Today,* VII (Autumn–Winter, 1942–43), 62; LS, "Dope with Lime" (*NGR,* Spring, 1939), in *From the Mountain,* 14.

9. Tindall, *Emergence of the New South,* 589; LS, "Comments for Maggie from L. S." [1964], typescript in autob. mats., LS Coll.

10. Autob. mats., LS Coll.

11. LS, *Christian Century* questionnaire [1962(?)], in LS Coll.; LS, "Dope with Lime," *NGR,* IV (Winter, 1939–40).

12. Richard H. King, *A Southern Renaissance: The Cultural Awakening of the American South, 1930–1955* (New York, 1980), 179; LS, "Wisdom Crieth in the Streets" (*NGR,* Fall, 1937), in *From the Mountain,* 40–46.

13. LS, "From Lack of Understanding," *Pseudopodia,* I (Fall, 1936); LS, "Regional Presses," *NGR,* II (Spring, 1937); LS, "Dope with Lime," *NGR,* II (Fall, 1937).

14. Autob. mats., LS Coll.

15. *Ibid.*

16. LS, "So You're Seeing the South" (*NGR,* Winter, 1939–40), in *From the Mountain,* 84–90.

17. LS and Paula Snelling, "Across the South Today," *NGR,* VI (Winter, 1941), 58–59, 66–67, 100.

18. *Ibid.,* 104–105.

19. *Ibid.,* 99.

20. LS, "He That Is Without Sin," *NGR,* II (Winter, 1937–38); LS, "Dope with Lime," *NGR,* III (Spring, 1938), IV (Spring, 1939), V (Summer, 1940), and V (Winter, 1940–41).

21. LS, "Dope with Lime," *NGR,* V (Spring, 1940), and V (Summer, 1940); LS and Paula Snelling, "Symposium on War" (*NGR,* Autumn, 1939), in *From the Mountain,* 333, 335.

22. LS, "He That Is Without Sin"; LS, "'Mr. Lafayette, Heah We Is—'" (*NGR,* Spring, 1939), in *From the Mountain,* 331–33; LS, "Dope with Lime," *NGR,* V (Winter, 1940–41).

23. LS, "Wanted: Lessons in Hate," *NGR,* III (Fall–Winter, 1938–39); LS, "In Defense of Life," *NGR,* V (Summer, 1940); LS, "'Mr. Lafayette, Heah We Is—'" in *From the Mountain,* 331–33.

24. LS, "Winning the World with Democracy," *South Today*, VII (Spring, 1942), 7–9.
25. *Ibid.*, 8; LS, "Portrait of the Deep South Speaking to Negroes on Morale" (*South Today*, Spring, 1942), in *From the Mountain*, 110–15.
26. Richard M. Dalfiume, "The 'Forgotten Years' of the Negro Revolution," *Journal of American History*, LV (June, 1968), 93; John Morton Blum, *V Was for Victory: Politics and American Culture During World War II* (New York, 1976), 208.

## Chapter III

1. Autobiographical materials in Box 1 of the Lillian Smith Collection, Special Collections, The University of Georgia Libraries, Athens, Georgia, hereinafter cited as autob. mats., LS Coll. For an idea of Lillian's discussions of race relations with Laurel Falls campers, see LS, "Behind the Drums" (*North Georgia Review*, Fall, 1939), in Helen White and Redding Sugg, Jr. (eds.), *From the Mountain* (Memphis, 1972), 69–83. *North Georgia Review* is hereinafter cited as *NGR*.
2. LS, "Growing Into Freedom," *Common Ground*, IV (Autumn, 1943), 50–51.
3. *Ibid.*, 51.
4. Autob. mats., LS Coll.
5. *Ibid.*
6. Autob. mats., LS Coll.; H. L. Mitchell, *Mean Things Happening in This Land* (Montclair, N.J., 1979), 188. Harry Golden, editor of the *Carolina Israelite*, wrote: "If anyone can be said to have 'discovered' the Negro writers of our country it was [Lillian Smith and Paula Snelling] in their magazine, *South Today*. Until they put this magazine together, no Southern newspaper had ever reviewed a book by a Negro novelist, no Negro poet had ever lectured to a local writing group, no professor or clergyman had ever discussed the meaning of Negro writing from his desk or pulpit" (*Mr. Kennedy and the Negroes* [Cleveland, 1964], 20–21).
7. Autob. mats., LS Coll.; LS, "A Southerner Talking," Chicago *Defender*, November 13, 1948.
8. Autob. mats., LS Coll.; Charles G. Bolté to the author, March 17, 1981.
9. Autob. mats., LS to Dear Mrs. . . . [September, 1942], in LS Coll. Arthur Raper thought that the first time Negroes visited Old Screamer as guests was when he brought Ira De A. Reid and Hale Woodruff and their wives to the mountain. Interview #3 with Arthur Raper, April 23, 1971, in Southern Oral History Program 4007, Southern Historical Collection, University of North Carolina Library, Chapel Hill.
10. LS, "Are We Not All Confused?" (*South Today*, Spring, 1942), in *From the Mountain*, 103.
11. Richard M. Dalfiume, "The 'Forgotten Years' of the Negro Revolution," *Journal of American History*, LV (June, 1968), 90–106; George Brown Tindall, *The Emergence of the New South, 1913–1945* (Baton Rouge, 1967), 711–16; John Thomas Kneebone, "Race, Reform, and History: Southern Liberal Journalists, 1920–1940" (Ph.D. dissertation, University of Virginia, 1981), 553–54; Morton Sosna, *In Search of the Silent South: Southern Liberals and the Race Issue* (New York, 1977), 106–107; LS to Eleanor Roosevelt, April 7, 1942, in Eleanor Roosevelt Collection, Franklin D. Roosevelt Library, Hyde Park, New York.
12. LS to Walter White, February 14 and 15, 1942, in NAACP Records, Group II, Se-

ries A, Library of Congress, Washington, D.C. See also LS to White, January 17, 1943, in NAACP Records.

13. LS, "Are We Not All Confused?" in *From the Mountain*, 103–109.

14. LS to Eleanor Roosevelt, April 7, 1942, in Eleanor Roosevelt Collection; Sosna, *In Search of the Silent South*, 107–111, 131; Tindall, *Emergence of the New South*, 718; Dalfiume, "The 'Forgotten Years' of the Negro Revolution," 101. For Virginius Dabney's response to Lillian's editorial, see Virginius Dabney to LS, August 1 and 20, 1942, in LS Coll.

15. LS, "Are We Not All Confused?" in *From the Mountain*, 103–106.

16. *Ibid.*, 107.

17. LS, "Two Men and a Bargain: A Parable of the Solid South," *South Today*, VII (Spring, 1943), 6–10. This was reprinted in the Winter, 1944–1945, issue of *South Today* and also appears in slightly different form in LS, *Killers of the Dream* (New York, 1949), Pt. 3.

18. W. E. Burghardt Du Bois, *Black Reconstruction: An Essay toward a History of the Part Which Black Folk Played in the Attempt to Reconstruct Democracy in America, 1860–1880* (New York, 1935); C. Vann Woodward, *Tom Watson, Agrarian Rebel* (New York, 1938); W. J. Cash, *The Mind of the South* (New York, 1941); H. C. Nixon, *Forty Acres and Steel Mules* (Chapel Hill, 1938); John Dollard, *Caste and Class in a Southern Town* (New Haven, 1937); Arthur F. Raper and Ira De A. Reid, *Sharecroppers All* (Chapel Hill, 1941).

19. LS, "Two Men and a Bargain," 13; LS, "Democracy Was Not a Candidate," *Common Ground*, III (Winter, 1943), 7–8; [LS], "Buying a New World with Old Confederate Bills," *South Today*, VII (Autumn–Winter, 1942–43), 17–18.

20. [LS], "Buying a New World," 22.

21. "Author of 'Strange Fruit' Sees the Race Question as a Problem Above Politics," New York *Herald Tribune*, October 22, 1944, Sec. 8, p. 20; LS, "Personal History of 'Strange Fruit': A Statement of Purposes and Intentions," *Saturday Review of Literature*, February 17, 1945, p. 10.

22. LS, "Putting Away Childish Things" (*South Today*, Spring–Summer, 1944), in *From the Mountain*, 137; LS, "Growing Into Freedom," 51.

23. LS, "A Letter from Lillian Smith Addressed to Members of the Blue Ridge Conference 1944," in LS Coll.; LS, "Putting Away Childish Things," in *From the Mountain*, 134; LS, "Addressed to White Liberals," *New Republic*, September 18, 1944, p. 332; [LS], "Addressed to Intelligent White Southerners: 'There Are Things to Do'" (*South Today*, Autumn–Winter, 1942–43), in *From the Mountain*, 121; Karl Menninger, *Love Against Hate* (New York, 1942), 129; LS, "Humans in Bondage," *Social Action* (February 15, 1944), 17–19.

24. [LS], "Addressed to Intelligent White Southerners," in *From the Mountain*, 118–28.

25. *Ibid.*, 120; [LS], "Buying a New World," 14. Organizations based in the South that Lillian recommended included the Southern Workers Defense League, the Southeastern Cooperative League, the Commission on Interracial Cooperation, the Southern Conference for Human Welfare, the Association of Southern Women for the Prevention of Lynching, and the Fellowship of Southern Churchmen. She also recommended the following national organizations: American Civil Liberties Union, Fellowship of Reconciliation, Federal Council of Churches, National Urban League, the NAACP, YWCA, and YMCA.

26. Sosna, *In Search of the Silent South*, 88–104, 140–45; Tindall, *Emergence of the New South*, 636–41; Thomas A. Krueger, *And Promises to Keep: The Southern Conference for Human Welfare, 1938–1948* (Nashville, 1967), 14, 29–31, 42, 54, 96, and *passim*.

27. LS, "Southern Conference?" (*NGR*, Spring, 1940), in *From the Mountain*, 91; LS to James Dombrowski, September 10, 1942, in Southern Conference for Human Welfare Records, Hollis Burke Frissell Library, Tuskegee Institute, Tuskegee, Ala., hereinafter cited as SCHW Records.

28. LS to James Dombrowski, May 7, 1945, in SCHW Records.

29. [LS], "Crossing Over Jordan Into Democracy," *South Today*, VII (Spring, 1942), 46, 48–49, 50; LS to James Dombrowski, May 7, 1945, in SCHW Records.

30. LS to James Dombrowski, May 7, 1945, and to Clark Foreman, May 9, 1945, in SCHW Records; Virginia Durr to the author, September 3 and 10, 1985; Myles Horton to the author, September 29, 1985; Krueger, *And Promises to Keep*, 67, 75, 82, 89–92. See also Thomas Krueger to LS, August 12, 1963, in LS Coll.; LS to the Board Members of the SCHW, May 18, 1945, in Julius Rosenwald Fund Archives, 1917–1948, Microfilm Edition, Amistad Research Center, New Orleans, Louisiana.

31. [LS], "Crossing Over Jordan Into Democracy," *South Today*, 48–49; LS to James Dombrowski, June 16, 1942, in SCHW Records.

32. Clark Foreman, "The Decade of Hope," *Phylon*, XII (Second Quarter, 1951), 143; Krueger, *And Promises to Keep*, 96–99; LS to James Dombrowski, October 28, 1942 (two letters), and May 7, 1945, in SCHW Records.

33. LS to Clark Foreman, May 9, 1945, and to James Dombrowski, May 7 and May 9, 1945, in SCHW Records. See also LS to the Board Members of the SCHW, May 18, 1945, in Julius Rosenwald Fund Archives, Microfilm Edition.

34. LS to the Board Members of the SCHW, May 18, 1945, in Julius Rosenwald Fund Archives, Microfilm Edition.

35. Krueger, *And Promises to Keep*, 29, 58, 115, 121, 148; LS to Clark Foreman, May 9, 1945, in SCHW Records. See also LS to James Dombrowski, June 23, 1944, in SCHW Records.

36. Tindall, *Emergence of the New South*, 718ff; Sosna, *In Search of the Silent South*, 118ff; Margaret Anderson to LS, January 27, 1944, in LS Coll.; LS, "Southern Defensive—II," *Common Ground*, IV (Spring, 1944), 43, 44, 45.

37. LS to Dr. Guy B. Johnson, June 12, 1944, in Julius Rosenwald Fund Archives, Microfilm Edition; LS, "Addressed to White Liberals," 331–33.

38. LS to Dr. Guy B. Johnson, June 12, 1944, in Julius Rosenwald Fund Archives, Microfilm Edition. See also LS, "Humans in Bondage," 8, 12, 27; LS, "Putting Away Childish Things," in *From the Mountain*, 133, 137.

39. I use the term *southern liberals* to refer to such persons as Jessie Daniel Ames, Will Alexander, Howard Odum, Virginius Dabney, Mark Ethridge, Jonathan Daniels, and Frank Graham. They worked in such organizations as the Commission on Interracial Cooperation and its successor, the Southern Regional Council; the Association of Southern Women for the Prevention of Lynching; and the Southern Policy Association. John B. Kirby, *Black Americans in the Roosevelt Era: Liberalism and Race* (Knoxville, 1980), 40, 71, 93, 232; Sosna, *In Search of the Silent South*, 172; Tindall, *Emergence of the New South*, 632–33; Kneebone, "Race, Reform, and History," *passim*.

40. [LS], "Buying a New World with Old Confederate Bills," 23, 25, 26–27.
41. Anthony P. Dunbar, *Against the Grain: Southern Radicals and Prophets, 1929–1959* (Charlottesville, 1981), 74. For evidence of Lillian's support of the STFU, see LS to Mr. Butler, December 20, 1939, and April 1, 1941, in Southern Tenant Farmers Union Papers, Microfilm Edition, Southern Historical Collection, University of North Carolina Library, Chapel Hill.
42. Autob. mats., LS Coll.; LS to Clark Foreman, May 9, 1945, in SCHW Records.
43. Rayford W. Logan (ed.), *What the Negro Wants* (Chapel Hill, 1944), 14; Kirby, *Black Americans in the Roosevelt Era*, 220, 232–35.
44. Gunnar Myrdal, *An American Dilemma: The Negro Problem and Modern Democracy* (New York, 1944); LS, "Growing Into Freedom," 51; LS, "Putting Away Childish Things," in *From the Mountain*, 137; LS to Editors of *PM*, January 16, 1943, copy enclosed in letter to Walter White, January 17, 1943, in NAACP Records, Group II, Series A. Lillian elaborated on her quarrel with the Myrdal book, comparing it unfavorably with Gilberto Freyre's *The Masters and the Slaves*, in her newspaper column, "A Southerner Talking," Chicago *Defender*, November 27, 1948.

## Chapter IV

1. LS, "Personal History of 'Strange Fruit': A Statement of Purposes and Intentions," *Saturday Review of Literature*, February 17, 1945, p. 10; "Miss Smith: Speaking from New York," *Northwestern University of the Air: Of Men and Books*, March 4, 1944, pp. 5–6.
2. LS, "A Trembling Earth," in Michelle Cliff (ed.), *The Winner Names the Age: A Collection of Writings by Lillian Smith* (New York, 1978), 123; LS to Lawrence Kubie, June 2, 1955, in the Lillian Smith Collection, Special Collections, The University of Georgia Libraries, Athens, Georgia.
3. LS to Walter White, February 14, 1942, in NAACP Records, Group II, Series A, Library of Congress, Washington, D.C.; LS, *Strange Fruit* (New York, 1944), 121, 49, 51.
4. LS, *Strange Fruit*, 176.
5. *Ibid.*, 30, 81, 82, 104–105, 110, 274.
6. *Lillian Smith answers some questions about Strange Fruit* [n.p., 1944], LS Coll.
7. Autobiographical materials in Box 1, LS Coll., hereinafter cited as autob. mats., LS Coll.; LS to Walter White, February 14, 1942, in NAACP Records, Group II, Series A; LS to Mr. Muller, October 17, 1959, in LS Coll.; LS and Paula Snelling, "Do You Know Your South?" *North Georgia Review*, VI (Winter, 1941), 100; LS, "Two Men and a Bargain: A Parable of the Solid South," *South Today*, VII (Spring, 1943), 13, 14.
8. Autob. mats., *Lillian Smith answers some questions about Strange Fruit*, both in LS Coll.
9. Edmund Wilson, "Briefly Noted," *New Yorker*, March 4, 1944, p. 81; "Fruit of the South," *Newsweek*, March 20, 1944, p. 77; H[enry] S[eidel] C[anby], "'Strange Fruit,'" *Saturday Review of Literature*, April 1, 1944, p. 14; Struthers Burt, "The Making of a New South," *Saturday Review of Literature*, March 11, 1944, p. 10; Edward Weeks, "The Atlantic Bookshelf," *Atlantic Monthly*, CLXXIII (May, 1944), 127; Richard H. Rovere, "The Rise of Adolf Hitler," *Common Sense*, XIII (March, 1944), 112; Orville Prescott, "Outstanding Novels," *Yale Review*, XXXIII (Spring,

1944), x; Florence Haxton Bullock, "Indian, Negro and White, Americans All," *New York Herald Tribune Weekly Book Review*, March 5, 1944, p. 1; J. Donald Adams, "Speaking of Books," *New York Times Book Review*, May 28, 1944, p. 2; Malcolm Cowley, "Southways," *New Republic*, March 6, 1944, p. 322; Diana Trilling, "Fiction in Review," *Nation*, CLVIII (March 18, 1944), 342.

10. Trilling, "Fiction in Review," 342.

11. William Du Bois, "Searing Novel of the South," *New York Times Book Review*, March 5, 1944, pp. 1, 20; Theophilus Lewis, "Shaking the Magnolias," *Crisis*, LI (May, 1944), 170; Lula Jones Garrett, "'Strange Fruit' Fine Foil for White Supremacy Lore," Baltimore *Afro-American*, March 18, 1944, p. 11; "People Who Read and Write," *New York Times Book Review*, August 5, 1945, p. 18.

12. Myra Page, "Southern Tragedy," *New Masses*, LI (May 30, 1944), 24; Cowley, "Southways," 320; Mike Gold, "Change the World," *Daily Worker*, May 29, 1944, p. 7.

13. Gwen Davenport, "Two-Way Traffic to Colored Town," Louisville *Courier-Journal*, March 12, 1944, Sec. 3, p. 8.

14. "Former Macon Woman Author of New Race Problem Novel," Macon *Telegraph*, March 1, 1944, p. 5; Marian Sims, "Georgia Novel Evokes Praise and Discussion," Atlanta *Journal*, February 27, 1944, Sec. C, p. 8; "Rosenwald Fund Under Embree Now Bearing 'Strange Fruit'," Hapeville (Ga.) *Statesman*, May 18, 1944, p. 1; Anna Greene Smith, "Strange Fruit," *Social Forces*, XXIII (October, 1944), 113–15.

15. "Feverish Fascination," *Time*, March 20, 1944, p. 99; advertisement in *New York Times Book Review*, April 30, 1944, p. 22; "The Best Selling Books, Here and Elsewhere," *New York Times Book Review*, May 14, 1944, p. 21.

16. New York *Times*, March 21, 1944, p. 17, April 5, 1944, p. 21, April 7, 1944, p. 21, April 27, 1944, p. 21, April 6, 1944, p. 21; autob. mats., LS Coll. In September, 1945, the Massachusetts Supreme Court upheld Isenstadt's conviction, declaring that *Strange Fruit* was "obscene, indecent and impure" and contained material that "would tend to promote lascivious thoughts and to arouse lustful desire in the minds of substantial numbers of the public into whose hands [it was] . . . likely to fall" (New York *Times*, September 18, 1945, p. 21).

17. New York *Times*, May 16, 1944, p. 1, May 17, 1944, p. 21; autob. mats., LS Coll.; Louise Blackwell and Frances Clay, *Lillian Smith* (New York, 1971), 37.

18. Autob. mats., LS Coll.

19. *Ibid.*

20. *Ibid.*; Blackwell and Clay, *Lillian Smith*, 56–57.

21. New York *Times*, October 18, 1945, p. 25; autob. mats., LS Coll.; "Strange Fruit," *New York Theatre Critics' Reviews*, December 3, 1945, pp. 82–85.

22. Autob. mats., LS Coll.

23. LS, "Personal History of 'Strange Fruit,'" 9; autob. mats., LS Coll.; Charles G. Bolté to the author, March 17, 1981.

24. LS, "Personal History of 'Strange Fruit,'" 9.

25. *Ibid.*; Walter White to LS, November 7, 1945, in NAACP Records, Group II, Series A; autob. mats., LS Coll. In his autobiography, *A Man Called White* (New York, 1948), 338–39, White took a much more positive view of *Strange Fruit* and Jane's role in it.

26. LS, "Personal History of 'Strange Fruit,'" 9; autob. mats., LS Coll.; Mike Gold, "Change the World," *Daily Worker*, May 15, 1944, p. 7; Samuel Sillen, "Books and

People: Comstockery in Boston," *New Masses*, LI (May 9, 1944), 24–25; Mike Gold, "Change the World," *Daily Worker*, May 29, 1944, p. 7; Page, "Southern Tragedy," 23–25.

27. Autob. mats., LS Coll.

28. *Ibid.*; John Chapman, "'Strange Fruit' Splendidly Staged, Honestly Written—But Episodic," New York *Daily News*, November 30, 1945, and Louis Kronenberger, "Less Power Than Purpose," *PM*, November 30, 1945, both reprinted in "Strange Fruit," *New York Theatre Critics' Reviews*, December 3, 1945, pp. 82, 83; Stark Young, "Strange Fruit, Etc.," *New Republic*, December 17, 1945, p. 839; Samuel Sillen, "Lillian Smith's 'Strange Fruit' Proves Disappointing as Play," *Daily Worker*, December 5, 1945, p. 11; Eugene Gordon, "'Strange Fruit' Worth Seeing Despite Weakness," *Daily Worker*, January 12, 1946, p. 11; Samuel Sillen, "'Strange Fruit' Publicist Offers Robeson's View," *Daily Worker*, December 15, 1945, p. 11.

29. Autob. mats., LS Coll.

## Chapter V

1. *New York Times Book Review*, March 12, 1944, p. 14; Helen White and Redding Sugg, Jr. (eds.), *From the Mountain* (Memphis, 1972), xi; New Yotk *Times*, February 7, 1943, p. 48.

2. Autobiographical materials in Box 1 of the Lillian Smith Collection, Special Collections, The University of Georgia Libraries, Athens, Georgia, hereinafter cited as autob. mats., LS Coll.; New York *Times*, March 7, 1945, p. 19, April 20, 1944, p. 17, March 1, 1945, p. 23, October 27, 1944, p. 22L, June 18, 1944, p. 28; Charles Bolté to the author, March 17, 1981; Irwin Klibaner, "The Travail of Southern Radicals: The Southern Conference Educational Fund, 1046–1076," *Journal of Southern History*, XLIX (May, 1983), 180; LS to Mr. Fleischman, May 9, 1946, in Socialist Party of America Papers—National Office Correspondence, William R. Perkins Library, Duke University, Durham, N.C.; Atlanta *Journal* clipping [October, 1944], in Margaret Mitchell Papers, Special Collections, The University of Georgia Libraries, Athens.

3. LS, "We Must Stop Mob Violence in America," *ADA World*, I (June 18, 1947), 1–2; LS, "Licking Scars an Old Southern Custom," *ADA World*, II (February 19, 1948), 2; LS, "Our Worst Luxury Tax," *ADA World*, II (March 31, 1948), 2; "Poll Tax Riddance Up to Congress: Lillian Smith," *ADA World*, II (March 31, 1948), 1, 4; LS to Mr. Hedrich, June 20, 1947, John F. P. Tucker to LS, July 23, 1947, LS to James Loeb, Jr., February 6, 1950, James Loeb, Jr., to LS, February 9, 1950, George P. Brockway to James Loeb, Jr., February 15, 1950, all in Americans for Democratic Action Papers, Microfilm Edition, State Historical Society of Wisconsin, Madison.

4. LS, "Building Christian Fellowship," *Methodist Woman*, V (February, 1945), 174–77, 182; LS, "What Segregation Does to Our Children," *Child Study*, XXII (Spring, 1945), 71–72, 90; "Author of 'Strange Fruit' Sees the Race Question as a Problem Above Politics," New York *Herald Tribune*, October 22, 1944, Sec. 8, p. 20.

5. LS, "Addressed to White Liberals," *New Republic*, September 18, 1944, pp. 332–33; LS, "How to Work for Racial Equality," *New Republic*, July 2, 1945, pp. 23–24.

6. LS, "How to Work for Racial Equality," *New Republic*, July 2, 1945, p. 24; New York *Times*, April 20, 1944, p. 17.

7. LS, "Burning Down Georgia's Back Porch," *Common Ground*, II (Winter, 1942), 69–72; LS, "It's Growing Time in Georgia," *Nation* CLXIII (July 13, 1946), 34–36.

8. LS, "Democracy Was Not a Candidate," *Common Ground*, III (Winter, 1943), 7, 10.

9. LS, "Pay Day in Georgia," *Nation*, CLXIV (February 1, 1947), 118–19.

10. LS to Edwin Embree, February 5, 1948, in Julius Rosenwald Fund Archives, 1917–1948, Microfilm Edition, Amistad Research Center, New Orleans, La.; Lillian Smith interview, December 8, 1943, in Arthur Raper Papers, Southern Historical Collection, University of North Carolina Library, Chapel Hill. Lillian had also been involved in Frank's campaign of 1942–43. This was at the same time that the Clayton and Atlanta postmasters were holding up the second-class mailing permit for the magazine and there was talk of an investigation of *South Today* and its editors by the Georgia legislature. Lillian wanted to avoid hurting Frank's political career. "He has done such wonderful things . . . that it breaks my heart to get him messed up in my affairs," she wrote James Dombrowski. So she was trying to prevent an investigation from taking place. But, she declared, if it couldn't be prevented, she planned "to make the most possible of it both for the magazine's sake and for the sake of democracy." She outlined her strategy at length:

> You see it can be made into an unusually good test case. In the first place it will be the first time that a well bred white southern "lady" has been investigated by the legislature. In the second place when they begin to ask me about my racial beliefs I shall not back down. . . . I shall give them straight full answers and unequivocal ones, telling them that I believe in full political, economic, educational, health, and social democratic rights for all people of the world including the Georgia Negro. That will be a new experience in Georgia and fairly new for the entire South. . . . The Monkey Trial killed out fundamentalism in the upper classes. This kind of trial might kill out racial prejudice in the upper classes also. However that may be, I think it would do the southern Negro good—help the whole group's morale—for a white southern woman to maintain firmly and publicly that he should have the same rights in every way that whites have.

As it turned out, the Georgia legislature did not investigate the magazine and Frank was reelected by a substantial majority of votes. LS to James Dombrowski, January 29, 1943, in Southern Conference for Human Welfare Records, Hollis Burke Frissell Library, Tuskegee Institute, Tuskegee, Ala. (See also *From the Mountain*, xxii–xxiii; LS to Walter White, January 17, 1943, in NAACP Records, Group II, Series A, Library of Congress, Washington, D.C.; Albert Deutsch, "Lillian Smith of Deep South Urges Negro-White Amity," *PM*, March 13, 1944, p. 9).

11. LS, "Life with a Best-Seller," *Atlanta Journal Magazine*, January 14, 1945, p. 6.

12. LS to Edwin Embree, February 5, 1948, in Julius Rosenwald Fund Archives.

13. Robert J. Donovan, *Conflict and Crisis: The Presidency of Harry S Truman, 1945–1948* (New York, 1977), 352–53.

14. *Ibid.*, 353–54; Atlanta *Constitution*, March 11, 1948, p. 5, March 13, 1948, p. 4, March 3, 1948, p. 1; Kenneth Coleman (ed.), *A History of Georgia* (Athens, Ga., 1977), 392.

15. "Southern Liberalism," New York *Times*, April 4, 1948, Sec. 4, p. 8.
16. *Ibid.*
17. *Ibid.*
18. LS, "A Southerner Talking," Chicago *Defender*, October 16, 1948.
19. *Ibid.*, October 23, 1948.
20. *Ibid.*, December 11, 1948, August 20, 1949.
21. *Ibid.*, December 25, 1948, April 2, 1949, August 13, 1949.
22. *Ibid.*, December 25, 1948, March 26, 1949.
23. *Congressional Record*, 81st Cong., 1st Sess., Vol. XCV, Pt. 2, pp. 2670, 2672.
24. LS, "A Southerner Talking," Chicago *Defender*, April 16, 1949, February 5, 1949.
25. *Ibid.*, March 12, 1949, July 9, 1949.
26. *Ibid.*, August 6, 1949.
27. *Ibid.*, February 5, 1949, October 16, 1948, June 25, 1949, February 12, 1949.
28. *Ibid.*, October 16, 1948, February 12, 1949.
29. *Ibid.*, February 12, 1949, June 18, 1949.
30. *Ibid.*, April 23, 1949, June 11, 1949, July 9, 1949.
31. *Ibid.*, June 18, 1949.
32. Autob. mats., LS Coll.
33. LS, *Killers of the Dream* (New York, 1949), 9–11.
34. LS, *Killers*, 17.
35. *Ibid.*, 88, 18–20.
36. *Ibid.*, 111.
37. *Ibid.*, 120, 121, 124, 130.
38. LS, "Why I Wrote 'Killers of the Dream,'" *New York Herald Tribune Weekly Book Review*, July 1, 1949, Sec. 7, p. 2. See also Richard H. King, *A Southern Renaissance: The Cultural Awakening of the American South, 1930–1955* (New York, 1980), 180–84.
39. LS, *Killers*, 234, 236, 240, 241, 244.
40. *Ibid.*, 227, 256.
41. LS, "Why I Wrote 'Killers of the Dream,'" 2.
42. Autob. mats., LS Coll.; Daniel Joseph Singal, *The War Within: From Victorian to Modernist Thought in the South, 1919–1945* (Chapel Hill, 1982), 374.
43. Homer P. Rainey, "The Mind of the South," *Saturday Review of Literature*, October 22, 1949, p. 21; Marguerite Pace Corcoran, "Killers of the Dream," *Catholic World*, CLXX (February, 1950), 399; Vincent Sheean, "Out of the Tempestuous, Impassioned Heart of the South," *New York Herald Tribune Weekly Book Review*, October 23, 1949, p. 1; R.E.C., "Hard Facts and Harder Truths," *Phylon*, XI (First Quarter, 1950), 81; "Sex, sin, and segregation," *Atlantic Monthly*, CLXXXIV (December, 1949), 96; William Pfaff, "Killers of the Dream," *Commonweal*, LI (December 16, 1949), 299; Bucklin Moon, "A Passionate Outcry for Brotherhood," *New York Times Book Review*, October 23, 1949, p. 3.
44. Sheean, "Out of the Tempestuous, Impassioned Heart of the South," 1; "Tract from the South," *Time*, October 31, 1949, pp. 84, 86.
45. Nina Ridenour, "Killers of the Dream," *Survey*, LXXXV (November, 1949), 613; Ellsworth Faris, "Sin, Sex and Segregation," *Christian Century*, LXVI (December 7, 1949), 1457. In a 1965 interview with Margaret Long, Lillian objected to *Killers* being called a Freudian interpretation. She said she admired Freud as a great mind, but thought that Jung had provided insight into the collective uncon-

scious, where Freud had failed. Anyway, she said, "Killers of the Dream is *my* knowledge and understanding of the South, the way I lived and studied and experienced and know the South to be. If it happened to coincide with some of Freud's theories, well, so it did" (Margaret Long, "Lillian Smith: A Match for Old Screamer," *Progressive*, XXIX [February, 1965], 37).

46. Tarver quoted in Redding S. Sugg, Jr., "Lillian Smith: A Prophecy of Strange Fruit," *Atlanta*, IX (February, 1970), 42; Ralph McGill, "Miss Smith and Freud," Atlanta *Constitution*, November 24, 1949, p. 18-B.

47. Harold Rosenberg, "The Orgamerican Phantasy," in *The Tradition of the New* (New York, 1961), 275, 278.

48. New York *Times*, December 31, 1949, p. 15; Louise Blackwell and Frances Clay, *Lillian Smith* (New York, 1971), 22–23.

49. George P. Brockway to the author, July 26, 1983; autob. mats., LS Coll.; John K. Hutchens, "On an Author: Lillian Smith," *New York Herald Tribune Weekly Book Review*, October 30, 1949, p. 2.

## Chapter VI

1. LS to Eleanor Roosevelt, July 11, 1954, in Eleanor Roosevelt Collection, Franklin D. Roosevelt Library, Hyde Park, N.Y.; LS, *The Journey* (New York, 1954), 7.

2. Anthony West, "Briefly Noted," *New Yorker*, May 1, 1954, p. 123.

3. LS, *Journey*, 6, 8.

4. *Ibid.*, 50–51, 46, 54; "Do You Know Your South?" *North Georgia Review*, VI (Winter, 1941), 100; LS, *Killers of the Dream* (New York, 1949), 99.

5. LS to Donald Seawell, November 14, 1959, in the Lillian Smith Collection, Special Collections, The University of Georgia Libraries, Athens, Georgia; LS, *Journey*, 51, 253, 256; autobiographical materials in Box 1 of the LS Coll., hereinafter cited as autob. mats., LS Coll.; *Christian Century* questionnaire [1962(?)], in LS Coll.; West, "Briefly Noted," 123.

6. LS, *Journey*, 255, 256.

7. LS to Mary Squire Abbot, August 13, 1955, in LS Coll.; Eleanor Roosevelt to LS, June 24, 1954, July 24, 1954, LS to Eleanor Roosevelt, July 11, 1954, in Eleanor Roosevelt Collection; LS to Dr. Horace Kallen, February 24, 1954, and to Keith Jennison, May 25, 1955, in LS Coll.

8. Frances Witherspoon, "The Pilgrimage of Lillian Smith," *New York Herald Tribune Weekly Book Review*, April 18, 1954, p. 1; Mary Stack McNiff, "The Journey," *America*, June 5, 1954, p. 281; Lucy Freeman, "Tears, Laughter, Understanding in 'The Journey,'" Chicago *Sun-Times*, April 18, 1954, Sec. 2, p. 4; Charles J. Rolo, "The Proper Study of Mankind," *Atlantic Monthly*, CXCIII (May, 1954), 80; Gerold Frank, "Lillian Smith Reaffirms Faith in Goodness of Man," Philadelphia *Inquirer*, April 18, 1954, Sec. SO, p. 10.

9. LS to Denver Lindley, December 10, 1955, in LS Coll.

10. *Ibid.*

11. LS to Eleanor Roosevelt, July 11, 1954, in Eleanor Roosevelt Collection.

12. Autob. mats., LS Coll.; LS, "'The Walls of Segregation Are Crumbling,'" *New York Times Magazine*, July 15, 1951, pp. 9, 31–32. The *New York Times Magazine* article was originally delivered as the commencement address at Kentucky State

College, Frankfort, June 5, 1951, and later published as "Ten Years From Today," *Vital Speeches*, XVII (August 15, 1951), 669–72.

13. LS, "The South as It Is—the Ideas That Stir Its People," *New York Times Book Review*, February 5, 1950, p. 3.

14. *Ibid.*; LS, "The South Reacts to Segregation," *New Leader*, September 3, 1951, pp. 4–5.

15. LS, "'The Walls of Segregation Are Crumbling,'" 31–32; LS, "The South Reacts to Segregation," 5.

16. LS, "Ten Years From Today," 671–72.

17. LS, "The South Reacts to Segregation," 3, 4.

18. *Ibid.*, 3; LS, "The Unanswered Question," *Confluence*, III (March, 1954), 108–10. In the *Confluence* article Lillian for the first time used the word *integration*, apparently as a synonym for *desegregation*. In later writings she continued to use the two words interchangeably, though she seemed to prefer the more precise *desegregation*. "Integration," she observed in 1965, "appeared on the scene very late: it actually was a word reporters made popular—not those of us who really knew about these matters. To me, it is semantically a mean, tricky word that makes little sense racially" ["In answer to questions from Joan Titus" ([July, 1965]), typescript in autob. mats., LS Coll.].

19. LS to the Editors, Atlanta *Constitution* [May 31, 1954], in LS Coll.

20. LS to the Editors, New York *Times*, June 6, 1954, Sec. 4, p. 10; LS to Halleck Hoffman, July 28, 1955, in LS Coll.; LS to Eleanor Roosevelt, July 11, 1954, in Eleanor Roosevelt Collection; LS to Jeffrey E. Fuller, [June, 1954(?)], in LS Coll.

21. Paul Bixler to LS, September 10, 1954, LS to Paul Bixler, September 13, 1954, in LS Coll.

22. LS to Mrs. Dudley Moore, June 6, 1954, to Frank Spencer, June 29, 1955, in LS Coll.

23. LS to Eleanor Roosevelt, September 30, 1954, in Eleanor Roosevelt Collection.

24. LS to Mrs. Dudley Moore, June 6, 1954, in LS Coll.

25. LS to Dr. Lawrence Kubie, June 2, 1955, to William B. Hart, August 24, 1954, to Keith Jennison, June 27, 1954, in LS Coll.

26. LS to Dr. Lawrence Kubie, June 2, 1955, autob. mats., LS Coll.

27. LS, *Now Is the Time* (New York, 1955), 21, 26, 11.

28. *Ibid.*, 71, 68–69.

29. LS to Dr. Lawrence Kubie, June 2, 1955, in LS Coll.

30. LS, *Now Is the Time*, 54, and see also 116–17. On the Eastland investigation, see Irwin Klibaner, "The Southern Conference Educational Fund: A History" (Ph.D. dissertation, University of Wisconsin, 1971), 136–59; John A. Salmond, *A Southern Rebel: The Life and Times of Aubrey Willis Williams, 1890–1965* (Chapel Hill, 1983), 229–41.

31. LS, *Now Is the Time*, 20, 75, 94–95, 15; LS to Keith Jennison, June 27, 1954, in LS Coll.

32. LS to Keith Jennison, June 27, 1954, in LS Coll.; LS, *Now Is the Time*, 83–85, 89, 87, 90–93, 81–82.

33. LS, *Now Is the Time*, 102–105, 110–11.

34. LS to Keith Jennison, June 27, 1954, in LS Coll.

35. LS to Keith Jennison, June 5, 1954, to Francis S. Harmon, June 5, 1955, Dr. Law-

rence Kubie to LS, June 1, 1955, LS to Dr. Lawrence Kubie, June 2, 1955, in LS Coll.

36. Austin Wehrwein, "A Crusader's Moderate Approach to America's 'White Democracy,'" Chicago *Sun-Times,* February 13, 1955, Sec. 3, p. 4; James Rorty, "A Unique Tract for Our Times," *New Leader,* March 4, 1955, p. 26; Brendan Gill, "Briefly Noted," *New Yorker,* March 5, 1955, p. 119; Robert R. Brunn, "Segregation Fades," *Christian Science Monitor,* February 10, 1955, p. 9; Hodding Carter, "Hope in the South," *Saturday Review,* April 2, 1955, pp. 29, 35; Ralph McGill, "A Matter of Change," *New York Times Book Review,* February 13, 1955, pp. 7, 32; Ralph McGill, "Lillian Smith Pens Segregation Theme," Atlanta *Journal and Constitution,* February 13, 1955, p. 8-E.

37. LS to Francis S. Harmon, June 5, 1955, and see also to Keith Jennison, June 5, 1955, in LS Coll.

38. LS to Charles Johnson, July 26, 1955, LS Coll. On Carter and McGill, see Ronnie J. Carpenter, "Hodding Carter, Jr., and the Race Issue" (M.A. thesis, Louisiana State University, 1983), 66–71; Harold H. Martin, *Ralph McGill, Reporter* (Boston, 1973), 132–33. Another southern moderate who shared McGill's and Carter's views was Jonathan Daniels, editor of the Raleigh *News and Observer.* See Charles W. Eagles, *Jonathan Daniels: The Evolution of a Southern Liberal* (Knoxville, 1982), 144, 159–60, 169, 171–75, 203, 232–33.

39. LS to Francis S. Harmon, June 5, 1955, to Charles Johnson, July 26, 1955, in LS Coll.

40. Autob. mats., LS to George Fredrickson, June 14, 1965, to Anna Hedgeman [June 10, 1956], to Dr. Lawrence Kubie, June 2, 1955, to Charles Johnson, June 10, 1955, to Mrs. Myrtle Weichman, [1954(?)], to Frank Spencer, March 8, 1956, to Patrick Malin, October 11, 1956, to Mozell Hill, March 7, 1957, in LS Coll. Social worker Anna Hedgeman was assistant to the mayor of New York City.

41. LS to Denver Lindley, December 10, 1955, to Keith Jennison, May 25, 1955, in LS Coll.

## Chapter VII

1. LS to Patrick Malin, January 28, 1956, to Frank Taylor, February 17, 1956, in the Lillian Smith Collection, Special Collections, The University of Georgia Libraries, Athens, Georgia; LS to Alan Reitman, February 15, 1956, in American Civil Liberties Union Archives, Princeton University Library, Princeton, N.J., hereinafter cited as ACLU Archives.

2. LS to Hazel F. Bailey, April 20, 1956, to Patrick Malin, January 28, 1956, to Patrick Malin and Alan Reitman, February 22, 1956, to Patrick Malin, October 11, 1956, in LS Coll.; to Alan Reitman, February 15, 1956, in ACLU Archives.

3. Patrick Malin and Alan Reitman to LS, February 20, 1956, Alan Reitman to LS, April 5, 1956, in LS Coll.

4. LS to Hazel F. Bailey, April 20, 1956, and see also to Anna Hedgeman, June 10, 1956, to Patrick Malin, October 11, 1956, in LS Coll.

5. LS to Patrick Malin, October 11, 1956, to Dorothy Norman, April 11, 1956, to Hazel F. Bailey, April 20, 1956, to Charles M. Jones, January 4, 1958, to Frank Spencer, March 8, 1956, in LS Coll.

6. LS to Dorothy Norman, April 11, 1956, in LS Coll.

7. LS to Wilma Dykeman Stokely, December 21, 1957, to Patrick Malin, February 22, 1956, to Mozell Hill, March 7, 1957, and see also to Ray Brewster, December 8, 1957, in LS Coll.; LS to William Warren, February 12, 1958, in possession of William Warren.

8. LS to Frank Spencer, March 8, 1956, to Wilma Dykeman Stokely, December 21, 1957, and see also to Dorothy Canfield Fisher, March 10, 1956, in LS Coll.

9. LS to Dorothy Canfield Fisher, March 10, 1956, to Dorothy Norman, April 11, 1956, to Frank and Lillian Spencer, April 5, 1956, in LS Coll.

10. LS to Frank and Lillian Spencer, March 8, 1956, to Frank Spencer, April 4, 1956, to Dorothy Norman, April 11, 1956, to Bevan C. Glover, March 8, 1956, to Mary Francis Baral, March 29, 1956, in LS Coll.

11. William Faulkner, "A Letter to the North," *Life,* March 5, 1956, pp. 51–52; LS to Helen Bullard, March 10, 1956, to Frank Spencer, March 8, 1956, to Dorothy Canfield Fisher, March 10, 1956, May 30, 1956, to Frank and Lillian Spencer, April 4, 1956, to Bevan Glover, March 8, 1956, to Gilbert Harrison, March 15, 1956, to *Life* [n.d.; 2 drafts], to Sir [n.d.; 2 drafts], in LS Coll. For the reviews of Faulkner in *South Today,* see Helen White and Redding Sugg, Jr. (eds.), *From the Mountain* (Memphis, 1972), 153–58, 208–10.

12. *Time,* March 26, 1956, p. 10; LS to Editor, *Look Magazine,* March 24, 1956, to Eric Sevareid [n.d.], to Editor, New York *Times,* October 6, 1957, Louise Polk Huger to LS, October 9, 1957, LS to Lawrence Kubie, October 10, 1957, in LS Coll.

13. LS to Lawrence Kubie, October 10, 1957, to Wilma Dykeman Stokely, December 21, 1957, to Jeffrey E. Fuller, October 5, 1957, to Mrs. Ed A. Albright, October 3, 1957, in LS Coll. For Lillian's prepared statement, see "Addressed to the South. By Lillian Smith," (typescript in Paula Snelling to Dear Friend, October 9, 1957), in LS Coll.

14. Paula Snelling to Dear Friend, October 9, 1957; LS to Richard McCutcheon, October 3, 1957, to Donald Seawell, October 3, 1957, to Jeffrey E. Fuller, October 5, 1957, in LS Coll.

15. Dorothy Canfield Fisher to LS, March 5, 1956, LS to Dorothy Canfield Fisher, March 10, 1956, April 6, 1956, Dorothy Canfield Fisher to LS, May 28, 1956, LS to Dorothy Canfield Fisher, May 30, 1956, in LS Coll.

16. LS to Helen Bullard, March 10, 1956, in LS Coll.

17. LS to Robert Evett, January 11, 1958, LS Coll.

18. See, for example, Frederica Mead Hiltner to LS, March 22, 1956, LS to Mrs. Walter G. Hiltner, March 29, 1956, to Mary Francis Baral, March 29, 1956, R. David Daniel to LS, October 13, 1957, LS to R. David Daniel, October 15, 1957, to Irwin Ross, November 27, 1957, to Morris Rubin, December 2, 1957, to Alfred Hassler, March 3, 1959, in LS Coll.

19. LS to Dr. Jack, August 28, 1956, in LS Coll.

20. LS to Chloe Fox [February (?), 1956], in LS Coll.

21. *Ibid.*

22. Telegrams: LS to O. C. Carmichael, Governor Folsom, Thurgood Marshall, George Mitchell, President of Student Legislature [February (?), 1956], in LS Coll.; LS to Dr. O. C. Carmichael, March 12, 1956, in LS Coll.

23. LS to President Dwight Eisenhower [September (?), 1957], in LS Coll.

24. LS to Gilbert Harrison, November 19, 1957, in LS Coll.; LS to Eleanor Roosevelt,

March 3, 1957, in Eleanor Roosevelt Collection, Franklin D. Roosevelt Library, Hyde Park, N.Y.; LS, "The Right Way Is Not A Moderate Way," *Phylon*, XVII (Fourth Quarter, 1956), 335–41; LS, "The Price of Silence," *Congress Weekly*, February 25, 1957, pp. 5–7; LS, "The Right Way is NOT a Moderate Way," *Fellowship*, XXIII (February, 1957), 13–19; LS, "Creative Extremists," *Community*, XVI (February, 1957), 3; LS, "'Until We Master Our Ordeal,'" *Civil Liberties*, No. 148 (January, 1957), 2; LS, "The Winner Names the Age," *Progressive*, XXI (August, 1957), 6–10; LS, "The Winner Names the Age," *New Leader*, August 26, 1957, pp. 12–14; LS, "The Winner Names the Age," *Phylon*, XVIII (Third Quarter, 1957), 203–12; LS, "No Easy Way, Now," *New Republic*, December 16, 1957, pp. 12–16.

25. LS to Gilbert Harrison, March 15, 1956, in LS Coll.; LS, "No Easy Way, Now," 13.

26. LS to Harry Golden, December 15, 1957, to Morris Rubin, November 24, 1957, in LS Coll.

27. LS, "No Easy Way, Now," 16; LS to Harry Golden, December 15, 1957, in LS Coll.

28. Morton Sosna, *In Search of the Silent South: Southern Liberals and the Race Issue* (New York, 1977), 168–69; Charles W. Eagles, *Jonathan Daniels: The Evolution of a Southern Liberal* (Knoxville, 1982), 191, 193–94, 198, 203, 233–35; Harold H. Martin, *Ralph McGill, Reporter* (Boston, 1973), 155, 157–58; Ronnie J. Carpenter, "Hodding Carter, Jr., and the Race Issue" (M.A. thesis, Louisiana State University, 1983), 45, 51–52, 58, 64, 70, 71; *Time*, March 26, 1956, pp. 10, 12; LS to Dorothy Canfield Fisher, March 10, 1956, to Gilbert Harrison, March 15, 1956, "Letter to New York *Times* or LIFE" [March, 1956(?)], in LS Coll.

29. LS, "The Right Way Is Not A Moderate Way," *Phylon*, 335, 338–41.

30. LS, "A Declaration of Faith in America," *New York Times Magazine*, September 21, 1952, pp. 13, 39–42; LS to Mrs. Ed A. Albright, October 21, 1957, LS, "'Demagoguery: A World-Size Danger. Have We World-Size Defences?' The Sidney Hillman Lectures, Nov. 16–19, 1954" (typescript), LS to Editor of the New York *Times*, October 6, 1957, to Ruth Nanda Anshen, October 8, 1957, to Lawrence Kubie, October 10, 1957, in LS Coll.; LS, "No Easy Way, Now," 12.

31. LS to Ray Brewster, December 8, 1957, to Ruth Nanda Anshen, October 8, 1957, to Lawrence Kubie, October 10, 1957, in LS Coll.

32. LS to Morris Rubin, April 4, 1956, to Martin Luther King, Jr., March 10, 1956, to Dorothy Canfield Fisher, April 4, 1956, to Mrs. Walter G. Hiltner, March 29, 1956, to Gilbert Harrison, March 15, 1956, in LS Coll. See also LS, "The Winner Names the Age," *Phylon*, 211; LS, "And Suddenly Something Happened," *Saturday Review*, September 20, 1958, p. 21; Homer A. Jack, "Lillian Smith of Clayton, Georgia," *Christian Century*, October 2, 1957, p. 1168.

33. LS, "Negroes in Gray Flannel Suits," *Progressive*, XX (February, 1956), 34–35.

34. LS to Morris Rubin, November 24, 1957, to William C. Allred, October 14, 1959, in LS Coll.

35. LS to Irwin Ross, November 27, 1957, to Charles J. Williams, November 21, 1957, to Ray Brewster, December 8, 1957, in LS Coll.

36. Aubrey Williams to LS, December 17, 1956, in LS Coll.

37. John A. Salmond, *A Southern Rebel: The Life and Times of Aubrey Willis Williams, 1890–1965* (Chapel Hill, 1983), 223, 236, 240, 244–45; Irwin Klibaner, "The

Southern Conference Educational Fund: A History" (Ph.D. dissertation, University of Wisconsin, 1971), 124, 145, 155, 177–84.

38. LS to Aubrey Williams, December 18, 1956 [first draft], in LS Coll.
39. *Ibid.*
40. *Ibid.*; Irwin Klibaner, "The Travail of Southern Radicals: The Southern Conference Educational Fund, 1946–1976," *Journal of Southern History*, XLIX (May, 1983), 180; Klibaner, "Southern Conference Educational Fund: A History," 170, 183–84. See also LS to Harry Barnard, June 26, 1958, in LS Coll.
41. Salmond, *A Southern Rebel*, 235–40; Virginia Durr to LS, December 6, 1956, in LS Coll.
42. LS to Virginia Durr, December 8, 1956, in LS Coll.
43. LS to Mozell Hill, March 11, 1957, to Grace T. Hamilton, May 7, 1956, to Doris V. Wilson, November 28, 1956, in LS Coll.
44. LS to Mozell Hill, March 11, 1957, in LS Coll.

## Chapter VIII

1. LS to Irita Van Doren, September 8, 1959, in Irita Van Doren Papers, Manuscript Division, Library of Congress, Washington, D.C.; LS to Dan Wickenden, November 1, 1959, and to Sidney M. Greenberg, August 15, 1956, in the Lillian Smith Collection, Special Collections, The University of Georgia Libraries, Athens, Georgia. See also LS to Henry Pratt Fairchild, July 16 [1956(?)], and to Denver Lindley [October 27, 1956], in LS Coll.; LS to Eleanor Roosevelt, August 15, 1956, in Eleanor Roosevelt Collection, Franklin D. Roosevelt Library, Hyde Park, N.Y. For Alger Hiss's reported reaction to the novel ("he loved the book, said it had deeply moved him"), see LS to Sidney Greenberg, October 25, 1959, and to Ruth Nanda Anshen, December 29, 1959, in LS Coll.
2. LS to Richard V. Moore, October 12, 1956, in LS Coll.
3. LS to William B. Hart, September 14, 1956, to Denver Lindley, March 19, 1957, in LS Coll.; LS, *One Hour* (New York, 1959), 5, 260, 419–20, 289, 438, 406.
4. Winthrop Sargeant, "Briefly Noted," *New Yorker*, September 26, 1959, p. 191; Cecilia Bartholomew, "The New Books—Mark Channing Has His Terrible Hour," *San Francisco Sunday Chronicle This World*, October 11, 1959, p. 28; Edmund Fuller, "Sins and Sorrows," *Saturday Review*, October 3, 1959, p. 22; Carter Brooke Jones, "Novel by Author of 'Strange Fruit' Has Strange and Haunting Power," Washington *Sunday Star*, September 27, 1959, p. C-5; Harold C. Gardiner, "Undeserved Praise," *America*, October 10, 1959, p. 49; Coleman Rosenberger, "Lillian Smith's New Novel of Love, Guilt and the Hour We Live In," *New York Herald Tribune Weekly Book Review*, September 27, 1959, p. 5.
5. Leslie A. Fiedler, "Decency Is Not Enough," *New Republic*, January 4, 1960, pp. 15–16.
6. Dr. Lawrence Kubie to LS, October 2, 1959, in LS Coll.
7. LS to Maxwell Geismar, January 1, 1961, to Joan Daves, December 31, 1960, to Dr. Leeper, June 1, 1960, in LS Coll.
8. LS to William Jovanovich, August 4, 1960, in LS Coll.; LS, *One Hour*, 73.
9. LS to Joan Daves, June 29, 1960, to William Jovanovich, December 7, 1959, to Gordon Bartineau, February 17, 1960, to Ruth Nanda Anshen, May 5, 1958, in LS

Coll. In addition to the writers mentioned, Lillian's reading during the 1950s included the following: Franz Kafka, Werner Jaeger's *Paideia*, psychologists Erik Erikson and Carl Rogers, the novelist Charles Williams, C. S. Lewis, Dorothy Sayer's *The Mind of the Maker*, Rudolf Otto's *The Idea of the Holy*, Elizabeth Sewell's *The Orphic Voice*, and Michael Polanyi. In 1959 she began to read the works of Pierre Teilhard de Chardin, who had considerable influence on her thinking (LS to Rev. Nathanel E. Parker, Jr., March 9, 1957, to Dorothy Norman, October 18, 1959, to Dr. Paul Adams, July 6, 1960, to Rollo May, September 18, 1960, in LS Coll.; see also "Books and Authors Who Have Meant Much to me since 1955" [October 4, 1965], in autobiographical materials in Box 1, LS Coll., hereinafter cited as autob. mats., LS Coll).

10. LS to Maxwell Geismar, January 1, 1961, in LS Coll.

11. On Brooks and MacLeish, see Charles C. Alexander, *Here the Country Lies: Nationalism and the Arts in Twentieth-Century America* (Bloomington, 1980), 245–52.

12. LS to Dorothy Norman, October 18, 1959, to Dr. Paul Adams, July 6, 1960, Dr. Lawrence Kubie to LS, October 2, 1959, Rollo May to LS, December 11, 1959, Paul Tillich to LS, October 8, 1959, LS to Paul Tillich, November 17, 1959, to Dorothy Norman, September 2, 1960, to Hal Bowser, December 1, 1960, in LS Coll.

13. LS to Dorothy Norman, October 18, 1959, and September 2, 1960, to Henry H. Crane, October 14, 1959, in LS Coll.; Ruth Ballentine, "Good Vs. Evil Vie in Novel," Memphis *Commercial Appeal*, October 4, 1959, Sec. 4, p. 10; Margaret Long, "Miss Smith Delves Deep Down Into Lives of Southern Town," Atlanta *Journal*, October 12, 1959, p. 23; Eddie Barker, "They Won't Carry This Book Around Town in Paper Sacks," Atlanta *Journal*, September 28, 1959, p. 25; Sam F. Lucchese, "Evil and Ignorance Plots Smith Novel," Atlanta *Journal*, September 27, 1959, p. 2E. Another review that pleased Lillian was by W. W. Stout in the Hattiesburg, Mississippi, *Petal Paper*, August 25, 1960, p. 1 (LS to P. D. East, July 20, 1960, in LS Coll.).

14. LS to Denver Lindley [October 27, 1956], to Dan Wickenden, September 30, 1959, to George L. White, October 1, 1959, to Henry H. Crane, October 14, 1959, in LS Coll.

15. LS to William Jovanovich, December 7, 1959, in LS Coll.

16. LS to William Jovanovich, December 7, 1959, and January 24, 1960, to Denver Lindley, June 30, 1957, to Ruth Nanda Anshen, December 29, 1959, to Henry H. Crane, October 14, 1959, to Florence and Rollo May, May 5, 1961, in LS Coll.; to Irita Van Doren, September 8, 1959, in Irita Van Doren Papers. *One Hour* sold 29,141 copies of 30,600 printed (Aaron A. Borovoy to the author, September 6, 1983).

17. LS to Henry H. Crane, January 25, 1960, to Paul Tillich, November 17, 1959, in LS Coll. Crane was a former pastor of the Central Methodist Church of Detroit.

18. LS to Sara F. Terrien, December 1, 1965, in possession of Sara F. Terrien; LS to Paul Tillich, November 17, 1959, in LS Coll.; LS, *One Hour*, 78, 179.

19. LS to Sara F. Terrien, December 1, 1965, in possession of Sara F. Terrien. According to Mrs. Terrien, the title of the sermon Tillich preached was "The Divine Name" (Sara F. Terrien to the author, April 20, 1981).

20. LS to Rochelle Girson, November 7, 1964, in LS Coll.; Margaret Long, "Lillian Smith, A Match for Old Screamer," *Progressive*, XXIX (February, 1965), 38.

21. LS, "Books and Authors Who Have Meant Much to me since 1955" [October 4, 1965], in autob. mats., LS Coll.; Roland N. Stromberg, *After Everything: Western Intellectual History Since 1945* (New York, 1975), 219; LS to Rochelle Girson, November 7, 1964, to Rollo May, September 18, 1960, to Maxwell Geismar, January 1, 1961, in LS Coll.; LS, "An Optimist Looks at the Human Race," *Chicago Tribune Books Today*, March 13, 1966, p. 1.

22. LS to Dorothy Norman, October 18, 1959, in LS Coll.

23. LS, "A Trembling Earth," in Michelle Cliff (ed.), *The Winner Names the Age: A Collection of Writings by Lillian Smith* (New York, 1978), 124; LS, "Novelists Need a Commitment," *Saturday Review*, December 24, 1960, p. 19; LS, *Killers of the Dream* (New York, 1949), 224–25.

24. LS to Paul Tillich, November 17, 1959, in LS Coll.; LS, "Novelists Need a Commitment," 18; LS, "Duels and Seductions," *Saturday Review*, November 11, 1961, p. 29; LS, "Poets Among the Demagogues," *Saturday Review*, October 2, 1965, p. 24 (*SR* changed the title of the speech).

25. LS, "Poets Among the Demagogues," 24, 35.

26. LS, "Poets Among the Demagogues," 24, 35; LS, "Novelists Need a Commitment," 18; LS, *The Journey* (New York, 1954), 256. For a perceptive discussion of Lillian's literary philosophy, see Margaret Sullivan, "Lillian Smith: The Public Image and the Personal Vision," *Mad River Review*, II (Summer–Fall, 1967), 3–21.

27. Autob. mats., LS to Henry H. Crane, March 6, 1956, to Harry Golden, December 15, 1957, and July 20, 1965, and see also to Mrs. Willa L. Currier, February 11, 1965, in LS Coll.

## Chapter IX

1. LS to William Jovanovich, January 24, 1960, in the Lillian Smith Collection, Special Collections, The University of Georgia Libraries, Athens, Georgia.

2. LS to William Jovanovich, January 24, 1960, to Dorothy Norman, October 18, 1959, to Ruth Anshen, December 29, 1959, in LS Coll.

3. LS to Joan Daves, December 31, 1960, to Maxwell Geismar, January 1, 1961, to Denver Lindley, June 30, 1957, "Writing and Events from 1955 on—" (typescript in autobiographical materials in Box 1, hereinafter cited as autob. mats.), in LS Coll.

4. "Writing and Events from 1955 on—," in autob. mats., LS to Rochelle Girson, November 7, 1964, to Lawrence Kubie, April 5, 1965, to Wilma Dykeman [Stokeley], October 30, 1965, in LS Coll.

5. LS, "Woman Born of Man," in Michelle Cliff (ed.), *The Winner Names the Age: A Collection of Writings by Lillian Smith* (New York, 1978), 202–203; LS, "No More Ladies in the Dark," *Saturday Review*, August 25, 1962, p. 24; LS to Gerald Sykes, August 8, 1959, to Frank Daniel, November 12, 1964, to William Jovanovich, July 30, 1959, to Dan Wickenden, October 16, 1961, in LS Coll.

6. LS, "Autobiography as a Dialogue Between King and Corpse," in Cliff (ed.), *Winner Names the Age*, 188; LS, "No More Ladies in the Dark," 24.

7. LS to Rochelle Girson, March 5, 1962, in LS Coll.

8. According to Esther Smith, the manuscript of "Julia" is no longer extant, having been destroyed in 1982 (Esther Smith to the author, September 29, 1983).

9. LS and Paula Snelling, "Man Born of Woman" (*South Today*, Winter, 1941), in

Helen White and Redding Sugg, Jr. (eds.), *From the Mountain* (Memphis, 1972), 240, 244.

10. *Ibid.*, 246.

11. *Ibid.*, 247–48.

12. Autob. mats., LS to Rochelle Girson, March 5, 1962, in LS Coll.; LS, "Autobiography as a Dialogue Between King and Corpse," in Cliff (ed.), *Winner Names the Age*, 188.

13. LS, *Strange Fruit* (New York, 1944), 206–207, 209–11.

14. LS, "One Hour" (typescript), Chap. 17, LS to Robert Coles, October 31, 1961, in LS Coll.; LS, *One Hour* (New York, 1959), 353–54.

15. LS, *One Hour*, 355.

16. Morton Sosna, *In Search of the Silent South: Southern Liberals and the Race Issue* (New York, 1977), 179; LS, "Dope with Lime," *South Today*, VIII (Spring–Summer, 1944), 4–6.

17. LS, *Strange Fruit*, 54–64; LS, *Killers of the Dream* (New York, 1949), 87–88, 115; LS, *The Journey* (New York, 1954), 67, 116.

18. LS, *Killers of the Dream*, 141, 139, 140.

19. *Ibid.*, 150, 153.

20. *Ibid.*, 143–47.

21. *Ibid.*, 118.

22. Richard H. King, *A Southern Renaissance: The Cultural Awakening of the American South, 1930–1955* (New York, 1980), 191.

23. LS, *Strange Fruit*, 247.

24. LS, "In answer to Eugene Moore's questions" (typescript in autob. mats.), LS to P. D. East, July 20, 1960, in LS Coll. My discussion of female characters in *Strange Fruit* and *One Hour* draws on Rose Gladney's "Lillian Smith's Hopes for Southern Women," *Southern Studies*, XXII (Fall, 1983), 278–79.

25. LS, "Woman Born of Man," 106; LS, *Killers of the Dream*, 141.

26. Gladney, "Lillian Smith's Hopes for Southern Women," 283; LS, "No More Ladies in the Dark," 24; Marynia F. Farnham, "The Pen and the Distaff," *Saturday Review*, February 22, 1947, p. 29.

27. LS, "Autobiography as a Dialogue Between King and Corpse," in Cliff (ed.), *Winner Names the Age*, 191; Homer A. Jack, "Lillian Smith of Clayton, Georgia," *Christian Century*, October 2, 1957, p. 1167; LS, "Notes for my article or letter to LIFE" [March, 1956], LS to Morris Rubin, December 2, 1957, to Irwin Ross, November 27, 1957, in LS Coll.; LS, *Killers of the Dream*, 153.

28. LS, "Too Tame the Shrew," *Saturday Review*, February 23, 1963, p. 34; LS, "Woman Born of Man," 209–11.

29. LS to Rochelle Girson, [January, 1963(?)], in LS Coll.

## Chapter X

1. LS, *One Hour* (New York, 1959), 232, 229; LS to George Brockway, July 3, 1965, in the Lillian Smith Collection, Special Collections, The University of Georgia Libraries, Athens, Georgia.

2. Autobiographical materials in Box 1 of the LS Coll., hereinafter cited as autob. mats., LS Coll. See also LS, "Glimpse of a Southern Writer," *Chicago Tribune Books Today*, April 10, 1966, p. 8.

3. LS to Cleveland Amory, November 22, 1965, to William G. Nunn, October 1, 1943, and to Dear Family, August 30, 1944, in LS Coll.
4. LS to Mrs. Donald D. Burr, March 1, 1965, in LS Coll.
5. Autob. mats., LS Coll. On Lillian's relationship with Esther prior to 1944, see Kathleen Atkinson Miller, "Out of the Chrysalis: Lillian Smith and the Transformation of the South" (Ph.D. dissertation, Emory University, 1984), 87, 107, 111–12, 244.
6. Autob. mats., LS to Lawrence Kubie, September 26, 1965, in LS Coll.; LS to Sara Terrien, July 18, 1961, in possession of Sara F. Terrien.
7. LS to Dorothy Norman [1956(?)], notebook, in LS Coll.
8. Margaret Long to LS, Friday & Saturday [December, 1963(?)], LS to Margaret Long, September 28, 1960, to Victor Gettner, October 14, 1960, in LS Coll.
9. LS to Dorothy Norman, October 18, 1959, to George Brockway, September 24, 1961, to Helen Bullard, March 8, 1957, Helen Bullard to LS, December 11, 1956, March 6, 1957, and to W. W. Norton, December 21, 1961, in LS Coll.; Atlanta *Journal*, July 20, 1979, Sec. C, pp. 1, 4; William Warren to the author, June 4, 1981, and August 20, 1985.
10. Paula Snelling to Louise Blackwell and Frances Clay, August 27, 1966, in LS Coll. See also, LS and Paula Snelling, "Yes . . . we are southern," *South Today*, VII (Spring, 1943), 41.
11. Autob. mats., LS Coll.
12. *Ibid.*
13. Paula Snelling to Louise Blackwell and Frances Clay, August 27, 1966, autob. mats., in LS Coll.
14. LS, "Concerning: Miss Paula Snelling" (typescript), LS to Virginia Durr, December 8, 1956, in LS Coll.
15. Paula Snelling to Louise Blackwell and Frances Clay, August 27, 1966, in LS Coll.; Glenn Rainey to the author, September 2, 1985; Joel Williamson, *The Crucible of Race: Black/White Relations in the American South Since Emancipation* (New York, 1984), 500; Joel Williamson to the author, October 4, 1985; George P. Brockway to the author, August 22, 1985; Faith Jackson to the author, August 31, 1985; confidential telephone interview, September 3, 1985; Barbara Livingston to the author, September 9, 1985; Rollo May to the author, November 15, 1985.
16. Correspondence between LS and Paula Snelling, autob. mats., LS to Morris Rubin, October 1, 1962, in LS Coll.
17. LS to Mimi Newcomb, September 7, 1962, to Paula Snelling, June 20 [1961], in LS Coll. See also LS to Margaret Long, December 3, 1961, in LS Coll.
18. LS to Paula Snelling, June 20 [1961], in LS Coll.
19. *Ibid.*
20. LS to Sara Terrien, December 1, 1965, in possession of Sara Terrien.
21. LS to Eleanor Roosevelt, April 7, 1942, LS and Paula Snelling to Eleanor Roosevelt, January 18, 1943, Eleanor Roosevelt to LS, July 3, 1944, in Eleanor Roosevelt Collection, Franklin D. Roosevelt Library, Hyde Park, N.Y.; Morton Sosna, *In Search of the Silent South: Southern Liberals and the Race Issue* (New York, 1977), 95.
22. Harvard Sitkoff, *The Depression Decade* (New York, 1978), 62, vol. I of *A New Deal for Blacks: The Emergence of Civil Rights as a National Issue;* LS to Mary McLeod Bethune, December 11, 1943, in LS Coll.; Helen White and Redding Sugg, Jr. (eds.), *From the Mountain* (Memphis, 1972), xii–xxlii; Joseph P. Lash, *A World of Love: Eleanor Roosevelt and Her Friends, 1943–1962* (Garden City, N.Y., 1984), 99.

23. LS, "A Southerner Talking," Chicago *Defender*, August 27, 1949.
24. Eleanor Roosevelt to LS, June 24, 1954, LS to Eleanor Roosevelt, July 11, 1954, Eleanor Roosevelt to LS, July 24, 1954, in Eleanor Roosevelt Collection.
25. LS to Eleanor Roosevelt [December, 1956(?)], in Eleanor Roosevelt Collection; LS, "A Southerner Talking," Chicago *Defender*, August 27, 1949.
26. Sara Terrien to the author, August 18, 1985.
27. Barbara Livingston to the author, September 9, 1985; LS to Dorothy Norman, [1956(?)], in LS Coll.; George P. Brockway to the author, August 22, 1985; Glenn Rainey to the author, September 2, 1985; autob. mats., LS Coll.
28. LS, "Facts about Friends, Etc. Jotted down in July, 1963, by L.S." (typescript), in LS Coll.
29. Autob. mats., "Chronology: Lillian Smith" (typescript), LS to Maxwell Geismar, January 1, 1961, to George Brockway, September 24, 1960, "Comments, etc. etc. for Maggie from L.S." (typescript), in LS Coll.
30. LS to Denver Lindley, June 5, 1955, in LS Coll.
31. LS, "Woman Born of Man," in Michelle Cliff (ed.), *The Winner Names the Age: A Collection of Writings by Lillian Smith* (New York, 1978), 206–207.
32. George Brockway to the author, August 22, 1985.
33. LS to Lawrence Kubie, September 30, 1954 and August 15, 1956, in Lawrence Kubie Papers, Manuscript Division, Library of Congress, Washington, D.C.; LS to Dorothy Norman, October 18, 1959, in LS Coll. For Kubie's evaluation of Lillian's writing see, e.g., Kubie to Storer Lunt, October 17, 1949, to LS, July 30, 1954, September 17, 1957, December 17, 1962, November 11, 1964, all in Lawrence Kubie Papers.
34. Rollo May to LS, December 11, 1959, LS to Rollo May, December 26, 1959, Rollo May to LS, January 19, 1960, LS to Rollo May (telegram) [January (?), 1960], LS to Rollo May, January 26, 1960, Rollo May to LS, September 25, 1961, LS to Harry Firestone, December 1, 1961, in LS Coll. Firestone was a professor at North Carolina Woman's College.

## Chapter XI

1. LS to Paul Tillich, November (?), 1960, in the Lillian Smith Collection, Special Collections, The University of Georgia Libraries, Athens, Georgia. LS, "The Moral and Political Significance of the Students' Non-Violent Protests," in Michelle Cliff (ed.), *The Winner Names the Age: A Collection of Writings by Lillian Smith* (New York, 1978), 91–99; LS, "Are We Still Buying a New World with Old Confederate Bills?" (typescript in LS Coll.). The All Souls Unitarian Church speech was published as "The Crisis in the South," *New Leader*, September 19, 1960, pp. 12–14, "The South's Moment of Truth," *Progressive*, September 1960, pp. 32–35, and "Behind the Sit-Ins," Hattiesburg, Mississippi *Petal Paper*, August 25, 1960, pp. 1–4, September 8, 1960, pp. 1, 3.
2. Atlanta *Constitution*, October 20, 1960, p. 1; Stephen B. Oates, *Let the Trumpet Sound: The Life of Martin Luther King, Jr.* (New York, 1982), 161–62; LS to Marvin Rich, October 20, 1960, in LS Coll.
3. LS to Jane Stembridge, October 22, 1960, in LS Coll.
4. LS to Richard Rich, October 20, 1960, in LS Coll.

5. LS to Frank Neely, October 20, 1960, to the Honorable William B. Hartsfield, October 20, 1960, in LS Coll.

6. LS to Eugene Patterson, October 22, 1960, to Dale Clark, October 22, 1960, in LS Coll.

7. LS to Henry H. Crane, October 23, 1960, to Dale Clark, October 22, 1960, to Paul Tillich, November (?), 1960, in LS Coll.

8. Oates, *Let the Trumpet Sound*, 162–65; David Levering Lewis, *King: A Biography* (2nd ed.; Urbana, 1978), 121; LS to Paul Tillich, November (?), 1960, in LS Coll.

9. LS to Paul Tillich, November (?), 1960, to Eugene Patterson [December 21, 1960], in LS Coll. Georgians Unwilling to Surrender (GUTS) was organized by restaurant owner Lester Maddox and other extreme segregationists in the fall of 1960 to boycott stores that changed their racial policies in response to the sit-ins. Numan V. Bartley, "Part Six: 1940 to the Present," in Kenneth Coleman (ed.), *A History of Georgia* (Athens, Ga., 1977), 369.

10. LS to Chloe Fox Zerwick [September (?), 1960] and September 27, 1960, in LS Coll.

11. LS to Chloe Fox Zerwick, October 5, 1960, to Julian Bond, August 4, 1960, to Eugene Patterson, October 22, 1960, in LS Coll. In his telegram to the sit-in groups, sent from his Washington headquarters, Kennedy said: "The human rights for which you strive are the definite goal of all America. I pledge that if elected president we will move to make the freedom guaranteed in our constitution a living reality for all our citizens" (Atlanta *Constitution*, October 15, 1960, p. 3).

12. LS to George Brockway, July 25, 1960, [October] 23, 1960, October 18, 1960, to Kurt Enoch, July 24, 1960, in LS Coll.

13. LS, *Killers of the Dream* (Rev. ed.; New York, 1961), 15–17, 20.

14. LS to George Brockway, October 18, 1960, in LS Coll.; LS, *Killers of the Dream* (Rev. ed.), 237–40, 249, 250.

15. LS to Marianne Fink, May 2, 1961, to Rev. Charles Cooley, September 23, 1961, to Marvin Rich, December 1, 1961, to Rev. Herbert M. Hugo, September 24, 1961, to Dr. Robert M. Frehse, June 24, 1961, in LS Coll.

16. LS to Marianne Fink, May 2, 1961, to Mary Abbot, July 23, 1964, to Marvin Rich, June 22, 1961, to Robert Louis Shayon, February 1, 1963, to Edna Dunlap, June 23, 1961, in LS Coll. Lillian also wrote the introduction to James Peck's *Freedom Ride* (New York, 1962).

17. LS to Eugene Patterson, October 22, 1960, to Dale Clark, October 22, 1960, in LS Coll.

18. LS, "The Moral and Political Significance of the Students' Non-Violent Protests," in Cliff (ed.), *Winner Names the Age*, 92–94.

19. LS to Jane Stembridge [November (?), 1960], in LS Coll. Clayborne Carson, *In Struggle: SNCC and the Black Awakening of the 1960s* (Cambridge, Mass., 1981), 28, 52, points out that several leftist groups attended the October sit-in groups conference in Atlanta, including the Young People's Socialist League, Students for a Democratic Society, the SCEF, and the Highlander Folk School; and that especially close ties developed between SNCC and SCEF. Irwin Klibaner, "The Southern Conference Educational Fund: A History," (Ph.D. dissertation, University of Wisconsin, 1971), 355–58, documents a close relationship between Jane Stem-

bridge and SCEF field director Anne Braden. For a similar warning to the executive director of the Atlanta Human Relations Council regarding its school desegregation project, see LS to Eliza Paschall, May 3 and 10, 1961, in LS Coll.

20. LS, "The Moral and Political Significance of the Students' Non-Violent Protests," in Cliff (ed.), *Winner Names the Age*, 94, 97; LS to the editor of the Atlanta *Journal*, September 5, 1960, to Frank Neely, October 20, 1960, in LS Coll.

21. LS, "The Ordeal of Southern Women," *Redbook*, CXVII (May, 1961), 44–45, 81–85; LS, *The Changing Heart of the South* [(n.p., n.d.) text of an address for delivery at the twelfth annual Prize Awards luncheon of the Sidney Hillman Foundation, May 3, 1962, in New York City], LS to William B. Hart, January 16, 1961, to Marianne Fink, May 2, 1961, in LS Coll.

22. LS to Edna Dunlap, June 23, 1961, to Frank McCallister, October 25, 1961, and see also to George Brockway, September 24, 1961, and Marvin Rich, December 1, 1961, in LS Coll.; LS, "Now, the Lonely Decision for Right or for Wrong," *Life*, October 12, 1962, p. 44. On Atlanta school desegregation see Alton Hornsby, Jr., "A City That Was Too Busy to Hate," in Elizabeth Jacoway and David R. Colburn (eds.), *Southern Businessmen and Desegregation* (Baton Rouge, 1982).

23. LS, "Now the Lonely Decision for Right or for Wrong," 44; LS to Robert H. Frehse, September 24, 1961, in LS Coll.

24. LS to Mimi Newcomb [July, 1962(?)], to Helen Fuller, September 6, 1962, and see also telegrams to Senator Carl Sanders, Governor Ernest Vandiver, and Attorney General Robert Kennedy [July, 1962(?)], in LS Coll.

25. LS, "Now, the Lonely Decision for Right or for Wrong," 44; LS, "The South Speaks Softly, *Saturday Review*, February 2, 1963, p. 29; LS, "A Strange Kind of Love," *Saturday Review*, October 20, 1962, pp. 18–20.

26. LS, "A Strange Kind of Love," 20; LS to All of You at SNCC [January, 1963(?)], in LS Coll.

27. LS to All of You at SNCC [January, 1963(?)], in LS Coll.

## Chapter XII

1. LS to George Brockway, November 20, 1960, in the Lillian Smith Collection, Special Collections, The University of Georgia Libraries, Athens, Georgia.

2. Eugene Patterson to LS, January 16, 1961, and February 24, 1961, LS to George Brockway, November 20, 1960, in LS Coll.

3. LS to Ashley Montagu, February 9, 1965, to Page Wilson, October 9, 1962, in LS Coll.; LS, "The Ordeal of Southern Women," *Redbook*, CXVII (May, 1961), 44–45, 81–85; LS, "Memory of a Large Christmas," *Life*, December 15, 1961, pp. 90–94; LS, "Now, the Lonely Decision for Right or for Wrong," *Life*, October 12, 1962, p. 44; LS, "A Strange Kind of Love," *Saturday Review*, October 20, 1962, pp. 18–20; LS, "The Day It Happens to Each of Us," *McCall's*, XCII (November, 1964), 124–25, 166, 168. Lillian was given the $500 Sidney Hillman award at the twelfth annual Prize Awards luncheon of the Sidney Hillman Foundation, May 3, 1962, in New York City. Illness prevented her from attending the luncheon; her acceptance speech was read for her by Eugenia Rawls, who had played the role of Harriet Harris in the stage production of *Strange Fruit*.

4. LS to P. D. East, May 1, 1961, to Marvin Rich, December 1, 1961, to Rochelle Gir-

son, November 7, 1964, to Arthur Raper, March 9, 1965, to Marvin Rich, June 22, 1961, to John B. Bennett, September 15, 1961, in LS Coll.

5. LS, *Our Faces, Our Words* (New York, 1964); LS to George Brockway, November 1, 1963, to Rochelle Girson, November 7, 1964, in LS Coll.; LS to Frank Daniel, September 15, 1964, in Frank Daniel Papers, Special Collections, Robert W. Woodruff Library, Emory University, Atlanta, Ga.

6. LS to Rochelle Girson, November 7, 1964, to Wilma Dykeman Stokely, February 24, 1965, to George Brockway, September 18, 1964, in LS Coll.; LS, "The Author Comments on Our Faces, Our Words" (typescript for Frank Daniel [November 11, 1964]), in LS Coll.

7. LS to Bruce Galphin, January 9, 1965, in LS Coll.

8. LS to George Brockway [November 2, 1964(?)], to John Mack Carter, November 9, 1964, to Leslie Dunbar, November 16, 1964, in LS Coll.

9. LS to John Mack Carter, November 9, 1964, to George Brockway, October 30, 1964, to Mary Abbott, August 1, 1964, in LS Coll.; Saunders Redding, "In Freedom's Cause," *New York Times Book Review*, February 21, 1965, p. 34.

10. LS to Frank Daniel, November 23, 1964, in Frank Daniel Papers; LS, *Our Faces*, 123; LS to Marvin Rich, September 10, 1961, in LS Coll.; Clayborne Carson, *In Struggle: SNCC and the Black Awakening of the 1960s* (Cambridge, Mass., 1981), 61–67ff., 95, 164; August Meier and Elliott Rudwick, *CORE: A Study in the Civil Rights Movement, 1942–1968* (New York, 1973), 374–76, 397, 399.

11. LS, *Our Faces*, 123.

12. *Ibid.*, 115, 188, 126, 127.

13. LS to Marvin Rich, September 10, 1961, in LS Coll.; LS, *Our Faces*, 121; LS to Warren Austin Smith, II, March 3(?), 1962, in LS Coll.

14. LS to Marvin Rich [1963(?)], to Robert Louis Shayon, February 1, 1963, to John Howard Griffin [January, 1963(?)], in LS Coll.

15. LS, *Our Faces*, 73, 99–100.

16. LS to Hoke Norris, January 20, 1965, in LS Coll.

17. LS to Joan Daves, January 10, 1965, to William B. Hart, March 17, 1965, to Marvin Rich, December 11, 1964, to Paul Anthony, December 31, 1965, in LS Coll.

18. LS to Rochelle Girson, November 17, 1964, and November 20, 1964, in LS Coll.

19. LS to Lawrence Kubie, April 5, 1965, to Harry Golden, July 20, 1965, in LS Coll.

20. Felicia Geffen to LS, September 30, 1965, LS to Felicia Geffen, October 4, 1965, in LS Coll.

21. LS to George Brockway, November 30, 1965, in LS Coll.

22. LS to Donald Seawell, October 3, 1965, in LS Coll.

23. LS to Donald Seawell, October 4, 1965, in LS Coll.

24. LS to George Brockway, December 1, 1965 [November, 1965(?)], and December 19, 1965, in LS Coll.

25. LS to Alice Shoemaker, October 30, 1965, in LS Coll.

26. LS to Ruth Nanda Anshen, January 9, 1966, to Lewis Mumford, November 24, 1965, and November 13, 1965, in LS Coll.

27. LS to Norman Cousins, March 3, 1966, to Ruth Nanda Anshen, January 9, 1966, in LS Coll.

28. LS to Ruth Nanda Anshen, January 9, 1966, to Lewis Mumford, November 24, 1965, and November 13, 1965, to Alice Shoemaker, October 30, 1965, in LS Coll.

29. LS to Norman Cousins, March 3, 1966, in LS Coll.

30. LS to Sue Thrasher, December 8, 1964, to Alice Shoemaker, October 30, 1965, to Zoë Cloak, October 4, 1965, in LS Coll.

31. LS, "Old Dream, New Killers," Atlanta *Constitution*, January 14, 1966, p. 4; Atlanta *Constitution*, January 7, 1966, p. 1; Carson, *In Struggle*, 188; "SNCC: Statement on Vietnam War," in Massimo Teodori (ed.), *The New Left: A Documentary History* (Indianapolis, 1969), 251–52.

32. Atlanta *Constitution*, January 7, 1966, pp. 1, 12.

33. Atlanta *Constitution*, January 7, 1966, pp. 1, 12; Carson, *In Struggle*, 189.

34. LS, "Old Dream, New Killers," Atlanta *Constitution*, January 14, 1966, p. 4.

35. *Ibid.*

36. LS to Arthur Raper, February 14, 1966, to Karl Menninger, February 7, 1966, to David Maness, February 5, 1966, to Daniel Patrick Moynihan, February 4, 1966, to Norman Cousins, February 3, 1966, to Bruce Galphin, January 22, 1966, to Harry Golden, January 28, 1966, in LS Coll.

37. LS to Karl Menninger, February 7, 1966, to David Maness, February 5, 1966, to Norman Cousins, February 3, 1966, to Arthur Raper, February 14, 1966, in LS Coll.

38. LS to Norman Cousins, February 3, 1966, to Karl Menninger, February 7, 1966, to Harry Golden, January 28, 1966, in LS Coll.

39. LS, "Old Dream, New Killers," Atlanta *Constitution*, January 14, 1966, p. 4; LS to Harry Golden, January 28, 1966, to George Brockway, March 7, 1966, to Norman Cousins, February 3, 1966, to Arthur Raper, February 14, 1966, in LS Coll.

40. LS to Margaret Sullivan, January 22, 1966, in LS Coll.

41. Eugene Patterson, "Here We Go on a Red Dog's Back," Atlanta *Constitution*, January 11, 1966, p. 4. On the reorganization of SNCC, see Carson, *In Struggle*, 30, 40, 67, 69, 139, 145, 146, 155.

42. "SNCC: Loss of Faith, Loss of Vision," Atlanta *Constitution*, January 7, 1966, p. 4; Carson, *In Struggle*, 160; LS to Karl Menninger, February 7, 1966, to Daniel Patrick Moynihan, February 4, 1966, in LS Coll.; LS, "Old Dream, New Killers," Atlanta *Constitution*, January 14, 1966, p. 4.

43. Andrew Kopkind, "New Radicals in Dixie: Those 'Subversive' Civil Rights Workers," *New Republic*, April 10, 1965, p. 15; Carson, *In Struggle*, 180–83, 188–89.

44. LS to Arthur Raper, February 14, 1966, to Karl Menninger, February 7, 1966, Ivan Allen to LS [January, 1966], in LS Coll.

45. LS, "Orpheus and Roast Pig" (typescript), Norman Cousins to LS, March 1, 1966, in LS Coll. For a different version of the Bond affair, see Roger M. Williams, *The Bonds: An American Family* (New York, 1972), 219–34.

46. LS, "Orpheus and Roast Pig" (typescript), in LS Coll.

47. *Ibid.*

48. *Ibid.*

49. *Ibid.*

50. LS to Floyd McKissick, July 5, 1966, in LS Coll.; Meier and Rudwick, *CORE*, 414–15. For Lillian's views on Black Power, see George B. Leonard, "Not Black Power, But Human Power: An Interview with Lillian Smith," *Look*, September 6, 1966, pp. 40, 42–43.

51. LS to Dorothy Bromley, January 14, 1966, to Mary Abbot, July 2, 1964, in LS Coll.

52. LS to Dorothy Bromley, January 14, 1966, in LS Coll.

## Epilogue

1. LS, "Acceptance Speech for the Charles S. Johnson Award," in Michelle Cliff (ed.), *The Winner Names the Age: A Collection of Writings by Lillian Smith* (New York, 1978), 101–102. Lillian died September 28, 1966.
2. Autobiographical materials in the Lillian Smith Collection, Special Collections, The University of Georgia Libraries, Athens, Georgia. LS, "How to Work for Racial Equality," *New Republic*, July 2, 1945, pp. 23–24.

# Index